ROMAN CATHOLICISM
The Search for Relevance

ROMAN CATHOLICISM

The Search for Relevance

WILLIAM McSWEENEY

St. Martin's Press · New York

ISBN 0-312-68969-1

Library of Congress Catalog No: 80-18476

For Mary

Contents

Introduction

One thing is certain about modern Catholicism: it has changed. It is not what it was. Roman Catholics routinely behave and think today in ways that would have seemed extraordinary in the 1950s. A transformation has taken place, but no one seems sure what has happened. Everyone agrees that the Church is not the same, but few are confident that they can define the difference or explain how it occurred.

Catholicism is an intriguing subject for Catholics and non-Catholics alike. Non-Catholics are amazed at the persistence of medieval values and organization so far into the twentieth century and curious about the power struggles within the Church which will determine its survival or decline. Committed Catholics, accustomed by faith and tradition to a more reverential view of their Church and its government, are finding that faith tested by the exposure of human weakness, division and uncertainty at the highest level of authority. What will be the future of Catholicism? That is the question uppermost in the minds of most observers and it cannot be answered—if it can be answered at all—until we have a clearer definition of the change which has occurred and a clearer picture of the conditions which brought it about. For all the energy expended in debating and writing about the crisis of modern Catholicism, we know little about its nature and its origins.

It is widely accepted that the Second Vatican Council was a key event in the emergence of the modern Church. Typically, Catholicism today is contrasted with the Church before the Council; and, while theologians and laymen differ in the priority given to some changes over others, there is general agreement that the period of the Council has made available to Catholics an unprecedented degree of religious freedom. It is now possible to behave and express oneself publicly in ways which, before Vatican II, required considerable courage and submission to ecclesiastical and social penalties. Theologians can dispute the official interpretation of a point of doctrine, Catholics can refuse to obey a directive of the Pope, priests can abandon their ministry—and they can do these things while continuing to retain membership of the Church and the respect of the social community to which they belong.

But the new freedom is a mixed blessing, even for those who wish to avail themselves of it. There are many who regard religious liberty as an evil and the Vatican Council as an unqualified disaster for the Church. There are others for whom a degree of emancipation from ecclesiastical authority was an overdue development bringing the Church in line with Christian principles, but for whom the price paid was too high. Catholicism has become fragmented to the point that the label 'Roman Catholic' is no longer a safe indicator of beliefs or ethics. Among those claiming to be Catholics, one can now find a bewildering variety of competing and incompatible values, doctrines and moral attitudes, and these divisions extend even to the leadership of the Church. The beliefs are so varied and the divisions so manifest that it is becoming increasingly difficult for Catholics to retain a strong motive for commitment to the Church, even to see the point of their membership.

Still others regard the essence of the Catholic crisis as the failure of the Church to carry out the reforms implicit in the documents of Vatican II and to extend to all Catholics the full liberty of conscience proper to a Christian community, while at the same time committing the Church to an ethical programme consistent with Christ's command to evangelize the world.

The views of commentators on modern Catholicism seem to divide on much the same lines as those outlined. Catholicism is a subject largely restricted to initiates—Catholics or ex-Catholics whose background has given them an indispensable familiarity with the trappings of the Church: its rules and rituals, piety and customs, which are the pieces that make up the jigsaw of the Roman Church. (If they venture at all into this field, non-Catholics frequently feel obliged to apologize for intruding.) It is not easy to stand aside from the deep impressions of one's upbringing and subject the Church to unbiased scrutiny. As a consequence, the analysis of Catholicism tends to be either vindicatory or dismissive; it carries too many theological over-tones of praise or condemnation to be useful as a description of the modern Church and an explanation of its origin.

Despite the difficulties and pitfalls attendant on any attempt to put aside prejudice and to analyse fairly and objectively, the attempt must be made. There is need, I feel, for an account of Roman Catholicism which is not rooted in one or other of the major theological attitudes to the reforms of the Second Vatican Council. This is not a book about the Holy Spirit, nor is it written from the point of view that assumes his divine presence and guidance in the Church, though it is not inconsistent with that belief. One does not necessarily disbelieve in divine guidance if one expresses dissatisfaction with divine explanations. Religious change is never 'totally the work of the Spirit', as one of the Cardinals interpreted the election of Pope John Paul I after the Conclave. Decisions about doctrine, organization or discipline in the Church are inescapably decisions about power and politics, and one does not have to impute unworthy motives—or even political awareness—to the decision-makers in order to explain their actions as the outcome of social and political factors.

This is a book about the interrelation of politics and theology in the development of the Roman Catholic Church and about the effect of changes in the one upon the options for change in the other. It seeks to provide a detached account of the emergence of modern Catholicism and to identify the major religious and secular factors which have contributed to it. Like any satisfactory explanation of social change, it will attempt to describe the condition of the contemporary Church in terms which are theologically neutral and to situate its development within a social context sufficiently specific to account for its occurrence. I am concerned, therefore, with the historic conflict between the Church and the world—not only in the particular sense in which this dispute was consciously articulated by both sides but in the general sense of the effect of secular ideas and politics on the teaching of the Church and the changes in its structure which followed.

The search for an adequate description and explanation of modern Catholicism gives rise to certain problems and necessitates certain assumptions. In the first place, it is clear that the Roman Catholic Church—or any other comparable organization—does not have an objective unity corresponding to the neat definition of an analyst or observer. Even before Vatican II, Catholics in Latin America differed considerably from their co-religionists in Holland or France, not only in trivial matters like the language or architectural setting of religious services but in their allegiance to the Church, in the intensity of their faith. Intellectuals fall easily into the temptation of discovering unity where there is evidence only of diversity and of constructing explanations which are so general as to be worthless. The trouble is, however, that the objection applies equally to Catholics *within* Holland, France and Latin America. They, too, manifest a substantial degree of diversity to the keen observer, making generalizations about Dutch or French Catholicism as suspect as those on a more global level. Where is one to draw the line and to risk the loss of information incurred at any level of generalization for the sake of the richer theoretical understanding gained?

There is no completely satisfactory solution to the problem. The assumption is made here that the Roman Catholic Church, for most of the period under consideration, had a degree of objective unity and of solidarity with its official leadership adequate for the purpose of general description and explanation. This assumption clearly places limits on what we can understand about the Church. On the other hand, respect for the differences between Catholic individuals and groups would make impossible the only kind of explanation which is intellectually satisfying for those who, like the author, are puzzled or perplexed by the rapidity of change in the Church.

There is some justification in Catholic history for treating the Church as an entity, comprehensible as a social force, without detailed reference to its diversity. There is statistical evidence that, until the late 1950s, the Pope and his Curial officials in Rome successfully controlled the beliefs and ethics of Catholics—in a particular sense which will be discussed later. For example, papal directives on contraception and official teaching on abortion since the 1930s in fact inhibited Catholics from exercising a free choice in these matters to the extent that the world-wide distribution of these practices was considerably affected by the presence of even nominally Catholic populations.

The Church was a unity at least to the extent that its leadership could prevent certain actions and inhibit the public expression of certain views. Only in this sense is the unity of Catholicism assumed. It will become clear, moreover, that this does not imply the assumption of a positive consensus among Catholics in matters of doctrine and morality.

Today, after the Second Vatican Council, no such assumption of unity is possible. A papal directive on, say, homosexuality, contraception or the sanctity of private property would not in itself authorize an observer to predict the future of Catholics' sexuality or political affiliations. How we are to interpret and explain this apparently sudden change is the object of this inquiry.

This leads to the second problem and another necessary assumption. Where does one begin this inquiry without appearing to make a purely arbitrary judgement? It should be clear that the transformation of Catholicism which I am concerned with was not a sudden change. No social phenomenon of such complexity can be understood except in historical terms. The decade of the 1960s merely manifested a critical stage in a process of change, the beginning of which cannot be accurately dated; and one can no more understand it within the temporal boundaries of the sixties than one can understand the modern Church within the spatial boundaries of a parish or a diocese.

We cannot begin any story at the beginning. We can, however, choose a particular starting-point which begs less questions than others and leaves less unexplained. The strategy adopted here is to begin at the time when the world—understood as secular political institutions—first emerged as an independent entity and seriously challenged the hegemony and legitimacy of the Church. This dates the story from the end of the eighteenth century, around the time of the French Revolution. The first chapter, therefore, contains a broad sketch of the Church before this event; it discusses the medieval concept of the world and the interrelation of the social order with the supernatural which pervaded Catholic thinking prior to the emergence of a new world and a new problem of the Church's relevance to it.

Three periods are distinguished in the relationship of Catholicism to secular society. In the first—the stage of rejection—an official policy of aggressiveness towards the modern world was

implemented in reaction to secular demands which were perceived partly as a direct challenge to Catholic teaching and
property, and partly as a threat to political forces with which the
Church had formed alliances and on which it depended for some
of its privileges. In Chapter 2, which discusses this stage, the
term 'modern world' is seen gradually to focus on these
antagonistic forces, and the process of polarization between
Church and world as mutually destructive and irreconcilable
powers is clarified. In retrospect, the official policy of the Church
seems short-sighted. In the context of the changing and uncer-
tain political situation in Europe after centuries of relative
stability, however, the options open to the Vatican were severely
limited. The decisions taken were translated into dogmatic,
liturgical and organizational forms which would soon prove
redundant and embarrassing in a different and more modern
world.

The second period was that of competition, and it began with
the pontificate of Pope Leo XIII in 1878. This was the age of
Catholic Action: Leo's attitude towards the modern world was
competitive and antagonistic, if overtly accommodating, and his
policy was manipulationist rather than aggressive. Through
Catholic Action, he sought to use the new democratic institutions in order to recover for the Church an indirect form of the
power lost with the papal territories. His policies on the social
question and on philosophy and learning are shown, in Chapter
3, to have been dictated as much by the political exigencies of the
time as by the moral issues to which they were directed. This
second stage of the Church's relationship with the world, like the
first, left a legacy which future generations of Catholics, living in
a different world, would be forced to contend with.

Catholicism until the late 1950s can be interpreted as Leonine
in its structure and in the ideas which informed official policy.
But there were some in that period for whom the problem of
relevance could not be ignored or strategically redefined in the
interests of Catholic imperialism. Furthermore, the modern
world to which Catholicism was claimed to be irrelevant and
with which its future was now inescapably linked was becoming
increasingly indifferent to the Church and developing new
institutions which competed for the allegiance of Catholics and
threatened to reduce the function of the Church to the level of

ritual. In Chapters 4 and 5 I shall discuss the search for relevance within the Church and the conditions in secular society which stimulated it.

Chapter 6 concentrates on this search at an advanced and critical point: the Second Vatican Council. While it is clear from the documents that the Council was called to seek a new expression of the Church's teaching and liturgy, it was not clear what effect this would have on the beliefs and practices of Catholics throughout the Church. Neither was it easy to discern which of the two theological positions represented in these documents would emerge as the dominant intellectual force of the future Church.

The third and present stage of the Church's relations with the world begins after the Council with the victory of progressive theology (discussed in Chapter 7). This is the period of partnership, when the traditional definitions of the Church and its function lose their sharpness and merge within institutions of an established, secular kind. In Chapter 8, the contemporary situation is analysed in order to provide a theologically neutral description adequate for the purpose of explanation.

This explanation is contained in Chapter 9, in which the main threads of an argument implicit in the rest of the book are linked more formally into an interpretation of the emergence of modern Catholicism.

Throughout the book, the attempt has been made to avoid the rigid separation of technical from more discursive passages. The mingling of analysis and description is a little unconventional, but it will contribute, I hope, to the interest and readability of the end-product.

Finally, a word about the author's moral commitment to the subject-matter—or, rather, a note on why such a personal statement is not included. It seems unwise to many—an affront to some—that a writer on religion should claim the right to ideological anonymity. There is the risk that readers, confronted with views which disturb their own assumptions, will press quite inappropriate labels on the author in self-defence. It is fashionable for social theorists to say where they stand, to 'come clean' about their prejudices. But such confessions add nothing to the merit of a book; often the pressure to bare one's soul makes the authenticity of the confession highly suspect. It is premised on the false assumption that bias, lurking in the text to trap the unwary, is easily detectable by the writer whose frank admissions, therefore, save the reader the trouble of assessing the validity of a complex argument.

I hope readers will judge the argument for themselves. If they conclude that the author feels a strong sympathy towards those who grapple with the Church's problems and an ambivalence towards the solutions they propose, they will have guessed the substance that a personal statement would have contained.

Like most literary products, this one is the fruit of much revision following discussions with friends and colleagues. For their generosity in reading and criticizing parts of the manuscript, I am grateful to Colin Campbell, Robert Bocock, Pat Sills, Neville Symington, Bryan Wilson and James Walvin. I am happy to express my indebtedness also to the library staff at the University of York and to Mrs Mary Buck at the Catholic Central Library in London.

PART ONE

THE PROBLEM OF RELEVANCE

1
The World before Modernity

Catholics today take it for granted that the Church and the world are not separate and antagonistic universes, struggling for men's souls like primeval forces of good and evil. The distinction remains part of the language and framework in which most people speak and think about religion, but it no longer serves its traditional purpose of delineating moral boundaries and identifying moral communities whose values, goals and life-styles are radically opposed. For many theologians, the distinction has no meaning. The primitive notion that humanity was divided into chosen and regenerate, into religious society and secular, made sense only as long as membership of either had implications for salvation. This was certainly the case in the Middle Ages, when the doctrine *extra ecclesiam nulla salus* acted as a powerful justification of the Church in the eyes of Catholics and checked any tendency to wander to rival institutions. Taken literally, however, the belief that membership of the Roman Church was laid down by Good as a necessary condition for salvation could not survive the twentieth century. It was too crude to be rational; it was too arrogant to be ecumenical.

Theologians could not simply deny a belief because it was inconvenient, however. The burden of theological history weighed heavy on a Church, like the Roman Catholic, which stressed the unity and continuity of its beliefs. To be a Catholic, it was held, was primarily to assent to certain propositions about God and the Church, and secondarily to conform one's behaviour to the ethical and disciplinary requirements laid down for Church members. Modern theology has made it possible for Catholics to survive in a more rational and tolerant age without having to deny the proposition that the Church is necessary for salvation. By redefining 'church' in non-institutional terms—the phrase 'people of God' blurs the visible edges of the Church for this purpose—theologians can interpret the ancient formula to mean that all salvation is mediated through the presence of Christ in his Church. Not to be a member of the Church—to be of the world—does not mean that one cannot benefit from the supernatural gifts made available through the agency of the Church. Its *existence* is a necessary condition for salvation, but not membership of it in a formal sense.

Even as late as the 1950s, however, the traditional interpretation of the doctrine and the traditional polarization between the Church and the world dominated Catholic thinking. Forces of change were already astir and would have their dramatic impact in the Second Vatican Council, but their influence on official thinking and the wide diffusion of the new theology outside the pockets of liberalism that had generated it did not occur until the middle or late 1960s. Until then, Catholics had a powerful reason for remaining within the visible institution of the Church and for committing themselves to a variety of missionary activities aimed at the transformation and conversion of the non-Catholic world. The belief in the necessity of the Church for salvation was never as rigid as to exclude automatically all who were not members. Protestants, Jews, even atheists could still be saved, but Rome held the keys and it was safer to travel in the company of the elect than to risk it outside as an individual.

The idea of the 'world', in contrast to the Church, underwent a critical change in the nineteenth century, as we shall see in the following chapters. Until then, 'church' and 'world' were two realms as distinct in the Catholic mind as soul and body, light and darkness, good and evil; and the primacy of the Church in relation to the world was unquestioned. The Catholic lived between two trinities: the Father, Son and Holy Ghost on the one side, attracting him, through the Church, towards the devout life and salvation; the World, the Flesh and the Devil on the other, placing obstacles in his way, enticing him towards evil and damnation. On the face of it, this dispute for man's soul was rather one-sided, given the inherent superiority of the heavenly alliance. In an ideal universe, it was believed, men would be free to choose, and, naturally, they would opt for salvation. But original sin distorted that universe. Since the Fall, the balance of attraction had shifted—not because God was diminished, but because man had lost the capacity to choose of his own free will between good and evil.

According to this Augustinian theory of concupiscence, original sin inclined man towards evil, making him utterly dependent on divine grace for salvation. It may be that the unholy trinity doing battle for man's soul was crudely conceived, theologically exaggerated, erroneous.[1] The theologians' interest, however, lay in identifying factors considered to influence and limit free choice and personal responsibility, and, although they may have underestimated this influence and crudely explained its origins, they were not entirely mistaken about its existence and its effect. The World, the Flesh and the Devil have lost their titles and their supernatural status in secular society, but not their influence. The organization of modern behavioural science reflects the same threefold distinction of the determinants of action crudely depicted by the medieval theologians as the forces of evil: sociology, biology and psychology provide a secularized version of the old concerns of moral theology with the World, the Flesh and the Devil—now seen as the constraints on human freedom of the social environment and of physiological and mental conditioning.

The world we shall be concerned with in this book is not a concrete location or a particular institution. It is a theological concept, which can be defined as the ideas, values and patterns of behaviour not generated or controlled by the visible institution of the Church. The social environment which concerns the sociologist is not precisely the world as conceived in traditional Catholic theology. His interest is man as a social being; the network of social relationships that give rise to aspirations for power and security, stability and change, status and domination. Medieval Catholicism recognized that such worldly aspirations could flourish in the monastery just as they did in secular institutions, and it was not shy about organizing conquests and consolidating power on its own account. But such deviations from righteousness were not seen as endemic within

[1] Rahner (1961).

the Catholic institution itself. They were importations from that arena of life not under Catholic control. The world was the source of worldliness wherever it was found. It was a way of life, not a geographical area or a concrete institution; but it was typically in non-Catholic institutions that ideas and ideals were generated which distracted man from his true vocation—to work for the salvation of his soul. (The medieval concept of the world is similar in its fluidity to the idea of the Church in modern theology—not an observable institution, but a configuration of values and ideas which cluster in certain typical situations but are not to be identified with them.)

The Church and the world, therefore, defined each other and stood in a relationship of chronic tension to each other. The world constituted an arena of danger and opportunity: temptations to be avoided, territories to be evangelized, their evil exorcized, their people baptized. Catholics and non-Catholics, believers and non-believers, lived in the world—for want of anywhere else to live. But while they lived in it, they must not be of it; their lives must be guided by Catholic values and not by the standards of secular institutions.

The doctrine that salvation was unavailable outside the Catholic Church was first formulated by Origen and St Cyprian in the third century and formed a central part of Catholic teaching which survived more or less intact until the mid-twentieth. This doctrine formed part of a world-view or cosmology which located the Church at the centre of history as it located the earth at the centre of the universe. The Christian world-view which dominated thought and was reflected in the art and literature and institutions of the Middle Ages was a complex system of spiritual relationships linking three levels of the universe in a manner which expressed and legitimated the medieval social order. The heavens above contained the power of life, hierarchically organized with God at the pinnacle of a pyramid of beings descending by stages to the lowest rank, the heavenly proletariat of the saints. Below was the realm of death, darkness or annihilation, ruled by Satan and hierarchically structured like the kingdom of God. The earth in the centre was the stage of history where these two eternally fixed universes entered the temporal order of man and engaged in the dramatic struggle for his soul that constituted the historical process. Of its nature, the earth itself was a hierarchy, with man at its apex, qualitatively superior to the rest of creation and natural ruler of all that was not human. Humanity, from this point of view, was unique, privileged and equal; all men shared equally in its superiority, in its distinctive origins and in its ultimate purpose. In this sense, the belief that all human beings are equal in the sight of God, has always been a fundamental part of Catholic tradition and teaching and a crucial element in the theological interpretation of history which lent drama to human life and urgency to moral commitment. Religion was dynamic, not static. Christians were going somewhere—inevitably—and each person had equal opportunity to influence the course of that journey. Whereas Calvinists and the Lutheran tradition later stressed God's autonomy and freedom in bestowing grace, medieval Catholics underlined the need for good works and left the reasoning behind this apparently meritocratic view of salvation to the professional theologians.

The belief in man's fundamental equality before God was not, therefore, a vacuous acknowledgement of some embarrassing passages in the Scriptures, as was the case, for example, with the Catholic version of the doctrine of the universal priesthood. It was a basic element of Catholic cosmology on which the organization and moral structure of medieval religion depended. It served another function. The concept of hierarchy dominated medieval thought about the nature of the universe, about heaven and hell and the world of finite beings. The hierarchy of the natural order was not limited to man's superiority over the rest of nature, but included the social order itself. The belief in man's equality before God within a universal hierarchy served to justify the belief in men's inequality before their fellow-men within the social order, which, like every other order in the universe, was inconceivable except in hierarchic terms.

Most societies today are structured hierarchically, affording to the few the financial or political privileges of high rank, and to the many below them the disadvantages of lowly birth. Even in democratic societies, the problem of overcoming the heredity principle which transmits social rank from parents to children, allocating social and economic privileges by birth rather than merit, is an intractable one for social reformers. It would be silly, however, to pretend that nothing has changed since the Middle Ages. Hierarchy and stratification continue to exist as they did then, but they no longer constitute an opaque feature of social organization—the way things are of their very nature. They have become transparent, questionable. Social stratification is perceived no longer as an inalienable characteristic of social life but as an accomplished feature of social development and the outcome of historical contingencies. Modern Western society is characteristically one whose particular structure is perceived as changeable.

It is difficult for us to imagine the opaqueness of the social structure in the Middle Ages, the hard objectivity of the hierarchic social order which was immutable because it was considered natural, unquestionable because it was made in the image of God.[2] Johan Huizinga relates how the ideas of nobility and chivalry still impressed the medieval mind as the dominant forms of life even after the demise of feudalism:

There are, first of all, the estates of the realm, but there are also the trades, the state of matrimony and that of virginity, the state of sin. At court there are the 'four estates of body and mouth': bread-masters, cupbearers, carvers, and cooks. In the Church there are sacerdotal orders and monastic orders. Finally, there are the different orders of chivalry. That which, in medieval thought, establishes unity in the very dissimilar meanings of the word, is the conviction that every one of these groupings represents a divine institution, an element of the organism of creation emanating from the will of God, constituting an actual entity, and being, at bottom, as venerable as the angelic hierarchy.[3]

---

[2] According to the medieval conception of natural law, all created things—including the social order—are constituted by their Creator and governed by a rule of conduct which is knowable, in principle, by the light of unaided reason. The basic standard of right and wrong, therefore, is absolute, not relative to a human authority or to membership of a particular church. But original sin distorts the understanding and makes divine revelation a necessary aid to full and correct knowledge of the contents of natural law. Since the Church is the guardian of revelation, this means that what is natural and absolutely binding depends on the interpretation of the Church. The nature of society—and of the Church—is relative to the Church.

[3] Huizinga (1972), p.55.

It was not until the French Revolution that the social order was demystified and people could see what had always been too obvious to discern: the place of human greed and exploitation in the construction of allegedly divine and immutable institutions. The failure of the higher ranks of society to behave in a manner appropriate to their calling was not sufficient to pro-voke an attack on the old order. The sacredness of rank itself and the sanctity of the social order rather than the failure of individuals to live up to their noble vocation secured the stability of the hierarchic system in the Middle Ages. If religion was dynamic, the same could not be said for society:

> To the Catholic soul the unworthiness of the persons never compromises the sacred character of the institution. The morals of the clergy, or the decadence of chivalrous virtues, might be stigmatized without deviating for a moment from the respect due to the Church or the nobility as such. The estates of society cannot but be venerable and lasting, because they all have been ordained by God. The conception of society in the Middle Ages is static, not dynamic.[4]

The stability of the system does not mean that conflicts and wars were any less frequent and fierce than might be expected in a less stable or more dynamic society. Monarchs can dispute power, peasants can rebel against particular forms of oppression without any threat to the institutions by which they are governed. Despoiled by the Hundred Years War, plundered, exploited and ravaged by officials, bandits and famine, medieval peasants complained and rebelled, some churchmen supported them and the nobility characteristically expressed a sentimental compassion for their miseries. But always the solution was greater compassion. The social order itself was inviolate, sacred, intolerant of scrutiny. The theology of man's equality before God was a popular ideal, preached most eloquently by the nobility, the wealthy, and the Pope, who liked to hear the repetition of the humbling admonition 'sic transeat gloria mundi' as he staggered in procession under the weight of imperial jewellery and privilege.

Disparity of wealth in the Middle Ages, far from being a scandal of religion, was a demonstration of its value and a proof

---

[4] *Ibid.*, p.56.

of its validity. The equality of man was a moral ideal emptied of its modern implications by the exclusively religious context which conditioned its interpretation and which linked the social order to the other orders of the universe, created by God as unchanging manifestations of his glory. The political significance of the doctrine thus interpreted was to prevent the social order from being examined on its own merits, extracted from the religious cosmos and analysed in terms of its own internal mechanisms. The solution to suffering and poverty was to change men's hearts, not their institutions.

This doctrine of equality served to legitimate the material inequality which might otherwise have stimulated resentment and provoked revolution. Suffering varied in this life, according to men's station. But the ultimate suffering of death and the judgement of God restored the balance. In an age when death and judgement were to the forefront of men's consciousness, material inequality was but an indicator of God's inscrutable designs and a powerful stimulus to faith. The ethical obligations of Christianity centred on charity and prayer; the intellectual task was to understand the world, not to change it, and religion in many forms was the only source of legitimate explanation and understanding. Keith Thomas documents the power of the supernatural over the minds of medieval English peasants, their clergy and masters, and the necessity, even when social change was at issue, of finding some justification for it in a source of supernatural origin, religious or magical. Long after the Reformation, the physical and social world was still throbbing with supernatural life, permeated by the influence of saints and devils and witches. Even the Protestants, who did most to rid religion of its magical associations with material signs and omens, found the disenchantment of the world a more unpalatable idea than was anticipated in the reformers' theology:

A Protestant clergyman did not set out to promise health and worldly success to those who followed the word of God; he tried to bring spiritual consolation, not the hope of material prosperity. But until the end of the seventeenth century, and in many cases long afterwards, the overwhelming majority of clerical writers and pious laymen sincerely believed that there was a link between man's moral behaviour and his fortune in this world, whether in bodily health or professional success. It was impossible to reiterate the view that sin was the most probable cause of misfortune without conveying the implication that godliness was somehow linked with prosperity. Of course, the preachers would have explained that it was only spiritual prosperity with which they were concerned, and that God's promises related solely to the life to come. But their flock only too often took a cruder view, and so on occasions did the clergy themselves.[5]

If the cosmology or world-view which dominated Catholic thinking throughout the Middle Ages had the effect of including the social order among the other 'facts' of the universe and making it as impervious to questioning as the other hierarchies of the supernatural order, one would expect formal theology to reflect that view and to have little of substance to say on the subject of social justice. Theologians like Aquinas, Molina, Lessius and others were indeed preoccupied with the problem of justice. But their distinction between commutative and distributive justice, and the greater stress they placed on the former rather than the latter, slants their moral teaching towards the rights of the individual and the defence of private property. Even at the end of the nineteenth century, when events had shifted the Church towards a concern with distributive justice, the official moral teaching was still essentially Thomistic and medieval. It is instructive to learn from the official *Catholic Encyclopaedia* at the beginning of the twentieth century that the unemployed have no right in justice to work, nor the poor to be fed and clothed:

We sometimes say that the unemployed have a right to work, that the needy have a right to assistance, and it may be conceded that those phrases are quite correct, provided that such a right is understood as a claim in charity, not as a claim in justice.

There is no hint in this document that the medieval social order might be seen as a historical, social construction, as changeable as the territorial boundaries of monarchs. It is not a subject of moral inquiry, like slavery or the other social orders which preceded it, but an immutable fact of nature:

[5] Thomas (1977), p.103.

It is the function of the State to protect its subjects in their rights and to govern the whole body for the common good. Authority for this purpose is given to the State by nature and by God, the Author of man's social nature.

These rights of the citizen include the right to private property:

The right . . . to acquire property which is useful and necessary for an orderly human life is one of man's natural rights and it cannot be taken away by the State.

and the right to the profits of that property:

. . . increase in value, even unearned increment as it is called, belongs to the owner of that which thus increases. . . .

Clearly the theologians here were not entirely the politically neutral interpreters of God's revelation on the human condition which they purported to be. Societies, as moral persons, have the same rights as individuals, and:

The Catholic Church, founded by God Himself, is a perfect society and independent of the State. She has her rights, God-given, and necessary for the attainment of her end, and justice is violated if these are unwarrantably interfered with.[6]

Written in 1908, this teaching still carries echoes of the godless hordes of Italian nationalists clamouring for possession of Church property. Formulated in the Middle Ages, this moral theology is an ethic of medieval society, freezing man into the hierarchic order then established and wedding the Church indissolubly to that order. Sociologists since Emile Durkheim have explored the relationship between religion and society and the manner in which the worship of God tends covertly to support a particular structure of society, and traditionalist theologians, on the whole, tend to dispute that relationship or to locate it in the distance past or in someone else's religion. But no one could have put Durkheim's point more succinctly—if unwittingly—than the theologian of the *Catholic Encyclopaedia*:

[6] *Catholic Encyclopaedia*, London, 1910, Vol. 8, pp.571ff.; St Thomas Aquinas, *Summa Theologica*, 2a 2ae qq.57–8.

The Catholic doctrine of justice will be found one of the main safeguards of order, peace and progress. It gives the State ample authority for the attainment of its legitimate end, while it effectually bars the road to tyranny and violence . . . and when socialists and anarchists threaten to abrogate those laws and make new ones which will regulate men's rights more equitably, no rational defence of the old order is possible.

The defence of wealth and property, while it became a central feature of moral theology in the Middle Ages and remained unambiguously so until recent years, was not the last Catholic word on the subject. The early Franciscans, in particular, found much to criticize in the wealth of the Church and in the life-styles of its leaders. But for St Francis and his first disciples, the scandal was not poverty but wealth; and not the distribution of wealth but its possession. His admonition 'let us hate our body with its vices and sins' illustrates not only his own attitude to poverty as a necessary means of detachment from the world but also the dominant Catholic view of life as a war between matter and spirit, body and soul, the world and the Church. For St Francis, the command to follow Christ demanded poverty. But later Franciscans, notably St Bonaventure, modified this teaching and made life a little easier for Franciscans as well as for everyone else who found the vocation to poverty attractive in theory. Provided the Franciscans held property on trust from the Church—its true owner—their way of life was one of poverty even if appearances suggested otherwise. Charity replaced poverty as the ultimate virtue and material goods were—or could be—an important means of exercising it.

Thus, the beliefs of Catholics were informed and sanctioned by a moral theology which was individualist in its application and which conceived of a social problem only in terms of the threats to the social order posed by heretics and unbelievers. The idea of social reform as an ethical consequence of Christian belief did not occur to them because it was not an option within the system of thought that defined their universe. Parts of that system would be challenged by the Reformation, but Catholics would survive, depleted in number but cosmologically intact, until the twentieth century. Meanwhile, they struggled to save their own souls by charity and prayer and by the grace of a transcendent God mediated through the sacraments of the

Church, always assured that the inequalities of this world
would be corrected by an upward or downward passage to the
next. The terrifying prospect of God's judgement was a powerful enough image in the theological and devotional literature to
make the equitable distribution of wealth seem rather irrelevant. If the picture appears crude and 'medieval' to contemporary Catholics, this is a measure of the profound changes that
have affected Catholic beliefs and attitudes since the late 1950s
when the old Catholic theology still survived, with relatively
little modification, in its medieval form.

The political machinery of the medieval papacy was directed
towards the subjugation of the secular powers but its effectiveness never matched the rhetoric of the popes. The famous Bull
of Pope Boniface VIII, *Unam Sanctam*, issued in 1302, declared:

. . . there are two swords, namely the spiritual and the temporal. . . .
It is necessary that one sword should be beneath the other, and that
the temporal authority should be subjected to the spiritual power. . . .
Clearly we must acknowledge that the spiritual power excels any
earthly power both in dignity and in nobility, in as much as spiritual
things excel temporal. . . . Hence we declare, state and define that it is
altogether necessary for salvation for every human creature to be
subject to the Roman Pontiff.

The extent to which the reality of European politics corre-
sponded to the ideals of Boniface is a matter of historical debate
and historians today are generally agreed in regarding such imperialism in the late Middle Ages as papal posturing, a blend
of wishful thinking and myth-making. The secular rulers of
Europe were not trembling at the thunderings of the Pope nor
were their kingdoms dependent on his goodwill.[7] Prior to the
Reformation, papal power in the temporal sphere had been
considerably weakened and the Pope's spiritual authority had
declined. If the old claims were still being made, the purpose
was to strengthen the Pope's control of the faithful rather than
to strike fear in the hearts of the lapsed. The Reformation was
not caused by papal imperialism but by papal weakness. As
Geoffrey Barraclough notes, the medieval papacy had abdi-
cated its responsibilities:

[7] See Barraclough (1968), Chadwick (1964), Hay (1966).

. . . and it was only when, at the Council of Trent, the papacy put its house in order, and again took its religious responsibilities seriously, that it was able to compete, and to win back the leadership and esteem which the medieval papacy had forfeited.[8]

The Reformation, for all its ultimate religious and political consequences, had no immediate effect on the legitimacy of the distinction between Church and world which prevailed in medieval Catholicism. True, it abolished the institutional priesthood as the mediator of grace and elevated the status of lay activity in the world, thereby re-shuffling the contents of the two concepts by making holy some activities which were hitherto neutral, if not worldly. But the division of society into the religious and the secular, the contrast between holiness and worldliness and the conception of the Church as a distinctive community remained. God and the supernatural still dominated ideas and constrained behaviour, even if personal attachment to religious values may have been grudging or feigned. Neither before nor after the Reformation did religious commitment confirm the romantic notion of societies integrated into a moral unity by common bonds of religious beliefs and practices. The French historian, Jean Delumeau, has argued that Catholicism in pre-Reformation Europe was, in fact, a minority religion largely confined to the cities, leaving the massive populations in the rural areas free to practise their ancient paganism and superstition.[9] And Keith Thomas has shown that social and political pressure to conform tended to conceal the extent of scepticism and irreligion in post-Reformation England. Given the right conditions, an apparently orthodox and compliant society can soon manifest depths of disbelief previously unsuspected:

The relative freedom of the Interregnum brought much of this endemic scepticism into the open. In 1648 the authors of the Blasphemy Ordinance of that year found it necessary to prescribe punishments for those who denied immortality, cast doubt on the Scriptures, rejected Christ and the Holy Ghost, and even denied that there was a God or that he was almighty. . . . The Socinians denied

[8] Barraclough (1968), p.196.
[9] Delumeau (1978).

the divinity of Christ. The Ranters denied the immortality of the soul, the literalness of the Resurrection, the overriding authority of the Scriptures, and the physical existence of Heaven and Hell. Like the Familists, they still used such concepts, but chose to treat them symbolically: Heaven was when men laughed, ran one version, Hell was when they were in pain.[10]

But even in that heady period the scepticism released could not match the political and social significance of the religion it railed against. Political and social reformers during the English Civil War found that their proposals for change required justification in religious terms if they were to have any chance of success.[11]

The Council of Trent consolidated the authority of the Pope within the Catholic Church and in place of the lax and inefficient organization of the late Middle Ages created an effective weapon against any further decline of spiritual authority. The post-Tridentine Church was a bureaucratic machine intended to counter ideas and attitudes which deviated from official orthodoxy; it was a highly centralized communications system designed to transmit and receive information necessary to ensure compliance and to prevent any further erosion of Catholicism. Orthodoxy took on a new status and significance in a Church that was no longer carelessly confident of its control over its members' consciences. Hierarchy and clericalism were given a new prominence, in reaction to the reformers' demands for a universal priesthood and a sacerdotal democracy. New rules and schemes were drawn up to ensure the constant exposure of the laity to the traditional teaching of the Church and the Inquisitorial weapon was used with increasing zeal to defend the Church against heresy. The printing press became a means of diffusing orthodox doctrine contained in the official catechism drawn up by the Council, but it was also a vehicle for the spread of error in publications judged to endanger faith and morals. The Roman Index of banned books became a permanent institution, complementing the Inquisition in the purge of heresy and the defence of doctrinal integrity and rigidity. Besieged by the reformers' demands and

[10] Thomas (1977), p.202.
[11] *Ibid.*, p.164ff.

political threats, alarmed by the degree of ignorance and laxity among her own clergy, the Church was closing ranks. The Tridentine Reformation, or Counter-Reformation as it is called, was a renewal of the Church following the moral corruption and organizational ineptitude which characterized it during the later Middle Ages and which, in the eyes of the reformers, rendered it ineffective for the task of evangelization. In a sense, the Reformation and the Counter-Reformation were both caused by the same movement of spiritual renewal which links the Franciscans with the Calvinists, the Lutherans with the Jesuits—a movement which hitherto had been confined to the periphery of the Church and checked by its institutionalization in religious congregations and monasteries, only to explode into life at the charismatic touch of Luther. The Council of Trent was not called to give sympathetic consideration to Luther's proposition, but to define the truth and to ward off the threat of disintegration posed by Luther's doctrine. The bishops met at Trent in a spirit of militancy, not inquiry. Their attitude was one of alarm at the unforeseeable consequences for the Church if the spread of the new ideas was not halted. The historic decision of Trent was to close ranks against the world and to reform the Church by reconstituting it as a ghetto.

Looked at from the Catholic viewpoint, the world had shown its antagonism and had become an even greater threat to salvation. A spirit of worldliness had infiltrated the Church and the exhortations to prayer and the sacramental life embodied in the conciliar decrees were part of a general movement of spirituality aimed at combating this. But the real danger was the threat to the very existence of the Roman Church if the Lutheran teaching on priesthood and justification was not clearly exposed as heresy and vigorously expunged from the Catholic mind. Marriage, education and the family were important areas of concern for the Council in creating a social structure for Catholics that would best inoculate them against the world as it now loomed, larger and more dangerous than ever. New instructions were issued for the training of priests to re-evangelize the Catholic world in the Tridentine spirit. Regular attendance at Mass and a new stress on the sermon as a teaching instrument formed part of the drive to control beliefs. In matters of conscience the laity was encouraged to have frequent recourse to the priestly guidance, admonitions and absolution available in the sacrament of Penance. Allied to this was the development of a casuistic moral theology which gave teeth to the Church's injunctions and quantified sin and merit in the system of spiritual arithmetic which formed the Catholic ethic and which survived until the Second Vatican Council.

It is easy today to feel somewhat contemptuous of the ghetto mentality of the Catholic Reformation, as if the Pope and bishops faced the same conditions and options at Trent in the sixteenth century as their successors did in the 1960s. The decision of the bishops of the Second Vatican Council to embrace the world in a spirit of Johannine forgiveness and reconciliation was not one option among many; they could scarcely have acted otherwise in the circumstances, as I shall try to show, and for many sociologically-astute participants and observers their decision was a long-overdue act of resignation to social and political pressures, not the remarkable breakthrough of the Spirit popularly imagined. Similarly, the Council of Trent, faced with the same task of preserving what could be preserved of the structure of the Church in the face of the theological and political challenge to its integrity, adopted the only feasible policy in the circumstances.

The ghetto was inaugurated. From being a far-flung empire of indeterminate allegiance, the Church after Trent was moving swiftly in the direction of closed communities of the faithful, dotted throughout the globe, their members walled by rules, injunctions and sanctions from contact with the world outside, their eyes fixed on Rome as the centre of authority and the source of right thinking. The Church and the world had always stood in a relation of antagonism. The effect of the reformation and Counter-Reformation was to increase that hostility and to give it a new social and cultural expression.

Two features of the Counter-Reformation were crucial for the formation of Catholic attitudes to the world. Firstly, the spirit of militant orthodoxy, cultivated and fostered by the new congregation of the Jesuits, gave wide expression to the concern at Rome to strengthen papal authority by providing an unambiguous definition of the Catholic mind and promoting unswerving loyalty to Rome as the only safeguard against the world. The Society of Jesus was found in 1540 and rapidly spread in number and influence as the mainspring of the Tridentine reform. Jesuits took a special vow of obedience to the Pope and became his private army spreading the message of moral renewal and undertaking the theological instruction of clergy and influential laity that would consolidate the centralization of the Church and strengthen the authority of the Pope. St Ignatius, founder of the Jesuits, has these 'Rules for thinking with the Church' in his famous *Spiritual Exercises*, which was a manual of instructions for the Jesuit director of souls and intended to be used throughout the congregation as an instrument for the formation of the Catholic heart and mind:

We should put away completely our own opinion and keep our minds ready and eager to give our entire obedience to our Holy Mother the hierarchical Church, Christ our Lord's undoubted Spouse. . . . All the Church's commandments should be spoken of favourably, our minds being always eager to find arguments in her defence, never in criticism. . . . To arrive at complete certainty, this is the attitude of mind we should maintain: I will believe that the white object I see is black if that should be the decision of the hierarchical Church, for I believe that linking Christ our Lord, the Bridegroom, and His Bride, the Church, there is one and the same Spirit, ruling and guiding us for our souls' good.

The second feature was the so-called 'Devotio Moderna', the spirituality of simple piety and common-sense mysticism that originated in the Low Countries in the fifteenth century and expressed that rejection of worldliness and triumphalism which characterized the reforming spirit of Protestants and Catholics alike. Chief among the documents of the period which capture the new spirituality is the famous treatise, *The Imitation of Christ*, attributed to Thomas à Kempis.[12] In this little book, which has been a best-seller for centuries and which still remains a widely-read classic of devotional literature, the scandal of a Church steeped in worldliness and led astray by activism is contrasted with the simple mysticism of the pious Christian, who imitates Christ by retreating from the world into the sanctuary of communion with God. There is a stress on the transitory nature of this life, of its sufferings and petty vanities,

[12] Probably written by Gerhard Groot: see Hyma (1924).

an awareness of death and the life to come, and a general sense of the utter irrelevance of secular institutions and activities which distract men from the contemplation of their final end:

Turn with all your heart to God, and give up this miserable world, and your soul will find rest. Learn to despise outward things, and attend only to the state of your soul, and you will feel the coming of the kingdom of God within you. . . . It is certain that learned speeches do not make a man holy and just; it is a virtuous life that makes him dear to God. I would rather feel sorrow for my sins than be able to define it. If you knew the whole Bible by heart, and all that philosophers have said, what use would it all be to you without the love of God and grace? 'Vanity of vanities and all is vanity', except to love God and to serve him alone.

When a man values things as they really are, and not as the world says or thinks they are, he is truly wise and has learned from God, not men. He who knows how to live an inward life and to give little heed to outward things need not choose particular places or wait for particular times for his works of piety. . . .

The predominance of these two aspects of Catholic spirituality in the life and literature of the Church after the Reformation fashioned Catholic attitudes in accordance with the spirit of Trent and gave an essential spiritual dimension to the organizational and theological reforms of the Council. The 'Devotio Moderna' provided the Church with that moral and spiritual zeal which the reformers—both Protestant and Catholic—saw as conspicuously lacking in the medieval Church and, at the same time, radically reinforced the separation of the Church and the world as two antagonistic realms and ways of life. The militant activism of the Jesuits channelled this other-worldly spirituality away from the individualistic interpretation which might easily be placed on *The Imitation of Christ*—the book enjoyed immense prestige among Protestants, even though some passages show the author's traditional Catholic belief in, and respect for, the hierarchical system—towards the integral Catholicism centred on Rome. Traditional Catholicism since the Reformation is the offspring of this alliance between the pious, romantic Christianity of à Kempis and the Roman, bureaucratized Christianity of the Jesuits. Between them, Ignatius and à Kempis drew the Catholic map of the universe and defined the boundaries of Church and world as never before with such clarity. Catholics knew where the world began and where it ended, what mattered for salvation and what was irrelevant. They knew that the world was irrelevant to the Church. The antagonism which had always been their characteristic attitude towards the world was now given renewed life and significance, and when the political consequences of the Reformation took shape in the nineteenth century that antagonism would be even more marked. Democracy, nationalism and science would threaten Catholic theology and organization in a different way and would pose problems for the Church which ultimately would prove insuperable by traditional means. Until then, it seemed reasonable to pursue a policy of building and consolidating the internal unity of the Church and of resisting the world which had rejected it.

2
The Emergence of the Modern World

If anyone thinks that the Roman Pontiff can and should reconcile and accommodate himself to progress, liberalism and modern civilization, let him be anathema.

Pope Pius IX, *Syllabus of Errors*, 1864

When Pope Pius IX summarized, in eighty propositions, the ideas and attitudes gaining currency throughout Europe and challenging the basic assumptions of Catholic orthodoxy, a new phase had begun in the relationship between the Church and the world. The Pope's final condemnation, quoted above, is comprehensive almost to the point of being incomprehensible. It is not very illuminating to read theologians' attempts to capture its precise meaning. The denunciation of civilization was taken from an earlier document, *Jamdudum Cernimus*, issued in 1861 to condemn the anti-Catholic legislation enacted in Piedmont against monasteries, convents and the religious basis of education and marriage. This legislation was promoted explicitly in the name of modernity and progress. While the Pope's main concern was to defend the Church against this invasion of its territory, both he and the secular authorities in Turin in effect conspired to link the Church with an unchanging past and to identify all instances of social change as emanating from a phenomenon recently emerged: the modern world. The repetition of the *Jamdudum* formula in the more general context of the Syllabus of Errors shows a process of mystification at work in which the term 'modern' acquires a political and institutional significance over and above its meaning in everyday usage. The Pope was not condemning in 1864 the legislation he had already condemned in 1861; he was acknowledging the presence of, and, in part, helping to create,

a new force within the Catholic territories under his command—a climate of opinion which would crystallize against
the Church not simply in respect of *specific* Catholic beliefs and
practices but in respect of its *raison d'être* and of the legitimacy of
religion itself.

It is conventional to date the birth of the modern world at the
French Revolution of 1789. Before then, there was no world to
which the Church could conceivably be made relevant. The
Church itself was the measure of relevance, the creator of
standards, the court of appeal which assessed the validity of
thought and judged the propriety of the actions of most people
within Catholic territory. From its early brash entry into this
medieval land of gods and shrines, of cassocks and inquisitions,
the world would succeed, in the twentieth century, in wresting
this cultural and political hegemony from the Church—a
victory constitutionally recognized in most countries by the
formal separation of church and state—to such a degree that
the Church today can no longer credibly dispute secular claims
and must submit its policy and teaching to a new standard of
relevance. It is not the catechism that determines modern
Catholic consciousness, but the economic, political and scientific developments since the French Revolution which constitute modernity.

When we speak of the modern world, we are referring to a
specific revolution in thought, politics and economics which
radically altered the material and social conditions and the
consciousness of people whose way of life was structured by
them. This revolution created a disjunction between religion
and the demands of everyday life. The picture of the world
presented by the medieval church, elaborated in its teaching
and discipline and reflected in the institutions and organizations which formed the background of mundane activity—this
picture was no longer recognizable. People were no longer
living their beliefs. This is not to say that all, or even most, lived
piously in the Middle Ages. But the nature of their work, their
relationships, their political allegiances, their notions of truth
and falsehood were conditioned by religion and were subject to
validation by Church teaching and disciplines. Religion
determined their consciousness and measured the worth of
their social existence. Religion and the social order were inter-

woven to the point that it was never clear where one ended and the other began.

The modern world is a process, not a static institutional form, and its development was in train long before the French Revolution. That event was a dramatic sign of its presence—a manifesto of the movement of opinion and struggle for change which began at the Renaissance and which continues today to combat the vestiges of that old order in which the observable world is permeated by the supernatural. The unifying and dominant ideal which prevails throughout this process is the ideal of liberty. It is this which underlies the various antitheses which mark the struggle between the old order and the new, between the Church and the world: reason against tradition, science against dogma, tolerance against oppression, individualism against collectivism, self-determination against despotism. Democracy, capitalism and science were at war with authoritarianism, feudalism and dogma. The transformation of society from medieval to modern was an organic process of change in which the production and distribution of power, wealth and knowledge in the Middle Ages were questioned, ridiculed, or violently opposed by intellectuals and social groups whose revolutionary ideals and activities converged in a way that was never intended.

Hobbes, Mill and Locke in politics, Galileo and Newton in science, Adam Smith in economics did not conspire to synthesize their ideas and to promote modern Western society. But their revolutions were interdependent and their work converged, as fundamental changes in the political, economic and cognitive fields must always converge and stimulate change in the other areas of society. We are not free to choose one without the others. As Max Weber has shown—and as John Wesley earlier noted with regret—the Protestant revolution in theology had the ironic and unintended effect of stimulating acquisitiveness and the growth of capitalism. What people are prepared to believe, and on what authority they are to believe it, is not a decision which can be made independently of the type of economy and government which control the rest of their lives. The Enlightenment philosophers, Voltaire and Montesquieu, who argued passionately for freedom of thought and expression, neither imagined nor desired the social and political revolutions that followed in the name of that freedom. They were opposed to the Church, not to the authoritarian governments of their time:

The men of the age had an unlimited belief in the powers of human reason and in the possibility of an immediate social transformation if only the legislature could be won over to the cause of reason and progress. But they had no desire for political or social revolution and little sympathy with democratic ideals. Almost to a man the philosophers, like their predecessors the English Whigs, were on the side of property and order . . . 'I doubt', writes Voltaire, 'if the populace has either the time or the capacity for education. . . . It seems to be essential that there should be ignorant beggars . . . We have never pretended to enlighten shoemakers and servant girls. . . .'[1]

It is a popular belief today that there is some natural affinity between capitalism and Catholicism and that the actual, historical conflict between the Church and socialism stems from some intrinsic contradiction between the two systems. Until the eve of the French Revolution, the Church was opposed not only to scientific and political freedom but to that freedom in the economic sphere also—to the capitalist system. The Church tolerated capitalism only when it was politically expedient to do so and when there was no apparent alternative if the Church authorities were to salvage their property and their control of Catholic beliefs. The medieval guilds which inhibited industrialization, the idealization of poverty and the condemnation of usury were features of a Catholic type of society conducive to religious compliance, but it was not a society in which capitalism could develop. The economic developments in Protestant England and Holland were made possible only because the traditional social and political constraints on freedom of thought and movement had been overturned by the rising middle classes in order to create the conditions for the development of free trade. A feudal economy could not be replaced by capitalism until the feudal order itself was transformed and until those with money to speculate had the political power and moral freedom to do so.

The early leaders of the Enlightenment campaigned for a

[1] Dawson (1972), pp.28–9.

moral and intellectual revolution against the obscurantism of
the Church. They were not advocating democracy or, indeed,
any change in the political sphere that might mitigate the
intolerance and despotism of Louis XIV. But whereas in
England the Enlightenment ideas fell on the pious ears of
Protestant individualists and could be turned to economic
advantage by the new capitalist class which already enjoyed
political freedom to explore and expand, in France the
bourgeoisie was tightly controlled in its commercial activities
by the state. Trade and industry was under state control and
there were not the independent financial institutions to stimulate capitalist expansion like the Dutch and English East India
Companies, the Bank of Amsterdam and the Bank of England.
In England the middle classes had already won the necessary
political freedom for economic development in the Puritan
revolution. Protestant piety could co-exist with science, democracy and capitalism, and Voltaire and Montesquieu discovered
in England a vigorous individualism, economic and social
prosperity, and open anti-clericalism. The major opposition to
their attempt to introduce new ideas into France came from the
Church, whose claim to absolute authority over thought and
morals was opposed, with equal intolerance, by a complete
rejection of religion and a campaign of anti-clerical and anti-
Christian character which culminated in the blasphemous
celebration of the Feast of Reason in the Cathedral of Notre
Dame.

Freedom of trade, freedom of expression and thought, and
political liberalism are inextricably linked; the attempt to
liberate thought in sacred or secular affairs while at the same
time wishing to retain a feudal or despotic political system must
fail, as Luther learned after the Reformation, as Voltaire was to
learn when his campaign for a moral revolution was politicized
by Rousseau. The Church could not tolerate the moral transformation of society proposed by Voltaire. Since such a
transformation could not be confined to the arena of thought
and morality but carried in its train parallel revolutions in
the political and economic sphere, the Church would oppose
these with equal force. As political reactionaries, Luther and
Voltaire did not anticipate, and certainly did not desire, the
modern world that was born of their labours. Voltaire despised

the masses and had little sympathy with democratic ideals. The peasants who revolted against rising prices and new tax impositions in Germany and Holland and who looked to Luther for support must have found little for their comfort in his pamphlet 'Against the Murderous and Thieving Hordes of Peasants', in which he condemned their rebelliousness as 'poisonous, obnoxious and devilish' and assured the princes that it was God's work to slaughter them. If the Church opposed liberalism and capitalism it was not because the new political and economic systems as such were incompatible with religion but because the old order, the *Ancien Régime*, promoted an intellectual and moral subservience on the part of the laity which had become a constituent feature of Roman Catholicism. The modern world would not be born until it could wrest from the Church that control of beliefs that was crucial to its organization and essential to its structure as it had historically developed.

It was the work of Rousseau to translate the liberal ideas of the Enlightenment into an ideology that penetrated beyond the privileged classes and provided the spark that fired men's minds with the ideal of democracy. He preached the cause of the poor against the rich, of the individual against a society which he saw as an artificial constraint on the essential goodness of men. The source of evil in the world, of poverty and injustice, was not original sin but the corrupt structure of society. Rousseau's aim was to free men from an oppressive political and economic order and in its place to institute a society in which the fullest political participation was available to all. This could only be possible if the economic conditions were provided not by capitalism but by a form of peasant socialism in states small enough to facilitate democracy.

Thus Rousseau extended the logic of the Enlightenment to the political sphere; freedom of thought was to find its political expression in democracy and, he hoped, its economic expression in the agrarian distributivism of peasant society. But if Voltaire was horrified by Rousseau's political interpretation of his Enlightenment ideas, so too was Rousseau's economic ideal to be frustrated and his movement for democracy to be taken up by bourgeois leaders who had little interest in poverty or justice or, for that matter, in the rights of man.

The victory of democracy in the American revolution—of a

social order based on an ideal of fraternity and equality—was the justification of liberalism for French idealists who returned from America, no longer to preach liberty as a moral ideal, but to demand its embodiment in society and the abolition of the *Ancien Régime*. The distribution of wealth in France had changed the structure of power but not the system of government. The development of commercial and industrial capital had shifted the balance of economic power from the aristocracy to the middle classes. This change in the financial system was irreconcilable with the political structure which excluded the middle classes from the control of taxation and from the participation in government which were necessary if risks were to be taken and capital invested. The new wealth of the bourgeoisie gave them prosperity without social status, economic power without political control. A government of nobles and priests was not relevant to bourgeois aspirations nor adequate to the new demands of capital. Norman Hampson gives this description of pre-revolutionary France:

There was not much in the organization of manufacturing industry to encourage radical thinking or a sense of change. Almost everywhere, production was controlled by guilds, whose *raison d'être* was the restraint of competition, to avoid over-production for a market assumed to be static. Guilds were semi-religious fraternities as well as economic organizations and their processions, banners and rituals were part of a medieval past. Guild relationships were very different from those of industrial capitalism. The journeymen and apprentices, sometimes living under their master's roof, did not regard themselves simply as his employees, and the economic interests of the whole team were more complementary than competitive. One reason for this was the fact that wage rates—like so much else—were often fixed by tradition.[2]

The French Revolution was the violent expression of the frustration of competing and often inarticulate interests: liberalism, democracy and capitalism were the forces of unrest which provoked the revolt; when joined by the peasant masses and the urban communes the Revolution took on a life of its own, beyond the control of any of its participants. It destroyed

[2] Hampson (1970), pp.57–8.

the rights and privileges of the Church which were protected by the *Ancien Régime,* divided the clergy between those who accepted the new state Catholicism of the Civil Constitution and those who remained loyal to Rome, enriched the wealthy with the spoils of the Church and impoverished the poor by the inflationary consequences of that enrichment and by the legislation dissolving their corporations and leaving them as a disorganized rabble with nothing to lose by violence. The state Catholicism of the 1790 Civil Constitution became the religion of nature, designed by Robespierre to provide a moral and political order appropriate to the economic and scientific changes of the modern world. The old religion had passed with the old state and a new order required its spiritual expression: 'All is changed in the physical order; all must change in the moral and political order. Half of the world revolution is already done; the other half has still to be achieved.' That other half—the religion of the Supreme Being—was intended to 'strike a mortal blow at fanaticism', according to Robespierre, and to be the moral justification of his reign of terror.

The effect of the Revolution was to identify republicanism with anti-clericalism and the revolutionary ideals in France with irreligion. The anti-clericalism of the Enlightenment became inextricably linked to the political liberalism and economic changes that followed it; to be 'modern' was to approve of the new order and to reject the *Ancien Régime* and its religious base. Modernity came in a package; it was not available in its separate components. The modern world was seen as incompatible with Catholicism because the history and fortunes of the Church were for so long and so closely wedded to the *Ancien Régime* that any attack on the one was perceived inevitably as a threat to the other.

The economic and material consequences of the Revolution were disastrous for the Church. In Germany and in France, the Church had been reduced to complete dependence on the secular power, its privileges abrogated, its priests and religious in France and elsewhere persecuted, exiled or executed. Liberalism, the spirit of the age, had won the battle with tradition, but there were few liberals to rejoice at the victory. The course of the Revolution was fatal to the hopes of almost every party, as wave followed wave of destruction in the cause of liberty.

The whole period from 1789 to 1870 was an age of violence and revolution that shook the foundations of the Catholic Church with a force that had not been achieved by the Reformation. The world that was born of this explosion was a challenge to Catholicism of the most traumatic kind. In medieval days, dissent, even heresy, might go away or be tamed in a monastic institution—or at least be geographically contained in an area whose boundaries were relatively clear and stable. How could the Church respond to the wholesale persecution of its officials and attacks on its property as the bandwagon of liberalism careered through the post-Revolutionary years into the nineteenth century, manned by successive groups whose interests conflicted with those of the old order; now by frustrated capitalists, now by inflamed workers; later by socialists and communists and finally by nationalists—all in search of freedom and, in France and Italy, all identifying the Catholic Church as a major source of their frustration?

It is a recurring and basic theme of this book that the response of the Church to the modern world at any particular point in history cannot be understood at the level of the theological and philosophical accounts later constructed to justify that response. The history of the modern Church—as distinct from the Church of the Middle Ages—can be shown to be one of repeated attempts at accommodation to a variety of powerful secular movements and institutions whose instability left the Church politically and theologically compromised in a manner which has been progressively more difficult for the Church to assimilate. The history of the Church is not simply its past; sociologically, at least, the Church *is* its history, and contemporary Catholicism cannot be understood except in its historical depth. We cannot comprehend the Church's organizational structure, its theology, or its development since the 1960s without searching the past for the key to the interpretation of Catholicism today. The Church today does not have the same autonomy and freedom to respond to the secular world as it had in any other period of its history. Its response to the world of the sixties was already conditioned by its response to the French Revolution, and one can only understand the contemporary Church in the context of successive crises throughout the period since that event and before.

The extent to which theological reflection or political interest was the dominant factor in the major decisions of policy and doctrine during that period varied and, obviously, cannot be determined with any precision. But it can be shown that many of the most significant decisions—even some of a most innocently religious kind, like the Marian dogmas or the fostering of the lay piety of the nineteenth century—were not what was claimed for them. They were 'contaminated' by political interest, not only in the sense that all ideas are necessarily so in some degree, but in the sense that the Church was no longer taking the initiative and these decisions were being forced upon it by circumstances outside its control. The theology was a gloss on the political strategy, and the effect, finally, was that the Church was robbed of its capacity to make any statement of substance on the subject which legitimated its existence: theology. But that is the end of the story. In the immediate aftermath of the French Revolution, the Church was still a long way from that position, and Catholics were not yet witnessing to its effects on their commitment.

From the desperate material situation of the Revolution, the Church was first rescued by the Concordat with Napoleon which restored the life of the Church in some measure and struck the first blow for papal supremacy over national bishops and clergy. Bonaparte and the Church were forced into an alliance. He could not rebuild France without the Church; the Church could not recover its authority and possessions without Bonaparte. In the Concordat, Roman Catholicism, though not defined as the official religion, was recognized as that of the majority of the people of France, thereby strengthening the position of Rome and inhibiting the development of a French national church in opposition to it. Church property was restored in part and the Pope was free to depose bishops nominated by the state. Seminaries were reopened to replace the losses of ten years and the revival of the Church under the protection of a new political system began. In 1803, Napoleon's uncle, Mgr Fesch, was created one of four new French cardinals by Pope Pius VII. Pope and Emperor, rivals at one level, were partners at another: the restoration of the Church was bartered for the support and legitimation of the new state. The Church's moral authority was harnessed to the task of creating order and stability after the chaos of the Revolution and the state's power, in turn, was employed to reconstruct the shattered framework of the Catholic organization—though it was a partial reconstruction and a tamed organization compared with the old order; the balance of bargaining power lay decidedly with the French ruler. In 1804, Napoleon was anointed Emperor by Pius VII and a monarchy as absolutist as the *Ancien Régime*—if considerably less Catholic—began its alliance with the Church. This increased the Pope's prestige with other states of Europe, notably Prussia, Russia, Piedmont. The Catholic catechism was revised to link obedience to God with loyalty to the French Emperor and it became part of the school curriculum. The protests of some of the French clergy—notably Lamennais—at this subjection of the Church to the secular powers passed unnoticed.

The Response of the Church

The restoration of the European monarchies in 1815, accomplished on a tide of widespread anti-revolutionary opinion and of romantic longing for the revival of medieval ideals and of harmony between Church and state, gave the Church spectacular opportunities to re-establish itself after the horrors of the Revolution and to recover its life, its status and its influence in secular society throughout the continent. One of the Church's most valued resources for this work of reconstruction was unavailable—still in exile awaiting recall after its suppression in 1773. The restoration of the Jesuits would, in the words of the papal bull *Sollicitudo*, by which the suppression was rescinded, restore to the Church '. . . ceaselessly tossed by the billows, those strong and experienced rowers who would conquer the might of the waves'. With the help of the Jesuits, and through a succession of concordats struck with the conservative governments throughout Europe, Rome secured not only a *modus vivendi* with secular states which gave freedom to teach, worship and organize the hierarchy in countries where the Church had previously been harassed or suppressed but, by obtaining state recognition of the Holy See, ensured that the revived Catholicism would be unambiguously Roman. Between 1789 and 1820, the number of state officials accredited to the Holy See almost doubled. The tension between Rome and national hierarchies, which had beset the Church since the Reformation, was resolved by diplomacy. The nineteenth century would see the fruits of this diplomatic achievement in the ultramontanist movement which elevated the status of the Pope and his Curial organization throughout the Catholic world and helped to centralize the Church and to increase its bureaucratic control over clergy and laity as never before.

The new alliance of throne and altar was the religious and civil expression of the Romantic Movement, which reached a peak of fervour at the end of the eighteenth century. The contrived medievalism of nineteenth-century Catholic piety, liturgy and philosophy was facilitated by the general yearning of Romanticism for the spiritual unity of the Middle Ages:

Those were beautiful, brilliant times, when Europe was a Christian country, and a single Christian faith dwelt in this humanized region of the world; one great communal interest united the most distant provinces of this vast realm of the spirit.[3]

The discovery of the harmony of the Middle Ages in contrast to the chaos of the Revolution, the aesthetic approach to ideas in contrast to the rationalism of the Enlightenment, the stress on inner experience and the reasoning of the heart in contrast to logic and scientific method . . . these characteristically Romantic attitudes are implicit in the writings of influential Catholic conservatives like Maistre and Bonald as they are explicit in Chateaubriand. Their revulsion towards the Revolution and its consequences drove all three to become passionate advocates of law-and-order Catholicism—that peculiarly French blend of authoritarian government and medieval religion which has been a significant feature of Catholicism in France down to the present day. It is difficult to avoid the conclusion of George Brandes that it was a bogus movement in spiritual terms, desiring more the restoration of a political tradition than the salvation of souls, seeking a panacea for lawlessness rather than

[3] Novalis, *Die Christenheit oder Europa*, 1799, quoted in Thorlby (1969), p.157.

a revival of religion.[4] The Romantics made good ideologues, but bad historians. They saw the Middle Ages as the golden age of spiritual health, of unity of faith and social solidarity. But the bliss of the Middle Ages was not obvious to the romantics of that period, like Thomas à Kempis. Conjuring an image of religious fervour out of the mists of early Christianity, he contrasted the laxity and sloth of medieval religion with that golden age:

O how great was the earnestness of all religious in the beginning of their holy institution! What a love of prayer they showed, what a zeal for victory! What perfect discipline was observed, what reverence and obedience to the rule of the superior shone in all! Abundant evidence to this day remains that these were indeed holy and perfect men, who fought so bravely, and trampled all the world beneath their feet! . . . O the lukewarmness and carelessness of our lives; how soon do we fall away from our first fervour; how soon do we even grow tired of life, for very sloth and tepidity! (*The Imitation of Christ*)

The restoration of Catholicism after the French Revolution was continued and consolidated by the man who dominated the Church and occupied a prominent place in European politics for over thirty years. Pius IX began his pontificate in 1846, after the corrupt and inefficient administration of Pope Gregory XVI had failed to use the political opportunities available to increase the Church's moral influence or to strengthen its alliances with the European powers. Gregory left the Church weak and discredited, and his departure was an occasion for general relief and reasonable expectation that his successor would provide firmer leadership. Pio Nono was not a disappointment in that respect. He was greeted enthusiastically, not only because his predecessor was dead but because, in his own right, Pope Pius IX gave every sign of sympathy with popular liberal ideas and with Italian nationalist aspirations. He gave its own government to the city of Rome and established an elective chamber in the Papal States with power of veto.

But he lacked the imagination to carry through a liberal policy when nationalists looked to him for leadership in bringing about the unification of Italy. Against their pleading for support against Austria, and against his own judgement of the

[4] Georg Brandes, quoted in Thorlby (1969), p.127.

justice and legitimacy of their cause, Pio Nono refused military aid and declared his neutrality, under threat of Austrian retaliation against the Church if he should do otherwise. The man who had caused wonder throughout Europe for his promotion of liberal ideas—'a pretty state we are in altogether', Robert Wilberforce had written in 1848, 'with a radical Pope teaching all Europe rebellion'—was now to cause similar wonder for his growing opposition to liberalism and his total commitment to papalism. His career as Pope became one of unmitigated conservatism and papal authoritarianism. The nationalists responded and, under Mazzini and Garibaldi, forced the Pope into exile at Gaetà. By 1860, all that was left of the Papal States was a small strip of land along the Western coast of Italy. Pius IX, who likened the Papal States to 'the robe of Jesus Christ', and who shared the view of most Catholics that they symbolized and made possible the exercise of spiritual leadership throughout the Catholic world, found himself presiding over a savage dispossession of the Church. His response was to tighten the reins by which he controlled that organization and to attack the world with the only power left at his command. By 1870, the Italian troops had virtually destroyed what remained of the Papal States and the Pope was imprisoned in the Vatican. The loss of his temporal power made the preservation and exaltation of the spiritual authority of the Pope seem all the more necessary. If the enemies of the Church had lost all fear of the papacy and could not be cowed by threats of physical force or damnation, then there was all the more reason for the Pope to protect what remained of the Church, to close its ranks and to control its membership more rigidly and intransigently than ever before. The Church and the world were implacable enemies; there could be no reconciliation with a world which had proved itself so unmistakably anti-religious. As Wilfred Ward expressed it: 'Pius IX took up the position that Christendom had apostatized. The appropriate action of Catholics was intense loyalty to the central power, unity among themselves, and separation from the outside world.'[5]

The Church in the nineteenth century faced a critical dilemma. The medieval order which Europe had known, which

5 Quoted in Vidler (1971), p.153.

the Church had dominated, was still much more than a memory that lingered in the minds of monarchs and prelates whose wealth and influence were threatened by its passing. The modern world which was coming to birth was not yet so firmly and indisputably established as its successor that the medieval powers should yield their empire without a struggle. The Church had always dealt imperiously with its enemies and it is not surprising if its response to threats of annihilation was to denounce the world and to counter-attack with whatever resources it could command. Pope Pius IX was an autocrat, but he was not an inept autocrat like his predecessor. His style was majestic, even if his confidence was shaken, and his concern for the Church in pursuing his policy of papal aggrandizement and bureaucratic efficiency was beyond question. If the world would not submit, at least its invasion of Catholic consciousness might be prevented by strengthening the Church's control over its membership.

This process of centralization was begun at the Counter-Reformation and Pius IX, in accelerating it, was acting within the norms of a centuries-old tradition. But his task was more difficult in the mid-nineteenth century, in that the enemy was no longer a specific heresy embodied in a particular group which could be circumscribed geographically and removed from contact with Catholics by a combination of political and economic sanctions. The Pope could not depend upon physical boundaries to prevent the incursion of ideas and attitudes which threatened his authority and the legitimacy of religion. If the ghetto was to survive its boundaries must be internalized, moralized, clearly drawn within the minds of Catholics; and if its inmates were not to succumb to the temptations of worldliness they must be protected by something warmer than theology, more positive than the fear of hell. Catholic loyalty to the Church and Catholic loyalty to the Pope were one and the same thing in the mind of Pio Nono and his Vatican theologians and the political alliances of the Church with the European powers gave him the opportunity to spread that message and to promote the identification of Church and Pope in areas where, historically, there was little enthusiasm for it. The goal was ultramontanism—the creation of maximum cultural and moral dependence on Rome, leaving Catholics with minimal attachment to the secular institutions which governed their everyday lives. But this *Roman* Catholicism could not be demanded and could not be expected in the climate of political opinion in Catholic countries unless the Pope could offer some rewards for the intensely Catholic life he required. Loyalty to Church and Pope could not compete with the new attractions of the modern world in terms of the old Catholic sanctions which existed to foster it. Piety must be made attractive for the laity. Catholic liturgy was too impersonal and doctrine was too arid to ensure the compliance of a laity whose commitment to religion—still more, to Rome—was under increasing strain. From the mid-nineteenth century, a new piety was made available which would spread throughout the Catholic world, fix the eyes of its clergy and laity firmly on Rome and provide a religion of the heart in place of the rational apologetics which, since the Enlightenment, had preoccupied the Church and its members. The organizational base for accomplishing this was already firmly secured since the Counter-Reformation. This was the major achievement of the Council of Trent, according to Jean Delumeau.[6] It succeeded in bringing a literate Catholicism to rural areas attached to pagan beliefs and poorly served by medieval clerics whose lack of proper training and virtual illiteracy left them ill-equipped to nourish the faith of their parishioners. The post-Tridentine rural laity was provided with zealous priests and a catechism to direct their beliefs along orthodox channels.

Under the guidance of Pio Nono, Catholics were given a taste of medieval sentiment and splendour to encourage their allegiance to the Church and, it was hoped, to the political and social structure which the medieval Church found most compatible. The parallel cults of Mary and the Sacred Heart would personalize religion and grip the popular imagination by restoring sentiment to the practice of Catholicism and by offering a range of material and supernatural benefits in return for ritual observance in the form of novenas, invocations, litanies, confraternities, pilgrimages to officially-recognized shrines, prayers on special days, prayers in special places . . . something of the wonder and luxury of the Middle Ages was

[6] Delumeau (1978).

made available in the hostile environment of the nineteenth century.

Theologians and church historians tend to ignore or pay too little attention to this phenomenon, as if the fortunes of the Church could be charted and explained with reference only to the more conventionally political pronouncements and decisions of the Pope and his Vatican officials. Where reference is made to the lay practices which mark the revival of Catholicism in the nineteenth century, these tend to be seen simply as manifestations of the new religious fervour, almost as if they occurred spontaneously to give expression to a fundamental doctrinal commitment in the face of anti-Catholic and irreligious pressures.[7]

Catholic piety in the nineteenth century was a strategy carefully managed by Rome, not the spontaneous movement of the masses as people were encouraged to believe. It was a *cause* of Catholic compliance, not merely its effect and expression. The study of the daily rituals and practices of Catholics is important because it is through them that the Church exercises control and acquires that authority which makes official policy effective. It would be unrealistic, and lead inevitably to a subjective and misguided view of history, to presume that these rituals and practices were not, in some measure, orchestrated to produce their desired effect. The interesting question for both the Catholic and the historian is, surely, to what measure and to what effect? The politics of piety is not the whole picture of Catholic life, but it is an important angle from which to view it and an indispensable perspective for the interpreter of any period of church history. The official decrees of Pius IX condemning liberalism, progress and modern civilization might have evoked sympathy and stimulated resistance to modernity in some quarters where Catholic consciences were finely tuned to the meaning and significance of official documents. It is inconceivable that the erosion of Catholic authority and spirituality which was taking place in the cities, workplaces and homes throughout Western society could have been halted simply by the command of the Roman Pontiff. A religious

---

[7] Most Catholic historians take nineteenth-century piety at its face value in this way; see, for example, Daniel-Rops (1965); Dansette (1961).

revival on a massive scale was required if the Vatican was to check the systematic weakening of commitment to the Church which accompanied its decline in social and political status. The rediscovery of the cults of the Virgin Mary and the Sacred Heart played an important part in that revival.

In the Middle Ages, the cult of Mary the Virgin and of the saints was a central feature of popular religion. Reverence for their shrines, medals, scapulars and their relics of every conceivable kind was as instinctive and widespread as the readiness to see events and natural phenomena as signs from heaven and instances of God's providence.

The medieval Church thus appeared as a vast reservoir of magical power, capable of being deployed for a variety of secular purposes . . . a repository of supernatural power which could be dispensed to the faithful to help them in their daily problems. It was inevitable that the priests, set apart from the rest of the community by their celibacy and ritual consecration, should have derived an extra *cachet* from their position as mediators between man and God. It was also inevitable that around the Church, the clergy and their holy apparatus, there clustered a horde of popular superstitions, which endowed religious objects with a magical power to which theologians themselves had never laid claim.[8]

From the accounts of miracles and apparitions which survive, it is difficult to construct a picture of their pattern and distribution. In the Middle Ages, it appears, the heavenly hosts had no strong political bias, did not favour one particular society over the others and were not excessively attached to any particular social class. On the whole, their intrusions into the natural sphere were as random as one would expect, given the belief in the equality of all before God and the random distribution of piety and impiety which that belief implies. If any class prejudice was detectable, it was directed towards the wealthy and the nobility. As the Elizabethan Reginald Scot wrote sardonically of the Pope: 'He canonizeth the rich for saints and banneth the poor for witches.'[9]

[8] Thomas (1977), pp.51 and 35.
[9] Reginald Scot, *The Discoverie of Witchcraft*, 1584, ch.xxiv, noted in Thomas (1977), p.56.

At the beginning of the nineteenth century, devotion to the Virgin Mary was at its lowest for centuries. This was due, in part, to the general demoralization of Catholics before the restoration, in part also to the effect of the Enlightenment on certain devotional practices of the Middle Ages which were easy targets for attacks on the Church. At a time before the Reformation, when Church authorities and theologians were preoccupied with matters of state and metaphysics and experienced no anxiety about the purity of popular religion, the clergy could afford to be indulgent about the superstitions and pagan cults which formed a sizeable part of the beliefs and practices of the masses. As Catholicism came under threat at the Reformation, laxity gave way to control in matters of doctrine and discipline and the old luxuries which made medieval Catholicism almost a syncretic religion could no longer be tolerated. Shrines, medals, pilgrimages, indulgences and the cult of the saints were regulated, if not positively discouraged, for fear of enlarging the target for reformers and secularists and exposing a weak organizational front to the temptations of heresy. In the new situation of the nineteenth century, Pope Pius IX faced the task, not simply of defending the post-Reformation Church —its membership, influence and property—but of restoring it after the ravages of the Revolution. Shrines, medals, indulgences and the rest began to make their reappearance in a new fervour which contrasted sharply with the two centuries before. It was Pio Nono's policy to win back the Church and strengthen the allegiance of its members, not by making the Church relevant to the spirit of a secular age but by restoring to Catholics the devotional practices they had lost from a previous age. His policy, it could be said, was to offer to Catholics a counter-attraction to secular society and to make the world irrelevant to their real needs and aspirations. His problem was to define these needs for the people at a time when competing definitions of human needs and aspirations were rapidly gaining ground throughout Europe.

The belief that Mary was conceived without original sin—the doctrine of the Immaculate Conception—had been the subject of vigorous debate in the Church for many centuries. In the twelfth century Anselm of Canterbury denied it, as did St Bernard, St Thomas Aquinas and his Dominican followers. The Franciscans, following Duns Scotus, argued for a sinless conception and in 1483 Pope Sixtus IV found it necessary to intervene in the quarrel and silenced those who protested too much. Neither side was to be accused of heresy; both beliefs should be tolerated since the matter had 'not yet been decided by the Roman Church and the Apostolic See'. The bishops of the Council of Trent in the sixteenth century treated the belief with great caution and, like Sixtus, decided neither one way nor the other.[10] As late as 1840, Pope Gregory XVI, despite petitions from a number of French bishops, did not feel that a dogmatic definition of Mary's Immaculate Conception was appropriate, given the strength of opposition from theologians and bishops in countries where Catholics were in a minority.[11]

Extreme reserve, therefore, marked the official attitude throughout the ages towards the belief that Mary was not born in sin. Why did Pope Pius IX break with that tradition in 1854? Why was that year considered appropriate when 1840 was not, nor was any other time since the twelfth century, when popular devotion to Mary was often more extensive and fervent than in the nineteenth century? No new theological evidence was brought forward in 1854 which was not already available, though considerable theological labour was expended in favour of the new dogma at the instigation of the Pope and under the direction of Fathers Perrone and Passaglia, two Jesuits whose ideas were known to be in accord with the Pope's on this matter and on the question of infallibility. Another question arises from the manner in which the new dogma was proclaimed: why did the Pope choose to break with precedent by making his solemn pronouncement on Mary's Immaculate Conception without formal consultation with the bishops?

To the third question, Pio Nono himself gave the answer in his preamble to the new dogmatic definition. He acted alone 'by the authority of Our Lord Jesus Christ, of the blessed Apostles Peter and Paul and by our own authority', and for that reason he did not see fit to summon a council or include the bishops of the Church in his deliberations. The Pope was providing for the

[10] Bettenson (1963), p.271.
[11] See Heyer (1969), p.179.

bishops of the Church compelling theological evidence to support their acceptance of the dogma of papal infallibility which they would be asked to affirm at the First Vatican Council sixteen years later. As Cardinal Manning wrote, a practical demonstration of papal infallibility was considered at Rome to override considerations of the role of the episcopate in the teaching authority of the Church.[12] There was widespread opposition in the Church to the definition of papal infallibility which the Pope and his Curia considered to be politically necessary, and the Marian dogma would make it difficult for this opposition to be effective. Since his frightening experience of the political turmoil of 1848 and his period in exile which followed it, Pope Pius IX had embarked with determination on a policy of authoritarian control over that area of public affairs which was still under his influence. His temporal authority was rapidly coming to an end. The only hope for the Church, in the Pope's view, was to increase his bureaucratic control in the spiritual sphere in order to compensate for the loss of temporal kingship by asserting his power as Vicar of Christ and supreme ruler of the Church. To this end, papal infallibility seemed a sure means. By the end of the nineteenth century, the Roman Church would resemble a highly centralized state subject to the absolute authority of its monarch. While the Pope undoubtedly pursued his policy of centralization and papal supremacy 'in accord with his own deep spiritual aspirations', as Daniel-Rops concludes, it is only partly true to say that he was 'leaving political affairs more and more exclusively to Cardinal Antonelli', his Secretary of State.[13] The definition of papal infallibility was a political act, not only in the loose sense that any action of a religious leader is an exercise of power, but in that it was provoked by, and calculated as a counter-attack on, the political forces of secularism which were stripping the assets and undermining the authority of the Church. Like the defence of the Papal States against Garibaldi in 1860 and the Syllabus of Errors which followed it in 1864, it was not primarily theological reflection but political expediency which motivated Pio Nono to secure his own infallibility.

[12] Manning (1877), p.41ff.
[13] Daniel-Rops (1965), p.257.

The dogma of Mary's Immaculate Conception was, therefore, a stage in the process of papal absolutism within the Catholic Church. It was employed by the Pope as the only means of attack against the modern world which it was now in his power and imagination to use. But it was not only a strategy by which papal infallibility could later be presented as a *fait accompli*. The form of the Marian definition was certainly crucial to the policy of the Pope, as Mgr Talbot, an English prelate resident in the Vatican at the time, noted: 'You see, the most important thing is not the new dogma itself, but the way in which it is proclaimed.'[14] No less important was the content of the proclamation itself. There were other less contentious beliefs which the Pope might have chosen as a vehicle for promoting his infallibility had his enthusiasm for the Virgin Mary been secondary, as Talbot implies.

The Pope's intention to proclaim the dogma of the Immaculate Conception was announced during his period of exile at Gaetà. The brutality of the 1848 revolutions throughout Europe, particularly in Paris in June of that year, shook the Pope and sent the French Catholic world into a rapid retreat from a liberal position to a more sheltered place under the protection of Louis-Napoleon Bonaparte, who was elected president of the Republic in 1849. With the Italian nationalists desiring the destruction of the Church after the Pope's failure to live up to his earlier reputation, Pio Nono's liberal days were over. He let it be known that he intended to define the dogma and to appeal for the Virgin's intervention in order to 'calm the fearful storms buffeting the Church'. The Virgin's interest in the political situation in France was already well publicized by an event which took place nearly two decades earlier. In July 1830, a year of violence and insurrection in France which rivals the disorder of 1848, an illiterate novice of the Sisters of Charity in the Rue du Bac, Paris, was said to have seen an apparition in which the Virgin referred to the calamitous state of society, gave certain messages to the young girl—later revealed to have included a prophecy of the attacks on clergy and Church in the Paris Commune of 1870—and asked that a medal be struck to her likeness. Those who wore it and were faithful to their

[14] Quoted in Heyer (1969), p.186.

prayers would form a world-wide campaign of prayer for the restoration of peace to society and to the Church. The 'miraculous medal', as it became known, was inscribed to 'Mary conceived without sin', and its popularity spread throughout Europe, helped by stories of miracles wrought and favours received through the intercession of the Virgin.

Pope Pius IX was, therefore, well aware that his political concerns were echoed in heaven. It would be quite false to conclude, however, that he had only a cynical interest in the Virgin Mary as a means of manipulating the masses in the pursuit of his political interests. All his biographers and many historians of the period attest to his personal attachment to the cult of Mary and to his personal piety in every respect. Since his childhood he had retained a deep and particular devotion to her. His obvious sincerity, however, does not exclude the political role she was called upon to play in his policy of centralization and papal absolutism, which he conceived as the work of God against the secular enemy of the Church. He was impressed by the success of the miraculous medal, with its political connotations and its potential for restoring to millions of Catholics the simple, devout piety of a past age, and was said to have remarked: 'It is of divine inspiration. It will be a resource for the Church.'[15] The proclamation of the dogma of the Immaculate Conception served to confirm the validity of Zoé Labouré's apparition in 1830 and the authenticity of the sentiments expressed to her by the Virgin Mary. Whatever its place in the development of theology, it was a key event in the political campaign against the modern world, a buffer against socialism and an instrument of papal absolutism. In 1858, four years after its proclamation, another apparition of the Virgin occurred at Lourdes, in southern France, this time confirming the Pope's definition of the Immaculate Conception just as the first apparition in 1830 had anticipated it. As Pope Pius XII said in the Lourdes centenary encyclical in 1958: 'Certainly the infallible word of the Pope, the authentic interpreter of revealed truth, required no endorsement from heaven to be valid for the faithful; but with what emotion did Christian people and their shepherds receive from the lips of Bernadette this answer which

[15] St John (1903), p.60.

came from heaven.' Sandwiched between two well-publicized arguments for its orthodoxy, the belief in the Immaculate Conception was revived, enlarged and translated into a world-wide movement of prayer in place of revolution, of pious consideration of the next world in place of angry protest about this one. The miraculous medal, linked to a network of prayer-groups, enjoyed astonishing popularity within a short period. By the 1880s, the Archconfraternity of Prayer had an estimated twenty-five or thirty million members.[16] The apparitions at Lourdes were no less successful and served to establish child-like simplicity as the model of Catholic virtue and the character ideal of Catholic societies.

Between 1830 and 1876, the Catholic world was visited by five apparitions of the Virgin. As in any other period of the modern Church, there were countless other claims to heavenly visitation from all over the Catholic world, but the claims were not upheld by the Church authorities. Only these five appari-tions were officially recognized and they are the first recorded occasions on which the Virgin's communications with earth-bound creatures were given hierarchic approval. In the Middle Ages, visions and shrines proliferated and the clergy's attitude to them was generally indulgent. Notable differences occurred in the nineteenth century. Apparitions were now a matter for legislation and the official criteria by which some were approved and the others rejected included the detailed and objective examination of the evidence for their authenticity. Celestial spirits moved where they willed throughout the world, it was held, and the Church was anxious to protect the unpredictability of their travels and the authenticity of their landings on earth; the authorities must be seen to be capable of detecting fraud and of making objective judgements free of personal bias. It is difficult to avoid the conclusion that the apparitions and the shrines whose cults were officially approved and encouraged during the nineteenth century were political accomplishments of the Catholic hierarchy rather than the dramatic and spontaneous supernatural events they purported to be and to which the hierarchy was forced to give its approval after scrutinizing the evidence. The five appari-

---

[16] *Ibid.*, p.94 and Daniel-Rops (1965), p.466.

tions of the Virgin which gave rise to approved cults and pilgrimages to their shrines took place in France. Their dates are significant: 1830, 1846, 1858, 1871 and 1876. In all these cases the Virgin appeared, not to a random sample of Catholics, but to young illiterates, and their simplicity and illiteracy was advanced both as a model of virtue and as an indicator of the authenticity of their accounts. All five apparitions contained a reference to the political situation and to the need for prayer and repentance to restore order.[17] The fifty-year period of the apparitions coincides with the wave of revolutionary activity centred on France which originated in the French Revolution, but which now aimed at the emancipation of the proletariat whose socialist ideology was listed among 'the principal errors of our times' and condemned in the papal encyclical *Quanta Cura* which accompanied the Syllabus of Errors in 1864. (Socialism now headed the papal league of obnoxious ideologies and would continue to do so until the early twentieth century, when communism, its more doctrinaire form, took its place.[18])

There was another important difference between the piety of the nineteenth century and that of the Middle Ages which it resembled. Medieval piety came from the people and, in that sense, it was truly popular. While the clergy often exploited it when it suited them it would be gross to claim that they created it. On the contrary, many of the popular devotions and practices were so crudely magical as to be an embarrassment to the medieval clergy, particularly the more rationalist among them who were sensitive to informed theological opinion. In general, the attitude of the clergy was ambivalent: the credulities of the laity could be useful if they bound people closer to the true

[17] On apparitions in general and in the nineteenth century in particular, see St John (1903); Graef (1965), Vol. 2; Vassall-Phillips (1920); Rahner (1964).

[18] As we enter the 1980s, it is hard to imagine that democracy and liberalism once occupied a high place in this league. They have since been relegated, as far as official pronouncements are concerned, and their anti-religious character survives only in the catalogue of errors occasionally published by extreme traditionalist groups. Russian communism has stimulated its own visitations, the most famous being the apparition of Our Lady to three peasant children in 1917 at Fatima in Portugal, with the aim of bringing about the conversion of Russia through the recitation of the Rosary.

Church and enhanced their respect for the clergy, but the tendency to excess required constant vigilance.[19]

There is no evidence that the revival of popular piety in the nineteenth century came from the people. They did not recover, independently of the hierarchy, from the process that had virtually eradicated such practices since the Reformation. The devotional impetus and, in particular, the Marian revival, came not from the masses but from the Church authorities under the personal guidance of Pope Pius IX. When only French apparitions were selected for approval during a period of anti-clericalism and socialist upheavals in France; when only illiterate chldren were the subjects of visitation during a period of antagonism towards the rationalist ideas of the Enlightenment; when the known political concerns of the Pope found a sympathetic echo in the Virgin's communications to those children; and when, finally, the evidence produced to establish the miraculous nature of the apparitions and the authenticity of their message was, in each case, of breathtaking inadequacy and offered no grounds for accepting these claims and rejecting others—in these circumstances one must conclude that the mass movement of Marian piety in the nineteenth century was a carefully-planned campaign to transform the Church into a cultural ghetto in response to political threats. The world was being condemned and the institution of the Church was being strengthened, not only by the statements of its leaders, but by the miraculous interventions of heaven.

It should be noted, in passing, that belief in miracles is not logically excluded by an awareness of their political connection and function, any more than belief in God excludes acceptance of Freudian or Marxist theories of his human construction. But it does strain their credibility. It is not intrinsically repugnant to Catholic faith that the Virgin's interests and policies should coincide with those of the Pope. But in the light of the evidence it is difficult to explain the coincidence and, at the same time, to hold the orthodox belief that heaven is a reality transcending the politics of Church and world and that the Church's teaching is a consequence of theological reflection on that reality, not a strategy dictated by the world. Pope Pius XII clearly felt that

---

[19] Thomas (1977), p.54ff.

difficulty in his Lourdes Centenary Encyclical: 'Every Christian country belongs to Mary,' he wrote, countering the impression that might have been given that the French has acquired a
monopoly. 'But this truth acquires a touching significance if
one calls to mind the history of France. . . . Nevertheless, it was
to be the nineteenth century, after the confusion of revolution,
that was to be the century of the demonstration of Mary's
favour.'

Foremost among the champions of nineteenth-century piety
and among the architects of its diffusion were the Jesuits. From
their founder, Ignatius of Loyola, they inherited a particular
devotion to the Virgin and to the person of the Pope, whose
cause they were dedicated to serve by a special vow of obedience. Jesuit influence was not confined to the two great dogmatic definitions of the nineteenth century. The cult of Mary
was complemented by the cult of the Sacred Heart of Jesus, a
medieval practice nurtured within the Society of Jesus, encouraged in the writings of St Ignatius, and now, in due time,
revived with great effect for the Church and the Pope. From
1856, when Pope Pius IX commanded the feast of the Sacred
Heart to be observed throughout the Church, until 1956, when
Pius XII, in his encyclical *Haurietis Aquas,* urged this devotion
on the faithful 'to set a strong bulwark against the wicked
designs of those who hate God and his Church', the Sacred
Heart has been invoked as a defence against socialism and
communism and other evils afflicting the Church.

The popularity of the cult since the nineteenth century was
undoubtedly helped by the benefits believed to accrue to its
devotees. The modern devotion originated in the twelve promises made to the seventeenth-century French visionary, St
Margaret Mary Alacoque. Eleven of these promises were set on
record at the time of her mystical experiences and are of a vague
prayerful character, not likely to stimulate a popular movement of piety. The twelfth, called 'the great promise' was of a
different order and was recalled later by the saint and communicated after her visions had ended in a letter to her
superiors. Prefacing this with the diffident 'if I am not mistaken', St Margaret Mary remembered that the Lord had
promised the gift of final repentance to all who received Holy
Communion on the first Friday of nine consecutive months.

This is the stuff of a mass movement. After the elevation of the feast of the Sacred Heart in 1856, the 'Nine Fridays' became a staple diet of every Catholic diocese in the world. Indulgences were granted by Pope Pius IX to encourage the movement, while the theologians were left with the task of correcting the magical interpretation of the promise which alone could account for its popularity. As recently as 1956, the German theologian, Karl Rahner, found it necessary to appeal to priests not to allow this promise to 'become for many men the occasion, at least after they have made the novena of First Fridays, of sinning in irresponsible presumption on God's mercy'.[20]

Bainvell records the fact that since 1870 the image of the Sacred Heart became so popular in France that it was virtually a national flag, and serious attempts were made to have the French tricolour, with the Sacred Heart on its white centre, adopted as the symbol of France. At the end of the nineteenth century, Pope Leo XIII, Pio Nono's successor, noted the alliance between the Sacred Heart and conservative political ideals and wrote to the bishop of Marseilles: 'The future is indeed dark, but we are convinced that as long as your country keeps to the devotion of the Sacred Heart, which, please God, she will do always, she will have therein a precious pledge of salvation.'[21] After the disasters of the Paris Commune, Catholic France nourished the hope of restoring the monarchy and, in June 1873, fifty members of the Assemblée Nationale made a pilgrimage to the shrine of Margaret Mary at Paray-le-Monial with banners in hand and the Sacred Heart emblem on their breasts and dedicated themselves and France to the Sacred Heart of Jesus.[22]

The spread of the cult was greatly stimulated by the work of two Jesuits, Fathers Gautrelet and Ramière, who formed the Apostleship of Prayer to ground the new piety in organized activity, and they established a journal, *The Messenger of the Sacred Heart*, which rapidly became a Reader's Digest for pious Catholics throughout the world, its holy chatter and tales of

[20] Karl Rahner in Stierli (1956), p.154. On nineteenth-century devotion to the Sacred Heart see Bainvell (1924); Verheylezoon (1955); also (author unknown) *The Century of the Sacred Heart*, Burns Oates and Washbourne, 1924.
[21] Bainvell (1924), p.323ff., p.337.
[22] Heyer (1969), p.178.

wondrous benefits for devotees of the cult performing a valuable service in stimulating the sentimental attachment to the Church which was characteristic of the period. With the miraculous medal hung round the neck and the oleograph representation of the wounded heart of Jesus enshrined in the home, the nineteenth-century Catholic was armed to the teeth against the vicissitudes of life and the dangers of a sudden death.

At the end of the eighteenth century the Catholic Church was a sort of federal system: the powers of the Pope, though absolute in theory, were in practice restricted by local custom and the traditions of national churches. By the end of the nineteenth century, Rome was the centre of Catholicism. This was the case in almost every dimension of the Church's life. The liturgist, Dom Gueranger, who wanted an end to the multiplicity of idiosyncratic and liturgically unsound practices, became the unwitting agent of the abolition of local liturgies and customs and of world-wide conformity to the Roman Rite. Prior to Gueranger's reform, twelve out of one hundred French dioceses used the Roman liturgy; by the time of his death every diocese had conformed to Rome. The Vatican's control over the world-wide Church was aided by bringing in more foreigners to the College of Cardinals—a policy begun by Pius IX in 1850. About the same time, a bi-monthly Jesuit review, *Civiltà Cattolica*, was founded to promote orthodoxy among the Catholic laity and it became the Vatican's mouthpiece on doctrinal matters. In 1860, the Holy See had an official journal, *l'Osservatore Romano*, to disseminate and advertise to the world the thinking and intentions of the Pope. The Pope's long period of office gave him the opportunity of renewing almost the entire episcopate of the Church, thus ensuring personal loyalty. Pilgrimages to Rome were encouraged and several national seminaries were established there to instil that Roman bias in attitude and theology in the more promising clergy selected for Roman training by their national hierarchies. The medieval practice of Peter's Pence, a world-wide collection of funds to supply the needs of the Pope, was revived to give the laity a stronger sense of participation in the Church and orientation to Rome. By the end of the century the secular and religious priesthood was strictly under the control of the Vatican—the

Jesuits had been restored, the Dominicans and Benedictines reformed, the Redemptorists reorganized, and countless new institutes and congregations established with lines of authority centred on Rome.

The climax of this comprehensive policy was the definition of the dogma of papal infallibility at the First Vatican Council in 1870. The first indication that a General Council of the Church was in the offing was given in secret to Curial officials immediately after the publication in 1864 of the Syllabus of Errors condemning the modern world. While it was known that authority in the Church was to be the main issue, opinion among the bishops was divided as to the precise nature of the deliberations proposed and their likely outcome. Some felt that this First Vatican Council would give an opportunity to check the process of extreme centralization and ultramontanism which has developed since the beginning of the century. They read with mixed feelings in *Civiltà Cattolica,* some months before the Council, that papal infallibility was not only on the agenda but was already in the statute book, so to speak.[23]

The fall of Rome to Italian nationalist forces in September 1870—almost as the dogma on papal infallibility was being solemnly defined in the Vatican—created a paradoxical situation in the Catholic world. Humiliated as a temporal sovereign, the Pope ruled his Church with unprecedented powers over his subjects. He was deprived of a political outlet but exercised absolute dominance through the medium of theology. Hitherto, political concerns dissipated the energies of the Roman authorities and it was possible for bishops and theologians to act in their own sphere with some measure of independence. Now, with the political arm severed, all power was exercised through the spiritual. The extraordinary reverence for his person, which Pope Pius IX encouraged, expressed

---

[23] 'All genuine Catholics believe that the Council will be quite short. . . . They will receive with joy the proclamation of the dogmatic infallibility of the sovereign pontiff. It is not at all surprising that, from a feeling of proper reserve, Pius IX does not want to take the initiative himself in proposing what seems to concern him directly, but it is hoped that the unanimous revelation of the Holy Spirit, by the mouth of the Fathers of the ecumenical council, will define it by acclamation.' *La Civiltà Cattolica,* 6 Feb. 1869, quoted in Vidler (1971), p.155.

the extreme centralization of the Church which was to be its
notable feature for the next seventy years. Progressively during
his reign, as papal territory diminished, so papal authority
within the Church increased. As the Pope's direct political
power declined, so his control over his subjects was tightened to
the extent that papal control of the consciences of Catholics
would become an indirect source of political influence in the
developed countries in which Catholics were a sizeable
minority.

The Enemy Within

Like Britain after the Second World War, the Roman Church
at the end of Pio Nono's reign had lost an empire and had not
yet discovered a role. Pius IX had a clear idea what that role
should be. He was quite sure that it should be a political role, its
significance measured by the standards of the world which had
so humiliated the Church and diminished its leaders. But, at
the end of his life, he recognized his failure in making such a role
possible. He had attempted, by means of theology and piety, to
set apart the attitudes and the way of life of Catholics from
those of their non-Catholic neighbours and colleagues among
whom they lived and worked. That the Church survived in
ghetto form for so long is a measure of the Pope's commitment
and of the modifications to his policy made by his successor,
Pope Leo XIII. But the modern world, unlike medieval society,
was not a temptation which could be kept at bay by pious
practices, nor was it a distant enemy that could be recognized
at sight. The enemy was now within, attacking the foundations
of religion itself. The world permeated Catholic consciousness,
splitting life into the religious and the non-religious, the
Catholic and the worldly. In varying measure in different
countries, the Catholic world had undergone a revolution in
economics, politics and science, and, short of entering a monastery or abandoning their religion, Catholics could not avoid the
schizophrenia which became increasingly one of the characteristics of the Catholic mind. It was a major defect of ghetto
Catholicism that the Church could not prevent that contact
with the world of business, of education, of politics which

generated values and attitudes not in harmony with those of religion. The Vatican was well aware of these dangers and created a segregated education system to protect Catholics from the world. And where active participation in political life was not specifically forbidden, as in Italy, it was discouraged. Attempts in France, Germany and Italy to involve Catholics in political movements and parties met with suspicion in Rome, much to the disillusionment of the more progressive Catholic political leaders. Karl Von Aretin has argued:

Neither the French liberal Catholics nor later the leaders of the German Centre Party understood that what the papacy disliked above all was the position of Catholic parties as mediators between state and church, and that Rome preferred to keep control of diplomatic negotiations at all stages. The papacy looked upon the Catholic political parties as the successors of the hated episcopal power structures of the eighteenth century, and feared an alliance between the state and its Catholic citizens over which Rome would have no control and which would also be against its system of centralization.[24]

Ghetto Catholicism was an experiment which failed because, with implacable and powerful enemies outside the Church, the real enemy was inside, working from within the Catholic consciousness. The most effective secular weapons against the structure of the Church in the nineteenth century were not laws and alliances of an openly anti-Catholic kind. They were the values of a world which contradicted the medieval Catholic world-view and which were subversive of ghetto Catholicism in that Catholics themselves subscribed to them while at the same time trying to hold to the beliefs and discipline of a religion which they undermined.

Nineteenth-century Catholics lived—perforce—in the modern world of capitalism, democracy and science, and the infiltration of values and attitudes embodied in the new institutions had their price in religious terms. The pursuit of economic prosperity as a legitimate goal entailed a weakening of the other-worldly character of traditional Catholicism. Medieval Church leaders had never been slow to indulge their taste for material goods, but the teaching they disseminated and to

[24] Von Aretin (1970), pp.113–14.

which they subscribed idealized the situation of the masses
—poor, socially immobile, but honest and obedient to lawful
authority. The emergence of a new middle class throughout
Western Europe which established a new economic order in
place of feudalism would result in making life after death a
valued extra rather than the sole justification for a life of
poverty and social immobility and had the effect of raising
questions about the distribution of wealth and power which
previously did not arise in a world taken for granted.

The price of democracy is the authoritarian structure of the
Church and, ultimately, the hierarchic priesthood itself. When
Pope Gregory XVI, in his encyclical *Mirari Vos,* 1832, condemned what he called 'the senseless and erroneous idea, better
still, absurdity, that freedom of conscience is to be claimed and
defended for all men', he was attacking the religious implications of democracy in its nineteenth-century context.
Democracy, which is now generally conceived as a political
arrangement that tolerates and is acceptable to the Catholic
Church, appeared in the nineteenth century to be fundamentally anti-Catholic. The rights of man seemed to diminish the
rights of God; self-determination was counterposed to
hierarchic guidance; moral individualism challenged the whole
corpus of Catholic moral teaching. Referring to the early
Christians' submission to pagan emperors, the Pope exemplified how political and religious ideas were inextricably inter-
connected in the ideas of his time:

These fine examples of loyal submission to princes, which necessarily
derives from the sacred precepts of the Christian religion, condemn
the detestable insolence and malice of those who, incited by their
vaunting and unbounded ambition for licentious freedom, use all
their power to agitate against and upset the rights of rulers, whereas
they really enslave the nations under the mask of liberty.

Political freedom and freedom of conscience were linked in the
minds of revolutionaries just as they were linked also in the
conservative view of the social order and in the mind of the
Pope, who opposed democracy as a 'corruption of youth, a
contempt for sacred matters and laws spread among the
nations . . .'

Prosperous states have perished through this one evil, the immoderate freedom of opinions, licence of speech and love of novelties. Linked with this is that abominable and detestable freedom of publication which some dare demand with much noise and zeal.

The price of science is the decline in reverence for revelation and the weakening of a faith which transcends empirical knowledge. In terms of its content, science does not threaten belief in a transcendent God. The content of scientific truths neither supports nor contradicts the content of religious faith. Its attack on God and his revelation is indirect, more subtle and more damaging than the contradiction of specific beliefs, like the place of the earth in the universe, the origin of man, the nature of biblical truth. Galileo and Darwin ruffled theological feathers for a time, but their lasting effect was to enrich theology and to enlarge theologians' conception of God's providence, not to diminish it. Science subverts faith by demoting its status in the cognitive hierarchy; it inculcates a sensitivity to the existence of the boundary between knowledge which is testable and that which is not; and, by rewarding testable knowledge with valued economic goods, it elevates its status above that of traditional authority and faith. In a stimulating and provocative work on the revolution in knowledge which accompanied the political and economic changes that gave birth to what we call the 'modern world', Ernest Gellner argues that the effect of the cognitive change was to bring about a radical segregation of the natural order from the moral.[25] The quotations from Pope Gregory XVI above are characteristic of a medieval mentality which conceived of the social order within the physical universe as a timeless representation of the mind and will of God. The moral order was underwritten by the natural, and man's identity was unproblematic in a world which located him at the centre of a stable and harmonious universe. This harmony was shattered by the success and prestige of science. From now on, the world as it existed was the subject of scientific analysis, economic profit and political experiment. It would no longer present itself as the daily proof of God's existence and the justification of man's faith.

[25] Gellner (1974); see especially ch.8.

Faith—and morality itself, as Kant saw—if it was to be an option at all, could only be acquired by a mental shift from that arena of knowledge, that cognitive process, by which the modern world was perceived and by which men and women, Catholic and non-Catholic alike, made their living. The origin of Catholic schizophrenia lay in the victory of science over religious authority as the standard of valid knowledge and as the source of apparently limitless economic benefits.

It was not first in the nineteenth century that Catholicism was forced to tolerate a 'trojan horse' in its midst and the split in Catholic consciousness began. The works of Bernard Groethuysen and Lucien Goldmann document the beginning of this process during the Enlightenment, when those who attacked Christianity did so within a newly-emerging bourgeois ideology.[26] In the Middle Ages, thought and action required justification in the light of faith. By the time of the Enlightenment, faith demanded justification in terms of reason. The dominance of faith in everyday life was ended when a new ideology of rationalism was required and adopted by the bourgeoisie to legitimate a new economic and social order. By the time of the French Revolution, as Goldmann observes, the victory was achieved and the middle classes could revive religion in a new form to provide a social bulwark for a changed society. The new form of religion consisted of beliefs and practices clearly circumscribed and separated from the routine business of life. The ordinary professional and economic life of the new man was not Christian but secular:

Such a man may of course live modestly, he may even practise self-denial and give all his profits to the poor or to the Church; what he cannot do is to earn his living in a 'Christian' or a 'sinful' way . . . in a society based on market production, economic activity can no more be 'moral' or 'immoral', 'Christian' or 'sinful', than an odour can be square or round, or a colour sweet-scented or evil-smelling. . . . Economic life is secular, and therefore as totally alien to the categories of 'right' and 'wrong' as to 'Christian' and 'un-christian'. Its only essential categories are those of success and failure. It may perhaps give temporary acknowledgement to values recognized or condemned

[26] See Groethuysen (1968); Goldmann (1973).

by the custom of the time, but it throws these overboard at the first sign of conflict between them and economic advantage.[27]

From being basically religious, modern man became basically *human;* he became one whose actions were largely irrelevant to religion, though some of them might be pleasing to God and others sinful. He was not a sinner, though he sometimes sinned—the Augustinian notion of fallen man still featured in his catechism of beliefs but it had no place in his life and attitudes.

The Jansenists would have no truck with such modern ideas and held fast to the Augustinian concept of God and of man's total dependence on him. But already in the eighteenth century the Jesuits were attacking Jansenism, not in traditional religious terms, but by arguments drawn from the ideas of the Enlightenment—the modern, anti-religious thinking of the Philosophers. The Jansenist notion of God was repugnant to reason:

To judge by Quesnel, the love of God is the sole virtue which honours that sovereign Being, the only one he understands, the only one he rewards. . . . That's very fine. But what happens? What happens, after this fine statement, is that this God, the love of whom is the only licit virtue, and even the fear of whom is reproved by Quesnel, is according to him nevertheless a tyrant, who commands impossible things and who, not content with commanding them, proceeds to damn pitilessly those who have not carried them out. Seriously, is this a God one can love?[28]

Goldmann argues that it was only such a rationalist adaptation by the Jesuits, which gradually pervaded official Church thinking, that saved Christianity from collapse in the face of the Enlightenment philosophy and middle-class ideology. The Church saved God by transforming him into a figure more acceptable to the philosophers. Perhaps this is so, and theologians had no other option but to yield to secular pressure. But it was a short-term solution. The eighteenth-century secular world was content with the shift in religious thinking, but

[27] Goldmann (1973), pp.58–9.
[28] Groethuysen (1968), p.82.

that world would not stay in the eighteenth century for long; and once the Church had yielded to it the right to dictate the terms of debate Reason would increase its demands to the point that faith itself would be unreasonable and knowledge which could not be validated scientifically would be inadmissible.

This is an example of that instability of the world—already noted—with which the Church was forced to compromise and in relation to which the Church was repeatedly judged 'out of date', and more, 'irrelevant'. With the Enlightenment, the erosion of the Church may have been temporarily halted, but in the long term the concession to Reason by which this was accomplished would be followed by new demands for the Church to become relevant to the constantly changing world. For the progressive French priest, Lamennais, writing in the middle of the nineteenth century, the Catholic acceptance of the Enlightenment principle that reason is the criterion of truth was the root cause of the intellectual libertinism and social disintegration he witnessed around him:

I know several people who used to be Christian but have become unbelievers through reading apologies for religion. . . . Since reason has proclaimed itself sovereign one must go straight at it, seize it on its throne and force it, on pain of death, to prostrate itself before the reason of God.[29]

If it were possible to have the economic or political aspects of modernity without the scientific, then it is also conceivable that the confrontation between Church and world could have been less sharp and less damaging to traditional Catholicism. Science is the real enemy. It is fundamentally anti-authoritarian, anti-clerical and, in the sense employed by Max Weber, anti-religious. The concession to science made during the Enlightenment was the opening round of a long struggle which would culminate in the late 1960s, after the Second Vatican Council. It would be the key factor in the relationship

---

[29] Letter to Maistre in *Lettres et Opuscules du Comte Joseph de Maistre*, 1869, quoted in Reardon (1975), p.67. That the Jesuits were particularly active in promoting the shift from traditional authority to the authority of reason is further suggested by their hostility towards Lamennais's ideas on the role of reason. See *ibid.*, p.77.

between Church and world and in their rivalry over the control of beliefs. That control, which the Church continued to exercise during the nineteenth century, was vital if the Roman Church was to retain its continuity with history.

We have seen in this chapter how the Church responded to attacks on various elements of its structure by secular movements of thought, politics and economics since the Enlightenment. The policy of Pope Pius IX was intended to protect and to strengthen the Church's control of beliefs against an adversary which he perceived as more powerful and potentially more damaging than the traditional enemy of heresy. Heretics at least shared some common ground with orthodox theologians in their opposition to the Church. The modern world threatened to abolish the very concepts of heresy and orthodoxy and thus to make impossible the survival of a religious organization which was defined on those premises. Furthermore, heresy traditionally erupted in specific geographical areas where it could be confined or contained. The new adversary was everywhere, gnawing at the roots of Catholics' allegiance to the Church. Pio Nono had little alternative but to pursue a policy of entrenchment and of the reorganization of spiritual resources into a cultural ghetto, just as the Church in the Enlightenment period had little option but to yield to secular philosophy the right to define the terms of philosophical debate.

The policy failed. The world did not repent and submit to the Vicar of Christ and the teaching authority of his Church. Pius IX recognized this at the end of his life:

I hope my successor will be as much attached to the Church as I have been and will have as keen a desire to do good; beyond that, I can see that everything has changed; my system and my policies have had their day, but I am too old to change my course; that will be the task of my successor.[30]

His successor, Pope Leo XIII, was no less attached to the Church, but his strategy for ensuring its survival was more subtle and took account of the pressure for accommodation to

[30] Quoted in Vidler (1971), p.153.

the world that was being exerted by influential Catholics, lay and clerical. The Church in the eighteenth century had been forced to accommodate to the world of the Enlightenment and some of the difficulties experienced by the leaders of the Church in the nineteenth century was a consequence of that compromise. Ironically, Pope Pius IX, by his refusal to accommodate to the world and the policy decisions taken as a consequence of that resistance, left the Church even further compromised, though in a different way. He committed the Church to an inflexible bureaucratic and theological structure which would make virtually any proposal for change a threat to the foundations of Catholicism. The world would change and pose new problems for the Church, but theologians were powerless to respond to them imaginatively, as indicated by the monotonous repetition of nineteenth-century dogmatics in approved manuals of theology since Pius IX.

3

The Leonine Strategy

Tell your priests not to shut themselves up within the walls of their church or their presbytery, but to go to the people and to concern themselves wholeheartedly with the workers, the poor, and the men of the lower classes. In our time above all, it is necessary to combat their prejudices and to bridge the abyss between the priest and the people.

Pope Leo Xiii[1]

Pope Leo XIII was primarily responsible for the change of official policy that marked the end of the long pontificate of Pius IX and the beginning of a new stage in the Church's relationship to the modern world. His reputation has survived among Catholics as an innovator, a man of vision and courage who opened the minds of clergy and laity to a new dimension of Christian witness in the world and opened the Church to the world in a spirit of reconciliation and service. Leo is particularly remembered for his attempts to find a religious solution to the social question which, for nearly a century, had been posed in anti-religious terms. His other major achievement was the radical re-structuring of Catholic thought by the imposition of the philosophy and theology of St Thomas Aquinas as the sole system of ideas mandatory on all seminaries and colleges for the training of the clergy. The nature of Leo's strategy, the relationship between these two central aspects of it and their consequences for the Church and for individual Catholics—these are the questions to be discussed in this chapter.

[1] Quoted in Brugerette (1935), p.377.

Liberalism and Authority

The adjournment of the First Vatican Council in July 1870 put an end, for a time, to disputes within the Church on the question of authority. The victory of ultramontanism was the triumph of a Catholic movement for the spiritual regeneration of society through the exaltation of papal authority and the centralization of the Church. The Council crushed the spirit of liberalism which, for almost fifty years, had been a candidate for official acceptance by the Church. What might have been the fate of Catholicism if the ideas of Lamennais, Buchez and their associates had prevailed instead of those of Maistre, Veuillot and Pope Pius IX no one can know. When Catholic liberalism re-emerged in the twentieth century it owed little to the men whose writings inspired some and outraged others in the century before.

Two questions dominated Catholic debate in the nineteenth century and they were related, though frequently argued independently of one another: the structure of authority, which divided ultramontanes from liberals on the issue of papal power and freedom of thought and expression throughout the Church, and the social question which concerned the application of Church teaching to the distribution of wealth and income. Usually an ultramontanist position on authority was conjoined to a similarly authoritarian view of the social question—though the reverse was not always the case: the modernists, at the turn of the century, were liberals in the sphere of authority but showed no particular interest in the social problem.

Joseph de Maistre is commonly regarded as the founder of ultramontanism, and in his writings he provides clear evidence of the need in the conservative Catholic mind for the structure of the Church and society to reflect and complement one another. 'Man is too wicked to be free', he wrote in his major work on the Pope. For Maistre, the French Revolution was radically evil in attempting to shake off the authority of the old regime and to establish democracy in its place. Throughout his writings the religious is interwoven with the political in a way that led one commentator to describe them as 'a slightly cleaned up paganism'.[2] Maistre's aim was to secure the restora-

[2] Faguet, quoted in Reardon (1975), p.42.

tion of pre-revolutionary France and a Catholic monarchy in which the stability of the social order would be guaranteed by the primacy of the spiritual and the supremacy of the Pope. His reasoning was simple. In a letter to the Duc de Blacas he wrote:

Never forget this reasoning: no public morality and no national character without religion. No European religion without Christianity. No Christianity without Catholicism, no Catholicism without the Pope. No Pope without the supremacy which is his prerogative.[3]

The central figure in the Catholic liberal movement of the nineteenth century was Félicité de Lamennais, a Breton priest, whose defence of liberty and the Church brought him immense prestige in his early years and might have earned him high office had not changed political circumstances and the accession of Pope Gregory XVI determined otherwise. He died in obscurity in 1854, rejected by the Church and impotent to influence it in the revolutionary socialist direction taken in his later writings. But in his youthful *Essay on Indifference*, which won him acclaim within and beyond France, Lamennais argued as an ultramontane in terms very similar to those of Maistre and Louis de Bonald, Maistre's contemporary and fellow-reactionary. Lamennais too wanted a Catholic monarchy and viewed the effects of the Enlightenment and the Revolution as destructive. He advocated the theocratic doctrine of the Middle Ages, echoing Maistre:

Without the Pope there can be no Church, without the Church no Christianity, and without Christianity no religion and no society, which implies that the life of the European nations is solely dependent on the power of the papacy.[4]

Lamennais attacked the cult of reason and the spirit of Cartesian philosophy which had infected Catholicism. Individual reason cannot itself be the ground of certitude: its role must be confined to acknowledging the authority of faith to which it must submit. He stressed the need for authority, as Maistre and Bonald had done, but for Lamennais the task was not simply

[3] Dansette (1961), vol.1, p.214.
[4] *Ibid.*

one of reinstating the old monarchies but of creating a new order in which authority would function to protect and promote freedom. He wanted authority *and* liberty, and only a Catholic society could provide them. Lamennais began as a monarchist and a papalist, and his ultramontanism was wedded to liberalism with a style and idealism which won him fame and invigorated the Church in France.

It was an idealist position which he was soon forced to abandon as the political reality of monarchical government brought into relief the contradiction in Lamennais's teaching. He came to see monarchy as a form of despotism no better than that which had emerged during the Revolution. Only an alliance of a free Church with a free people could provide the spiritual resources for true liberty. Catholic struggles for freedom in Ireland, Belgium and Poland influenced Lamennais's shift from royalism. The only hope for the Church was to embrace liberalism, not to attack it, to baptize the Revolution, not to exorcize it, and to demand in the name of the Church the freedom of thought, conscience and expression which would encourage a return to authentic Christianity. As Lamennais's ideas changed and his liberalism took new form so the regard in which he was held at Rome began to cool. The French bishops, who still yearned for the old alliance between throne and altar, found much to complain about in Lamennais's attitude to the July revolution of 1830: 'Society as a whole is aware that a new order must take the place of the old and that the world is moving forward to a new destiny', he wrote; 'To suppose that the movement which impels it can be arrested is to wish to bring time to a stop.'[5]

Lamennais founded a liberal journal, *L'Avenir*, to promulgate his ideas and to promote liberal reforms throughout the Catholic world, but the increasing hostility of the bishops reduced its circulation almost to the point of bankruptcy and persuaded him to appeal directly to the Pope for support. Pope Gregory XVI was not a likely ally. Authoritarian by temperament, his susceptibility to the political pressure of conservative governments placed the idealistic Lamennais at a considerable disadvantage. The Austrian Chancellor, Metternich, who was

---

[5] *L'Avenir*, 1 July 1831, quoted in Reardon (1975), p.93.

instrumental in securing Gregory's election as Pope, instructed his Vatican representative Lützow to warn the Pope of 'this atrocious man' and the 'detestable amalgam of religion and politics' which Lamennais was teaching.[6] Lamennais's ideas were duly condemned and their author, one of the Fathers of Catholic liberalism, was isolated and effectively silenced. He had united the liberal and ultramontane movements in France and, for a time, they continued to work in harmony against a state which had become increasingly secular and indifferent to the interests and needs of the Church.

The main issue which united conservatives and liberals was education. Church freedom to have schools independent of the Napoleonic state system led to Catholic demands for freedom of education for all religions, Catholic, Protestant and Jewish. The violent aftermath of the 1848 revolution ended that alliance as it ended the liberalizing honeymoon which began the pontificate of Pope Pius IX. Conservatives and liberals parted company, with the conservatives taking ultramontanism with them as their distinctive cause which would eventually triumph in the definition of papal infallibility at the First Vatican Council. Nineteenth-century Catholic liberalism died in 1870. From then on, the concept of freedom in the Church would carry that special qualification which made it indistinguishable from authoritarianism. Error could have no freedom, no rights. Since the Church embodied the truth in its fullest degree, only a conscience informed by Catholic doctrine could be free.

The division in France between liberals and conservatives was paralleled throughout Europe and was focused, as in France, on the personalities of one or two key figures. In Spain the disciples of Diego Balmes and Donoso Corses continued their quarrel; in Belgium Dumertier and Deschamps were opposed by the conservative Cardinal Sterckx; in England Newman and Manning and in Germany the theological schools of Tübingen and Mainz contested the structure of authority in the Church and the measure of freedom of inquiry and expression permissible to its clergy and laity.

On the social question, the Church of the nineteenth century

[6] Metternich to Lützow, 19 May 1832, quoted in Woodward (1963), p. 265.

responded to demands for a social teaching adequate to the new industrial conditions somewhat more flexibly. Rome could not tolerate any relaxation of its control of beliefs but there was less intransigence on the issue of social justice in so far as the two problems could be separated and treated independently. The wholehearted commitment of the Church to socialism, as Lamennais demanded in his later writings, was out of the question, given the revolutionary context which defined socialism in the nineteenth century. Not until the pontificate of Pope Pius XI and his encyclical *Quadragesimo Anno* in 1931 would any concession be made to socialism, and then only to draw into sharper relief the anti-religious character of communism. But not all Catholic pressure for a solution to the social and economic problems of poverty and exploitation in the industrial revolution entailed a socialist programme of reform, nor did this pressure derive exclusively from those who held liberal ideas in the sphere of doctrine and authority.

The history of social Catholicism is not so much the story of an awakening of Catholic consciences to the plight of the poor, as of a new awareness of the plight of the Church and of the threat to its existence posed by socialism. As socialism progressed after 1830 and the protests against the condition of the industrialized masses grew to agitation for fundamental change in the economic system, echoes of that protest began to be heard in Catholic circles. Lamennais was an outspoken critic of the politics that held wages at a minimum to ensure the maximum gain in terms of profit and the supply of labour. Chateaubriand had earlier denounced the 'excessive inequality of conditions and fortunes'. Frederic Ozanam founded the Society of St Vincent de Paul in 1833 in an attempt to alleviate the sufferings of the poor and to calm the rising temper of the proletariat. His campaign for a Church relevant to the needs of the masses ended with the violence of 1848. Philippe Buchez took a more political view of the condition of the poor. His message for Catholics was to work for the structural reform of society, not charity, and for a reconciliation between the Church and the Revolution in order to conjoin the Christian hope of heaven with justice on earth.

Not until it was clear that socialism was something more than a passing phase—not until the 1870s, when the cause of the workers demanding a share in the wealth of nations had firmly impressed itself on governments throughout Europe —did these scattered appeals for a Catholic response to that cause receive official recognition. Foremost among those immediately involved in persuading the Vatican to take notice and to formulate a new teaching on the social question was Emmanuel von Ketteler, an aristocrat who exchanged the Prussian civil service for the priesthood and, in 1850, the bishopric of Mainz. Ketteler was sympathetic to the socialist ideals of Ferdinand Lassalle, the leader of the German socialist party, but he was careful in his writing to avoid the suspicion of being less Catholic than socialist, less religious than political. Only under the guidance of the Catholic Church could the aspirations of the workers be fulfilled. Ketteler's moderation, and the fact that the Vatican was not as politically sensitive to the German secular establishment as it was to the French, allowed him greater freedom to develop and preach his views than he might have had otherwise. Inequality of wealth must be tolerated for the sake of peace, he argued. 'On the other hand, the Church also sanctifies the idea of communism by rededicating the use property to the welfare of all.'[7] In his idea that the Church already contains all that is most human and liberal in the competing ideologies of capitalism and communism, the future Pope Leo XIII would find a strategy better adapted to the needs of his pontificate than the sweeping anathemas pronounced by his two predecessors. Ketteler's solution to the social question was a major influence on his thinking, and Leo acknowledged his debt to 'Our great precursor' in his famous encyclical *Rerum Novarum*.

The Leonine Approach to Knowledge

The pontificate of Pope Leo XIII continued the Roman struggle against the erosion of papal power and signalled a change of direction in Catholic thinking about the world in general and about the scientific and economic aspects of modernity in particular. The Pope chose an unlikely instrument for

[7] See Alexander (1953), p.541.

the recovery of his authority: the restoration of the philosophy and theology of Aquinas as the basis of Catholic teaching. The rediscovery of Thomism was not a purely cognitive affair, intended to provide an intellectually valid basis for the beliefs of Catholics in the face of widespread scepticism about the Church and religion in the nineteenth century. It was a policy designed to change more than the manuals on seminary desks, as the French-Canadian scholar, Pierre Thibault, has demonstrated.[8] Contrary to popular thinking, the revival of Thomism by Pope Leo XIII was not a matter of peripheral interest in Church history, affecting only clerics and their training like the later and uncharacteristic imposition of Latin in the seminaries by Pope John XXIII. It was the centre of a political strategy intended to bring about the restoration of a Christian social order, an organic hierarchic society united by common values and common faith under the temporal kingship of secular rulers and under the ultimate authority of the Pope.

Pope Leo XIII was not a liberal, either in theology or in politics. He was first and last an ecclesiastic, a man of the visible Roman Church who noticed, during his nunciature in Belgium, that the Church in a liberal society had opportunities for survival and growth not apparent in more Catholic and authoritarian countries, like Austria. The victory of ultramontanism over national churches and the growth of new democratic institutions in place of the old monarchies provided an opportunity to restore the power of the papacy—not directly in temporal affairs, but indirectly through the papal control of the beliefs of Catholics living in secular society. It was a form of secular and subversive ultramontanism, the doctrinal and philosophical basis of which could be found in the writings of the thirteenth-century Dominican friar, Thomas Aquinas. Its practical implementation would be achieved by encouraging Catholics loyal to the Pope to act as leaven—a Roman leaven—in the mass of secular society.

According to Pope Leo XIII, it was the analytical genius and encyclopaedic knowledge of St Thomas Aquinas which gave Thomism its significance in the history of the Church and

[8] Thibault (1972). I am indebted to this work for much of the discussion of Thomism which follows.

justified its restoration. The social and political evils of the modern world were rooted in philosophical and theological error. The revival of Thomism would protect the Church against the errors of secular philosophy and science, and show that no contradiction existed between the teaching of the Church and the findings of modern physics. Thomism would, above all, express the authentic teaching of Christianity on the questions of liberty, authority and the basis of civil power. 'Of all my encyclicals,' the Pope declared later, 'that which is closest to my heart and which gives me most consolation is the encyclical *Aeterni Patris* on the restoration of scholastic and Thomist philosophy.'[9]

At the beginning of the nineteenth century, Thomism was little more than an obscurantist relic of the Middle Ages. Even in official Church circles, according to Thibault, the writings of St Thomas were of peripheral interest. Their redemption from obscurity was not the achievement of Pope Leo XIII. He was responsible for elevating Thomism to the level of official Catholic teaching and for excluding all rival systems of philosophy whose co-existence with scholasticism before the Leonine period lent some status and credibility to Catholic scholarship. Contending systems of thought within the Church were not to the Pope's liking. 'A multitude of opinions,' he wrote in *Aeterni Patris*, 'easily leads to hesitations or doubts.' The movement to restore Thomism began about fifty years before the papal encyclical which gave it official sanction and it was led, not by Dominican friars, as might have been appropriate, but by a group of Italian Jesuits whose ultramontanist theology encouraged a search for a political theory which would re-establish the power of Rome in the conditions of modern society.[10]

The political role which Thomism was destined to play in the affairs of the Church had been outlined in the early articles in *Civiltà Cattolica*. Taparelli d'Azeglio and Matteo Liberatore, whose influence on the thinking of the future Pope Leo XIII has been documented by Thibault, were co-founders of this

---

[9] Thomas Pègues, *Revue Thomiste*, May 1901, p.132, quoted in Thibault (1972), p.146.

[10] Thibault (1972), p.101ff.

journal, the orientation of which, they declared, was politically neutral, accepting in principle all forms of government.[11] The only solution for modern society threatened by socialism, argued the *Civiltà*, was to return to a situation in which people and rulers submitted to the authority of religion. The evils of modern society had as their basis Protestant individualism, the consequence of which was universal suffrage, resulting in anarchy and communism. For the Thomists of the *Civiltà*, only the postulate of a natural, immutable and objective social order could remedy these evils, and they offered religion to the established rulers of the world as an instrument of political power and social stability in return for the state protection of the Church which would guarantee its privileges and enhance its social status and significance.

Contrary to his own disclaimers and those of his *Civiltà* advisers, Leo's decision to impose Thomism as the standard and guide of Catholic orthodoxy had politics as its source and the transformation of the political situation in Europe as its end. Even the philosopher Etienne Gilson, an ardent admirer of the Pope and supporter of Thomism, must interpret the Thomist policy of the Pope as an essentially political action intended to stem the tide of wars and useless revolutions which, in the view of Leo, resulted from the abandonment of the Catholic faith. If the cult of reason and the seemingly endless multiplication of philosophies were the main symptoms of society's ills, as the Pope understood them, then the restoration of the primacy of the word of God, *even in philosophy*, must be the first step towards effecting a cure.[12]

The elements of Thomist writings which attracted the attention of the Pope and his consultants were St Thomas's theory of knowledge and his political theory. Since their goal was to restore clerical and papal power in the Church and by means of that authority to regain the Church's influence in secular affairs, the promoters of the new policy needed to combat the theories of knowledge which, since Descartes and

---

[11] Leo echoed these sentiments in his encyclical *Sapientiae Christianae*: 'The Church rejects none of the various forms of state, provided only that religion and morality are protected.'

[12] Gilson (1960), p.246.

Kant, elevated reason as the *active* element of knowledge and, effectively, made the world as it is unknowable. If knowledge, therefore, is the activity of the subject, and if there can be no guarantee that the world as it is known exists in that form outside the knowing subject—if this is the case then all clerical authority is undermined. Clerical authority rests on a revelation about the world of which the clergy alone is the authentic interpreter. It tends to absolutism, since any multiplication of those with access to the truth increases the danger of dissent and increases the possibility of relativizing this truth of revelation to the experience and situation of the individual. In the context of Protestant subjectivism and the rationalism of the nineteenth century, Thomism appeared to provide the solution to all the problems of an ultramontanist Church. It stressed the *passivity* of knowledge and the capacity of the knowing subject to grasp the essence of things as they really exist. This capacity, however, cannot be exercised without the aid of a revelation from God who is the source of all essences, all created things. The knowledge of the objective world, which is proper to the faculty of the intellect acting passively to receive *things* in the form of *ideas*, is in fact impossible to achieve because of sin and the consequent need of the supernatural help of revelation. Because of sin, all intellectual competence depends upon the *magisterium* of the Church as the guardian of that revelation. In Thomism, reason is the slave of faith, as philosophy is subordinate to theology and civil authority to ecclesiastical. Clericalism is fundamentally anti-democratic. It is threatened by any attempt to democratize knowledge and locate the creative process of knowledge in the individual. Clerical power rests on the control of beliefs exercised in relation to a divine revelation. It was the genius of St Thomas to provide a rational support for the existence of such a revelation and for its political consequences: the belief in the subordination of civil authority to the *magisterium* of the Church. It was the genius of Pope Leo XIII to recognise in Thomism an instrument for the recovery of papal power from the world without the damaging consequences of opposing it openly as his predecessor had done. It was the grand strategy of the Pope to deploy the intellectual and moral forces at his command in order to shift the social order to that level on which St Thomas wrote his *Summa*—the level of 'pontifical theocracy', as Gilson has called it, 'which no longer demands the suppression of the temporal power of princes but its subordination to the kingship of the earthly vicar of Christ'.[13] Thomism provided the Church at the end of the nineteenth century with the most refined instrument of intellectual discipline and papal imperialism.

'I intend to pursue a grand policy,' Leo announced the day following his election, and he did so with a political goal clearly in sight.[14] The threat of socialism facing European governments offered him an opportunity for an exchange of services between Church and state, to their mutual benefit. Throughout his pontificate, Leo was deeply concerned, almost obsessed, by the evils of modern society which he saw embodied particularly in socialism. He was convinced that the Church had an essential political role to play in the modern world and that the Church alone was capable of restoring the ruins of society. The 'deadly propaganda of socialism', as he described it in the encyclical *Quod Apostolici*, was destroying civilization and could only be combated by a Church teaching which nurtured in citizens from their infancy a respect for private property and for the authority of the state. While the Church affirmed the equality of all men in nature and in their final end, it equally affirmed and defended their inequality of wealth and power. In a later encyclical on the missions, *Sancta Dei Civitas*, the Pope continued his overtures to civil authorities, pointing out to them the benefits, in terms of European influence throughout the world, that accrue from the Church's missionary activity.

Leo's anxiety to recover the papal states made him particularly affable towards the German government, which he saw as a possible ally against Italy, and he made similarly friendly approaches to France and to its President, Jules Grévy. Once again, socialism was the problem to be solved by the Church in return for the reintegration of the Church into French society. Grévy's response, while making it clear that he too desired such an exchange, pointed to the difficulty in coming to an agreement of that nature: the refusal of French Catholics to accept

---

[13] Gilson (1944), p.574.
[14] Daniel-Rops (1963), p.150.

French republicanism in good faith. In 1892, much to the distress of traditionalists, who shared the Pope's general ambitions for the Church, but not his political subtlety, French Catholics were instructed to rally to the republic and to transfer the energies expended in constitutional dispute to the arena of legislation for the good of the Church. The indirect power over secular society which Pope Leo XIII's strategy sought to achieve and for which Thomism provided the political theory was outlined in *Immortale Dei*, 1885: Church and state are both perfect societies, each sovereign in its own sphere. But the end of the Church is superior to that of the state. They have mutual interests requiring mutual respect and the Church can never tolerate subordination to any civil authority. The health of society and the stability of its institutions depend upon the health and sovereignty of the Church.

The effect of papal policy on Catholic philosophy and doctrine was to create a clergy, professoriat and hierarchy ignorant of all currents of thought other than a particular and solidified version of Thomism. For the rest of his life, the Pope defended his policy and insisted on adhesion to the letter, with increasing impatience and severity towards laxists and deviants. By 1892, no one could hold a chair at any Catholics institution who did not subscribe fully to the doctrine of St Thomas as interpreted by the Vatican authorities. This was followed by a purge of the theological faculties at Rome, removing dissidents, whatever their intellectual merit, and making Thomist orthodoxy a condition of employment. As Thibault reports, Thomists found themselves comfortably dispensed from doing any work other than to repeat indefinitely the facts, ideas and form of exposition of St Thomas Aquinas. This papal philosophy, which took a medieval system from its context and raised it to the level of official Catholic teaching, had the effect of freezing doctrinal tradition and imposing it, immutable and eternal, on the whole Church. As a consequence, Catholic scholarship was stripped of a historical dimension for three-quarters of a century.[15] (It would be restored—with interest—after the Second Vatican Council.)

---

[15] Thibault (1972), p.155ff. On the isolation of Catholic philosophers from influential secular ideas see Eric d'Arcy in Outka and Reeder (1973).

As a highly rationalized system of apologetics, if not philosophy, Thomism provided the Church with a defence against Enlightenment attacks of superstition and irrationality while at the same time ensuring the compliance of Catholic scholars with the judgements of ecclesiastical authority. The Church bowed to Reason, but it could not tolerate the individualism which was an essential part of the scientific ethos. The Church bowed also to the state, over which it no longer claimed direct power. But since the state, like the intellect, is wounded by sin, it requires the guidance of a sinless Church if it is to promote the common good. Catholics had nothing to fear and everything to gain by welcoming the modern world. Modern society offered the occasion and Thomism offered the ideological means of giving the Church a new political role without renouncing any of its intransigence. This was the basis of Leo's strategy. The new world and the old philosophy would enable the Church to emerge from ineffective protest and condemnation and move to the offensive and to the acquisition of indirect power.

The Leonine Approach to Social Justice

Pope Leo's approach to the social problem was more predictable and more obviously influenced by pressures within the Church to adapt its teaching to problematic conditions in the secular world than was his policy on philosophy and doctrine. Among the more immediate factors creating pressure for change was the campaign of the French industrialist Léon Harmel. Harmel operated a spinning factory at Val-des-Bois, near Rheims, on lines which, though paternalistic by contemporary standards, were in advance of their time. It embodied a radical critique of economic liberalism within a framework of orthodox Catholicism and became the prototype of a later movement among Catholic industrialists to model their factories on the teaching of Pope Leo XIII's *Rerum Novarum* and to demonstrate to the world the effectiveness of Church teaching in solving the problems of industrial society. In 1885, Harmel organized the first of a series of pilgrimages of employers and workers to the Vatican in order to influence the Pope to stimulate a movement of Catholic action which would give the

Church a role in resolving the social and economic conflict of the industrialized nations. During the same period, the Pope was in touch with a group of Catholic social leaders from several European countries who formed the Fribourg Union, under the bishop of Fribourg, Mgr Mermillod, and whose aim was to develop and promote an industrial strategy for the Church. The content of Pope Leo XIII's teaching on the social question was largely based on lengthy discussions with members of this group in 1888.

The encyclical *Rerum Novarum* was published in 1891, setting out the teaching of the Church on 'The Condition of Labour', as the English translation is called. It is a watershed in Catholic history. The document was welcomed by most Catholics at the time as a masterly account of the social problem in the context of Catholic doctrine and a significant departure from the policy of entrenchment and detachment from the world which had stifled all previous attempts by Catholics to come to terms with contemporary problems. Not all were convinced, it is true. Henry Scott Holland described it as 'the voice of some old-world life, faint and ghostly, speaking in some antique tongue of things long ago;'[16] but it was a voice, however faint, that addressed the modern world in a way that none of Leo's predecessors had done. For the first time the world was treated with respect and its relationship with the Church was acknowledged as being problematic for both parties. Hitherto, the Church had suffered the world, resisted its imperialism, built defences against its evils. That period was now over and Catholics were being encouraged to cooperate with secular institutions and to work for their improvement—cautiously, it must be added, but in a spirit of apparent reconciliation.

Chief among the reasons for the Pope's readiness to yield to the pressure of Catholic opinion was the threat of socialism and its challenge to the legitimacy of those governments on which the Vatican depended for the recovery of the Papal States. It was not until 1929 that the Vatican finally abandoned its claim to those territories over which the Pope previously exercised temporal power and formally accepted the constitutional posi-

[16] See Vidler (1969), p.127.

tion of the Italian state. In the late nineteenth century, the Popes regarded themselves as prisoners in the Vatican, monarchs deprived of their territory, the recovery of which was as much an issue with Leo XIII as it was with Pius IX.

The ideological aspect of Leo's anti-socialist policy has been discussed. At the level of social organization, his strategy was to demonstrate that the Church already had a solution to the problems posed by socialists and that the interests of the workers and their emancipation from enslavement to material conditions were better served by Catholicism than by the godless creeds of socialism or communism. The Pope did not mince words in defining the enemies of Church and state:

> the sect of men who are known by the diverse and almost barbaric names of Socialists, Communists and Nihilists. Spreading all over the earth and closely linked in an iniquitous pact . . . they are trying to bring to its culmination a long-standing design to overthrow the very foundations of the civil order. (*Quod Apostolici*, 1878)

The conservative German government, which, in the same year, was threatened by a wave of assassination attempts, allegedly socialist-inspired, and whose assistance against the new Kingdom of Italy Leo XIII was actively canvassing, was as much in the Pope's mind when he wrote that encyclical as the barbarian alliance he condemned. Leo XIII genuinely abhorred socialism with all the passion Gregory XVI reserved for liberalism and democracy. His world-view differed little from that of Gregory: private property was a right sanctioned by natural law, and the unequal distribution of wealth reflected in the stratification of societies into different social classes was an inviolable part of the God-given social order. It was the major error of socialism that it sought to tamper with and destroy this organic union of the different components of society.

Writing to the Emperor William II of Germany shortly before the publication of *Rerum Novarum*, the Pope outlined the service his forthcoming encyclical might render: 'Religion will teach the emperor to respect the worker's human dignity and to treat him with justice and equity. It will inculcate into the conscience of the worker the sentiment of duty and fidelity and will render him moral, sober and honest.'[17] Some months previously, he had addressed one of Harmel's pilgrimages of French workers on the importance of private property and of the stability of the social order, and appealed to them to turn away from socialism and to seek a Catholic solution to their problems:

Around you, dear children, thousands of other workers are agitating. Seduced by false doctrines, they imagine that they can find a remedy for their misery in the destruction and annihilation of the property which constitutes the very essence of civil and political society. What vain illusions! They will only run up against unalterable laws which nothing can suppress. They will spew the paths they travel with blood and will bring on ruin, discord and disorder.[18]

The defence of social hierarchy and the defence of private property ranked high among the motives which inspired *Rerum Novarum*. On the more progressive side, the encyclical introduced an element of distributive justice into Catholic teaching to supplement the individualistic tradition of charity:

Public institutions and laws set aside the ancient religion. Hence, by degrees it has come to pass that working men have been surrendered, isolated and helpless, to the hard-heartedness of employers and the greed of unchecked competition . . . so that a small number of very rich men have been able to lay upon the teeming masses of the labouring poor a yoke little better than that of slavery itself. . . . [It is] a dictate of natural justice more imperious and ancient than any bargain between man and man, namely, that wages ought not to be insufficient to support a frugal and well-behaved wage-earner.[19]

But the concern for social justice which the Pope advocated was conditional upon the retention of the economic system which exalted private property as a sacred institution. The worker was encouraged to 'practise thrift, and he will not fail, by

[17] Quoted in Camp (1969), p.81. The German Emperor was convinced of the need to placate the workers and formulated a social policy which forced the Pope to publish *Rerum Novarum* earlier than planned in order to retain the initiative.
[18] Pope Leo XIII to workers' pilgrimage, 20 Oct, 1889, quoted in Camp (1969), p.53.
[19] English translation, 'The Condition of Labour', in Gilson (1954).

cutting down expenses, to put by some little savings and thus secure a modest source of income. . . .'

We have seen that this great labour question cannot be solved save by assuming as a principle that private ownership must be held sacred and inviolable. The law, therefore, should favour ownership, and its policy should be to induce as many as possible of the people to become owners.[20]

The most surprising achievement of *Rerum Novarum* was its support of the right of workers to form trade unions and to take strike action if the situation demanded it. And provided the state did not impinge upon the rights of the family, the Pope supported state intervention to regulate wages and conditions of work. Not all trade unions were open to Catholic workers, however. *Rerum Novarum* is not precise on this point, but in a later encyclical in 1895 the Pope reminded Catholics that they could not join organizations run on anti-religious lines and should, wherever possible, pursue their legitimate aims in Catholic organizations supervised by the clergy.[21] Trade unionism, therefore, was required and intended by the Church to be a form of Catholic Action, not a neutral sphere of activity independent of Catholics' beliefs and religious commitments.

Catholic Action was a movement inaugurated by Leo XIII with the aim of encouraging the Catholic laity to shake off the ghetto mentality of the previous half-century and to take a fuller part in social and political affairs. Model factories, trade unions, cooperatives, youth clubs, credit associations—these were some of the organizations that were fostered to promote the new policy. Catholic Action was not intended to reduce hierarchic control over lay activity but, on the contrary, to increase it. As Von Aretin says, lay organizations before Leo XIII were fewer in number but they enjoyed a greater measure of independence from clerical control.[22]

Leo's solution to the social question was, in one respect, an illusion. It created a new sense of freedom for Catholics, of openness towards the modern world and concern for its prob-

[20] *Ibid.*
[21] Pope Leo XIII, encyclical *Longinqua Oceani*, 6 Jan 1895.
[22] Von Aretin (1970), p.186.

lems. But the reality was an integrist or totalist movement calculated to subject all areas of thought and action to the judgement and supervision of the Vatican through the local hierarchy. It was another form of ghetto—more subtle, less obtrusive, but with essentially the same objective as the ghetto it replaced: to recover the Church's dominance in society and regain control of every aspect of Catholics' lives and to shield them from the enticements of a world still perceived as unquestionably hostile to religion and to the Church. 'Our aspiration,' said one of the Pope's collaborators on *Rerum Novarum*, 'is to recreate the social order that the Catholic Church alone can give us and we ask, therefore, that the Church be restored to exterior, social liberty so that it may resume the government of society and civilization.'[23]

The intellectual and social policies of Leo XIII were designed for the same end: the restoration of the power and influence of the Church in the secular world through a disciplined laity. The aim was no different under Leo from that of his predecessor, Pius IX, nor was his awareness that the chief obstacle to its realization lay in the political, intellectual and economic developments that characterized the modern world. What was different was the strategy of dealing with these secular trends. Whereas Pio Nono's response was to build a psychological and moral fence between the Church and the world, feeding his flock on a mixture of sentimental piety and triumphalist theology, Leo XIII attempted to control the world by manipulating certain features of it. He stimulated Catholic scholarship—this was the desired impression, though, as we have seen, the reality was closer to censorship than scholarship—and encouraged Catholic involvement in political and economic institutions with a view to transforming them into agencies of Catholic values and clerical power. The Pope had no wish to make the Church relevant to the modern world. On the contrary, he sought to create a Catholic elite that would infiltrate society, make the world relevant to the Church and bring it once again under the subjection of the hierarchy. Pope Leo XIII's concern to promote scholarship and social justice in the nineteenth century can be compared to the tobacco indus-

[23] Giuseppe Toniolo, quoted in Houtart and Rousseau (1971), p.106.

try's concern for health in the present day: the interest is real, the gains to health are not inconsiderable, but the commitment is not what it seems.

A consequence of Leo's pontificate was to create confidence among the Catholic intelligentsia that a door had been opened to the world and some measure of liberty to experiment in both the intellectual and social spheres had been granted. He made Newman a cardinal, despite the English convert's known liberal views and opposition to papal absolutism; he opened the Vatican archives to scholars and gave some mild encouragement to biblical criticism. These were not significant changes but they served to create the general impression of liberalism and to encourage scholars and social reformers to tread less warily. It is an indication of the frustration of the Catholic intelligentsia that at the end of the nineteenth century they were prepared to see signs where there were only gestures and to hear in the words of the Pope not 'the voice of some old-world life, faint and ghostly' but the message of Catholic *aggiornamento* and Christian renewal. In a sense, one must conclude, Leo XIII betrayed the Catholic intelligentsia. He created an elite by his liberalizing strategy and opened a window to the world which permitted a whiff of secularity to drift through a Church that, for centuries, reeked of incense. It was left to his successor, Pope Pius X, to cope with the consequences.

The Aftermath of Leo's Liberalism

The modernist movement in the Catholic Church arose out of the general sense of confidence in the liberalism of Leo XIII and a sense of frustration with the state of Catholic scholarship. The study of the bible had not, for many centuries, enjoyed a high status in Catholic intellectual circles, and the long reign of Pius IX ensured that it would reach its nadir by the end of the nineteenth century. Liberal Protestants had adapted the tools of modern science to biblical criticism and an attempt was made by some Catholic scholars to engage in a similar enterprise in order to defend the Church against the implicit attacks of Protestantism.

The chief protagonists in this debate were the Protestant scholar, Adolf Harnack, and Alfred Loisy, a French priest who worked for a synthesis of Catholic doctrine and historical science and who suffered the fate of others before him, like Lamennais, who pushed too hard and too soon. Loisy's best-known work, *l'Evangile et l'Eglise*, was published in 1902 as a refutation of Harnack's *What is Christianity*, which had appeared two years earlier, and which attempted to strip Christianity of its Catholic accretions and display it in its essence as individual trust in the divine fatherhood. Harnack denied the scriptural basis of the Church as a divine institution. In his defence of the Church, however, Loisy offered an interpretation of dogma which contradicted the traditional Catholic view and opened a way to relativism. Theological truths did not fall from heaven—'divine though they may be in origin and substance, in structure and composition they are human': a healthy theology must face the problem of the relativity of dogma. For his theological views, which today are commonplace within the Church, Loisy was subjected to a storm of abuse from conservative Catholics. His work was placed on the Index in 1903 and he was excommunicated from the Church in 1908.

Alfred Loisy was not the only French Catholic to engage in critical analysis of the bible, nor was modernism an exclusively French phenomenon. In England, Italy, Germany and Belgium there were other Catholic scholars who rose to prominence and notoriety in the search for a scientifically-sound approach to Catholic theology and biblical studies. They had been encouraged by the aura of freedom emanating from the Vatican during the Leonine period. 'The younger generation don't seem to have realized what a pope, how great a pope, they had grown up under in Leo XIII,' wrote Edmund Bishop, one of the lesser-known English modernists. 'It is a wonderful thing to think that this great old man on his very deathbed, with all kinds of influences urgent upon him as the spirit was quitting the body, still resisted to the last the efforts to induce him to censure *l'Evangile et l'Eglise*. (Loisy's comment was more cynical, but still supports the point being made: 'There has been far too much praise of Leo XIII's generosity of mind; he was never more than a great politician.'[24])

[24] Letters to Dom Cuthbert Butler, 1903 and 1904, quoted in Vidler (1970) pp.138–9; Alfred Loisy (1931), p.578.

Modernism was not a school or system of theology. Condemned by Pope Pius X in his encyclical *Pascendi* in 1907 and described by him as 'a synthesis of all heresies', it never existed in a coherent form in the writings of the so-called 'modernists', who were, according to the Pope, 'lost to all sense of modesty', 'imbued with poisonous doctrines'. Most commentators are agreed that *Pascendi* was a caricature of the widely diverging views, aims and aspirations held by Catholic intellectuals who had little more in common than a desire to promote a Catholic scholarship ᴠ ⸴ich could withstand the scorn of the scientific world. The modernists themselves denied that they had ever formed a coherent body of thought or an organized school of theology. As Alec Vidler notes: 'What they had attempted to do was, while remaining sincere and loyal Roman Catholics, to forward such a revision and fresh presentation of the Church's teaching as would acclimatize it in the modern world.'[25] *Pascendi* was issued in 1908, and two months later the Pope decreed that anyone daring to contradict its teaching would be automatically excommunicated. He again attacked the modernists in the following month, accusing them of trying to undermine papal authority. In September 1910, he enjoined on all Catholic priests an anti-modernist oath against the beliefs alleged to constitute the heresy—an obligation which remained as a condition for the ordination of clergy until the 1960s and the close of the Second Vatican Council.

What moved the Pope and the Vatican Holy Office to this violent reaction was not any particular beliefs attributable to the modernists but the threat to the Church implicit in *any* attempt to make science rather than authority the arbiter of religious truth. Modernism did not exist before Pius X defined it. What did exist was an elite of Catholic intellectuals, created by Leo XIII, which did not belong within the ghetto of Catholicism, whose members moved easily within the world of secular learning and found the image of Catholicism within that world an embarrassment. Secular and Protestant advances in the historical-critical methods of study, on the one hand, and the near-fundamentalist state of Catholic studies on the other, had left Catholic intellectuals eager to grasp the

[25] Vidler (1971), p.180.

opportunities held out to them by the liberal gestures of Pope Leo XIII. For the first time since the Enlightenment, Catholic intellectuals felt not only free but called to reconcile Church teaching with the findings of modern science. But if Leo XIII provided the vocation, he did not provide the bureaucratic support for following it nor could he have done so without seriously endangering the structure of the Church which he had laboured to strengthen. There is no doubt that, had he lived to see Catholics take the opportunities afforded them by his liberalism, Leo XIII would have been forced to act in a way no less authoritarian than his successor. As many of the modernists knew well in their hearts, the intolerance of Pius X was, in the circumstances, the normal state of Catholic affairs, though some, like Antonio Fogazzaro, believed that the Church would change and that Catholic integrism—the moral totalitarianism that insists on the submission of the Catholic in every aspect of his life to the judgement of the religious authority—would disappear.

In the social sphere also, the consequence of Leo XIII's liberalism provoked a strong reaction from the Vatican authorities. It is not surprising that Pius X had little sympathy with ideas which smacked of socialism. Politically, he stood firm in a long tradition of papal conservatives who could not comprehend, much less entertain, the idea that the structure of society is a human accomplishment. For him, as for them, the social order was as natural as the human organism and it was blasphemous to tamper with the structure of either. 'The Church teaches that the different social classes remain as they are because it is obvious that nature demands it,' Leo XIII had written. 'It is in conformity with the order established by God in human society that there should be princes and subjects, employers and proletariat, rich and poor, instructed and ignorant,' wrote his successor, Pius X, a year later.[26] His condemnation of the Sillon was consistent with this teaching.

The Sillon movement was founded by Marc Sangnier in 1894 in response to the social teaching of Leo XIII in *Rerum Novarum*. With a group of young, middle-class Catholics who felt

---

[26] Pope Leo XIII, March 1902; Pope Pius X, December 1903—quoted in Houtart and Rousseau (1971), p.354.

inspired, both by conditions in France and by the teaching of the Pope, to work towards the twin goals of social justice and democracy, Sangnier founded study circles for young workers throughout the country as a means of changing Catholic opinion from its traditional conservatism to a new awareness of the religious dimensions of justice and democratic government.

In its beginnings, the Sillon was warmly welcomed by Church authorities who saw in the movement a group of ardent young Catholics anxious to promote their faith and to eschew politics. When the right-wing Catholic press criticized his activities, Sangnier requested and received the reassurance of the new Pope Pius X that the Sillon met with Vatican approval. But an increasing number of French bishops dissociated themselves and their clergy from the movement and the opposition from the right increased. Charles Maurras and his fascist party, Action Française, were active in trying to secure its condemnation in Rome. In 1910, Pius X condemned the Sillon and ordered its dissolution. He denounced its ecumenical character: 'What is to be thought of the promiscuity in which young Catholics will find themselves in company with the unorthodox and unbelievers of all sorts in a work of this character?', and he attacked the Sillonist approach to the social question, offering in its place a medievalism which echoed the ideas of Maistre and Bonald: '. . . the true friends of the people are neither revolutionaries nor innovators, but traditionalists.' The Sillon had plainly ignored the Pope's warning to the Italian Christian Democrats in 1903 that 'Catholic writers, in supporting the cause of the proletarians and the poor, must be careful not to use a language that can inspire in the people an aversion from the upper classes of society'.[27] The movement could continue in existence only if its members worked directly under episcopal control and in groups independent of each other. A mass movement of the laity for political ends could not be tolerated.

As the focus of Sillon activities shifted from the more religious to the more political so the opposition of the French hierarchy and the Vatican increased. When it was a religious movement no one insisted too much on clerical supervision; when it became a political movement the bishops and the Pope

[27] Quoted in Vidler (1969), p.138.

argued that it was really a religious movement and should, therefore, come under the direction of the clergy.[28]

By 1910, theological and social innovation in the Church had died. The elite which Leo XIII had encouraged was silenced and strict sanctions operated to discourage others from following their example. Leo formulated a modern strategy for a modern world. But the leaders who emerged in response to his call were not looking for a Church that would manipulate secular institutions for ecclesiastical ends. The world towards which Loisy and Tyrrell, Von Hugel, Buonaiuti and Sangnier were drawn and in which they lived and worked was not for them simply an obstacle to the expansion of Catholicism but the proper arena for the exercise of their Christian vocation. It remained to be seen whether their condemnation by Pius X and the command to retreat from that world would successfully quench the spirit of independent thought and action which, for good reason, so alarmed the Roman authorities. It remained to be seen also whether the social and political changes that had forced Leo XIII to encourage intellectuals as part of his liberal strategy would not continue to exert pressure for change on the Catholic hierarchy and for how long the ghetto which Pio Nono established in 1848, and which Pius X attempted to rebuild, could survive in the twentieth century.

Basically, a single issue underlies the two movements condemned by Pope Pius X: the freedom of the individual to think and act independently of clerical supervision and control. While it must be granted that Pope Pius X's depiction of modernism was a caricature and distorted the specific beliefs of the so-called 'modernists', he was nonetheless astute in his sociological assessment of the modernist trend. Given the commitment to the dogmatic, sacramental and hierarchic structure which constituted traditional Catholicism—and the Pope shared this commitment not only with his bishops but even with many modernists, including Loisy in his early years—the freedom implicit in the scientific ethic could not be

[28] See Camp (1969), pp.34–5 and 116ff. The firm stand of the Pope moved Charles Maurras to write a book in praise of Pius X, 'The Saviour of France'. The Pope reciprocated by not promulgating the Vatican condemnation of Maurras when his writings were censured by the Holy Office. See Von Aretin (1970), p.166.

tolerated. The refusal to submit the intellect to any authority other than that of scientific evidence is the unforgivable sin in Roman Catholicism, and modernism represented a serious threat to the status of that sin and to the integrity of the organization of the Church. The Church might adapt to the modern world of politics and economics; it might adapt to the content of modern science and modify its theology accordingly—that, after all, is what the development of Catholic doctrine entails. What it could never do without fundamental change of its structure is to permit the intellectual freedom of the individual which the scientific ethic requires.

Catholicism in the 1950s

The teaching of the Church was dominated by anti-modernism from 1908 until the death of Pope Pius XII in 1958. That period of fifty years—from the crushing of liberal hopes in the Church until their reawakening with the accession of Pope John XXIII—belongs to the stage of competition or rivalry with the world, inaugurated by Leo XIII. But the ethos of the period is essentially that of ghetto Catholicism, introduced by Pio Nono in the nineteenth century. Nothing dramatic occurred to shake the belief in the immutable and uniform character of Roman Catholicism, or to make visible the continuing and inexorable process of change which must one day be manifested. The world which set the context for the Church was changing at a bewildering pace. The Catholic Church—serene, medieval, triumphalist—seemed impervious to the scorn and antagonism of secular society. But already in the Enlightenment its social mechanism had been altered, and successive policies which failed to correct it—in medieval terms—only served to damage it further. During the first half of the twentieth century, the rumblings of malfunctioning were scarcely audible.

The year 1958 marked the end of old Catholicism—imperialist, authoritarian and totalitarian in action and intent. For reasons I shall argue, there is no parallel in the history of the Church to the crisis which followed the pontificate of Pope John XXIII. The Reformation, the French Revolution, Modernism—these were no trifling affairs and each in their turn seriously weakened the structure of traditional Catholicism. While each may be viewed and contrasted as a discrete phenomenon, they cannot be properly understood except as a process of which the Second Vatican Council is the climax. Forgotten seeds came to fruition in the 1960s, and the Council, though it took the religious and secular world by surprise at the time, was not the sudden eruption of spiritual forces that was thought. It was the culmination of a historical process reaching back into the late Middle Ages and it is as a climax, as a manifestation of that process, that it ranks above its historical antecedents.

The gaps through which Catholic intellectuals might converse with secular scholars and scientists were never entirely closed in the fifty years following the modernist crisis, but the circumstances of their dialogue were marked by such restrictions and inhibitions that Catholic life and teaching were not visibly different at the end of this fifty-year period from what they were in 1908. A limited freedom of inquiry was granted to biblical scholars in 1943 and a reform of the liturgy was announced four years later in the encyclical *Mediator Dei*. But any doubt about the official position of the Church in regard to modern scientific and philosophical movements—any suspicion that Pius XII might have softened on the modernist question was removed by his 1950 encyclical, *Humani Generis*, condemning 'false opinions that threaten to undermine the bases of Catholic teaching'. By proclaiming the dogma of the Assumption of the Virgin on the centenary of Pio Nono's definition of her Immaculate Conception and, in 1951, by the beatification of Pope Pius X, Pius XII indicated, as Von Aretin observes, that official Vatican policy in the 1950s was substantially in line with that of 'the two Popes who had been the most emphatic advocates of the Church's retreat from an encroaching world of science, politics and autonomous human development'.[29]

Pius XII was the last of the emperor-popes, and with him the modern form of papal absolutism, inaugurated by Pio Nono, reached its culmination and, probably, its end. He left Catholic scholarship where he had found it—under the control and

[29] *Ibid.*, p.225.

supervision of the Pope and his Curia; he exercised his powers with that sublime confidence that befits an infallible interpreter of God's revelation: 'When the popes explicitly pronounce judgement on a hitherto controversial question, it is a clear indication to all of us that, according to the intention and will of the popes, it should no longer be subject to free discussion by theologians' (*Humani Generis*). Catholic scholarship was effectively stifled under his rule, but he could not isolate some Catholic scholars from the pressures that forced them to think outside the framework of theology manuals; he could not cure the frustration of the French worker-priests, of theologians like De Lubac, Congar, Schell, Maier and Guardini who risked the wrath of the Roman Curia in order to adapt Catholic theology and practice to the realities of society in the early part of the twentieth century. There is not much evidence of a personal link between them and the modernists at the turn of the century. But they felt the same zeal as the modernists to answer the call of Leo XIII to bring their talents to bear on a solution to the world's problems; they felt the same frustration when their solutions were rejected if they deviated from those already available in Catholic tradition as interpreted at Rome. The vocation to be in the world yet not of it was difficult enough. In the sense in which it was demanded of Catholic intellectuals in the first half of the twentieth century it was impossible. But their sustained attempt to resolve this contradiction between the ideal of a Church oriented to modern society and its problems and the authoritarian practice of the Roman Curia was of great significance for later developments in the Church. It is the subject of the next chapter.

It is helpful at this point to construct a model of Catholic teaching in the 1950s which represents the orthodox position contrasting Catholicism with other Christian churches. It is not claimed that this set of core beliefs summarizes the content of faith consciously held by all or even the majority of Catholics. What Catholics believed at any period of history has never been more than a crude approximation of the official version of their faith. They believed what the Church taught, though probably most could not list the main tenets of that faith. They knew of its existence from infancy, even if they could not articulate its main elements. They were reminded of these beliefs, of their absolute, binding and specific character, not only by the usual channels of religious teaching but by the significance attached to any public deviations from them. In the sense in which I refer to it, the teaching of the Church consists of those beliefs which the Church shows its readiness and ability to defend against any public denial or modification by its own members. In this sense, the core beliefs of the Church at the end of Pius XII's reign can be summarized as follows:

(1) God is personal, loving and transcendent.

(2) Mankind exists in a sinful state because of a historic fall of Adam and Eve, and to this original sin, each of us adds actual sin for which we are individually responsible.

(3) Sin is an obstacle to salvation and without God's grace this obstacle cannot be removed. By a life of morality and good works, we can cooperate with grace and so merit the reward of salvation.

(4) Salvation is possible through the redeeming work of Christ, fully God and man, whose physical death and resurrection made atonement for sin and made available God's presence to man in the gift of the Holy Spirit.

(5) Christ founded his Church to continue his work of ruling, teaching and sanctifying. To the apostles, he gave the power, the strength and the guarantee to perform this work; this power has been transmitted to the bishops of the Church and the primacy has passed from St Peter to the Roman Pontiffs, by whose infallibility the teaching of the Church is protected from error.

(6) Grace is primarily made available through the sacraments administered by the hierarchic priesthood. We enter the sacramental life through baptism and share fully in it by participating in the Eucharist, which is the re-enactment of Christ's death and resurrection and in which bread and wine are changed into the body and blood of Christ.

(7) At the hour of death, each person must undergo a judgement by God determining the balance of sin and merit during his life, rewarding the just with heaven, consigning the unjust to hell and damnation, with purgatory as a temporal punishment for those not meriting hell and not yet purified for heaven; their time in purgatory could be shortened by the prayers of the living and especially by the offering of the Eucharist.

These, then, were the beliefs that mattered, the beliefs that defined orthodoxy, and until the end of the 1950s no successful attempt was made to sustain a public critique of these beliefs within the Church. They could not be formally denied or given mythical interpretation without incurring ecclesiastical penalties which, until the end of the 1950s, had the force of legitimacy and served to maintain the control of beliefs in the hands of the Roman authorities. There were other beliefs, of course—age-old formulations about the Trinity and its processions, about angels and predestination—but they had long disappeared from the theological battleground where the living faith was displayed and defended.

Catholic life in the 1950s differed little in outward appearances from the bustling routine that identified Catholics as a people apart in the late nineteenth century. The numbers were declining steadily, but not dramatically; the pious observances that marked Catholics off from others may have seemed even more peculiar in the context of the general decline of religion in the 1950s, but, on the other hand, the inwardness of Catholic culture was less exaggerated. Catholics still clung to otherworldly values and practices; but they felt a duty, that was increasingly easier to perform, to take this world seriously, with all its problems and its rewards. Gary Wills's account of the 'quaint legalisms' that made up his Catholic boyhood in the United States reflects well enough, to judge from other popular accounts of the period, the experience of most practising Catholic families in North America and Britain:

One lived, then, in contact with something outside time—grace, sin, confession, communion, one's own little moral wheel kept turning in the large wheel of seasons that moved endlessly, sameness in change and change in sameness, so was it ever, so would it always be, a repetition like that frequent 'always'—per omnia saecula saeculorum, through all the ages—roll of ages—punctuating our prayers. . . . We were, thus, a chosen people—though chosen, it seemed, to be second-rate. Still, in that uncompetitive mediocrity we found a certain rest denied to others, those who, choosing themselves, achieving by themselves, were driven and badly in need of being first-rate. Our mediocrity hid superior moral tone, obvious to us, concealed from others, a secret excellence, our last joke on the World (World, dignified by a capital letter, but dumb—Devil and Flesh knew what we were up to, but not blundering, dim-witted World). We were distinguished by spiritual favours that made us just a bit—we had to admit it—odd. . . . All these things were shared, part of community life, not a rare isolated joy, like reading poems. These moments belonged to a *people,* not to oneself. It was a ghetto, undeniably. But not a bad ghetto to grow up in.[30]

---

[30] Wills (1972), pp.18–19 and 37.

PART TWO

THE SEARCH FOR
RELEVANCE

4

The Search Begins

The Catholic Church in the 1950s—on the eve of the Second Vatican Council—still presented to the world an image of organizational strength and moral unity, of confidence in its past and in its future. Things had changed, undoubtedly. The political and theological battles of the nineteenth century had left their mark and were reflected in theology, discipline and piety. It was not the same Church, and some of the changes taxed the ingenuity of Roman theologians to define them in terms of Catholic tradition and strained the allegiance of others to breaking-point. (The defence of the Marian dogmas is a case in point and it brought to prominence in Catholic theology the two-source theory of revelation which was to be the subject of heated debate at the Second Vatican Council.) But the changes made were successfully assimilated without damaging the consciousness of unbroken continuity. It was still the one true Church whose essential features had *developed*, not changed.

If the reality of Catholic faith and allegiance did not match this public image and if an underworld of dissent was already threatening to break to the surface of the visible Church, most commentators and observers of the period were unaware of it. 'The Roman Catholic is trained to look to his Church not only for guidance and inspiration, but also for direction on how to live, how to work, and how to think,' wrote the historian Jaroslav Pelikan in 1959. 'Even in a complex modern society the long arm of the Church's power reaches into almost every province of his life.'[1] Catholic historians, too, felt no tremors and heard no warnings in the years which followed the Second

---

[1] Pelikan (1959), p.92.

World War—indeed some interpreted post-war events as omens of a Catholic revival:

The return of the French intellectuals to the Church, the English conversions, are today no longer seen as isolated, exceptional events. Now they appear as characteristic of a new atmosphere in society, as the early manifestations of a new epoch. . . . The secularist world is on the defensive; it has lost its self-assurance, for it is no longer certain that it has the future on its side. The twentieth century is not only the century of nihilistic despair and bitter disappointment; it is also a period of longing for faith and certitude beyond the ups and downs of social and political struggles.[2]

Pope Pius IX had tried to stimulate a 'longing for faith and certitude' in his systematic attempt to cope with the challenge of modernity, and failed. Pope Leo XIII failed also, but his policy institutionalized a channel of communication between the Catholic intelligentsia and the secular world which was to be a major source of tension within the Church until its resolution at the Second Vatican Council. Catholic intellectuals, encouraged by Leo XIII to promote the Catholic cause in secular institutions, were left marginal to the Church and, for the first half of the twentieth century, were obliged to work in the anti-modernist atmosphere of fear and suspicion which led the German prelate Albert Ehrhard, to write: 'The current Roman condemnations constitute a mortal threat to conscience and religious learning in the Catholic world. They are a sin against the Holy Spirit.'[3]

But the tension between the legitimate ideals and their illegitimate realization could not easily be resolved. The Roman Curia could set rigid limits to the production of knowledge on the basis of a particular Catholic understanding of the world and of its threat to the integrity of the Church. It could cope with a stable world, however hostile. It could not cope with a world which changed at confusing speed or with the new ideas generated by such a world, in which intellectuals were already at work to find Catholic solutions to its problems. In the aftermath of the cultural and social upheavals of the First World War, that world was disintegrating and the concept of

[2] Gurian and Fitzsimons (1954), pp.2–3.
[3] Quoted in Von Aretin (1970), p.144.

the 'world' which informed traditional Catholic teaching was beginning to lose its meaning and viability as a tool of theology. The significance of secular changes for the Catholic Church was not immediately apparent to the Curial sleuths who stalked the schools and seminaries in search of modernist intellectuals who, in the years following the modernist crisis, continued to press for an adaptation of Catholic doctrine, liturgy and morality to modern conditions.[4] The ambiguity of the 'world' was reflected in the ambiguity of the problems raised in relation to it.

In the atmosphere of Leonine openness to the world, the problem for the Curia was not simply one of greater vigilance in the proscription of heresy. The new situation of Catholic intellectuals, living in two worlds with different and incompatible criteria of merit and status, was reflected in the novelty of the questions they raised for the Roman authorities. In theology and liturgy, in relations with non-catholic Christians and in the organization of missionary activity, the Curia was forced to make decisions whose implications for orthodoxy were not immediately apparent. This ambiguity persistently dogged the attempts of conservative forces in the Church to stabilize the organization; it persisted throughout the twentieth century to the point when intellectuals could appeal to the ambiguity of language itself to legitimate proposals for doctrinal or organizational change which, in the nineteenth century, would have been instantly recognized and summarily dealt with as heretical. When that point was reached, too many concessions to ambiguity had already been made to permit an authoritarian solution to the new 'heresies', the new proposals for change. These ideas were already stirring in the first half of the twentieth century when, to outward appearances, the Church had recovered its poise, its stature, its immunity to change.

Towards a New Theology and Morality

The new ideas originated mainly in Germany, France and the Netherlands—the areas of Northern Europe most damaged by

[4] The Sodalitium Pianum was a secret agency of the Curia organized with the aim of eradicating modernism. See Von Aretin (1970), p.145.

the physical and social effects of war, and those in which the Church, in terms of membership, was most visibly in decline. In these countries, theologians began to speak a new language and to formulate new concepts and categories for theological discourse. Unlike the modernist scholars at the turn of the century, whose conflict with the Vatican centred on the study and interpretation of the Bible, the pioneers of the new theology were, for the most part, speculative theologians, drawing new insights from their knowledge of patristic and scholastic sources.[5]

In Germany, the speculative thrust came mainly from the University of Tübingen. In 1812, the Lutheran population of Württemberg was enlarged by the annexation of Catholic territory, and the faculty of Protestant theology at Tübingen was joined by a Catholic faculty drawn from the theological college at Ellwangen. From the outset, this close contact with Protestant theologians stimulated Catholic scholars to present the most acceptable side of Catholicism and to win the respect of their Protestant colleagues, particularly with regard to the question of academic freedom within the Church. Until the mid-nineteenth century, the school enjoyed a reputation for creative theological scholarship oriented towards a new synthesis of the inner life of the Church and its visible structure—a scholarship developed by reflection on Catholic tradition and by the bold application of scientific method to the interpretation of scripture. The ghetto policy of Pope Pius IX, however, pushed the Tübingen school to the periphery of Catholic thought and elevated the theology of neo-scholasticism, with all its resistance to biblical criticism and doctrinal development. Catholic teaching and science were incompatible and, in the words of Abbé Maignen, the Church was 'fully justified in not attempting to find a useless reconciliation between her dogmas and the provisional results of the sciences. . . .'

She has only to be concerned with her own teaching, which is dependent on faith alone and to alleviate the distress of souls by protecting them against all that may give rise to doubt and against dangerous and rash views. Science may constantly change, but faith is unchangeable.[6]

[5] For details of the historical theology which follows I am indebted mainly to O'Brien (1965) and to Schoof (1970).
[6] Quoted in Poulat (1962), p.205.

Modernism in its historical form did not occur in Germany. This was partly because German theologians already enjoyed a greater measure of freedom of research than their colleagues in France or England and the radical solution seemed less obligatory in the circumstances. The Vatican was sensitive to the Germans' demands for academic freedom, and the anti-modernist oath, imposed on all clerics in order to check the spread of modernist ideas and methods, was not enforced in Germany. Ironically, the new theology received its most systematic elaboration, not in Germany, where Catholic scholars were least inhibited by an inquisitorial Curia, but in France; it was from French theologians that the most compelling challenge to the official orthodoxy originated and was sustained in the theological debates which culminated in the Second Vatican Council.

In Germany, Romano Guardini and Karl Adam were two theologians of the 1920s and 1930s who helped to popularize a theology that can best be described as 'humanistic'—its appeal resting on the use of everyday experience as a sign of transcendence. To this existential respect for experience was added a concern, central in new theology, to stress the humanity of Christ as a means of inner conversion and to replace the conceptually static and arid style of neo-scholasticism with a more fluid and discursive approach.

In a more rigorous and less discursive fashion, the writings of Karl Rahner continued, after the Second World War, the work of theological renewal pioneered by Guardini and Adam. Rahner's theology, which he himself described as 'anthropocentric', defines man by his openness towards God. To speak of man involves God and nothing can be said of either without implicating the other. Our knowledge of God must be verifiable in human experience—this insistence on the theological status of everyday life posed a threat to scholastic objectivism, but in the work of a man so thoroughly versed in and respectful of Catholic tradition the implications for orthodoxy were not clearly visible to the Curial authorities who subjected Rahner's writings to critical scrutiny.

In France, in the latter half of the nineteenth century, the Church was engaged in a struggle with the state for its continued existence. Laicization laws had diminished the influence of the Church, particularly in education, and Leo XIII's call to French Catholics to rally to the Republic was a tactical manoeuvre in the face of state hostility and widespread anti-clericalism which could do little to promote an atmosphere conducive to speculative and progressive theology. It found no sympathy among French traditionalists. Just as the antagonism of the state towards the Church was both political and religious, so the militancy of traditionalist Catholics was oriented to political and religious ends. Their continued resistance to the Republic was motivated by a desire both for the re-establishment of Catholic influence in secular affairs and for the restoration of the political conditions in which such influence was exercised in the past and which, in their eyes, was inextricably linked to the fortunes of the Roman Church. Not until the condemnation of Action Française by Pope Pius XI in 1926 and the same Pope's reaffirmation of the official Catholic policy of support for the Republic and for the structure of French society was the Church in France liberated from its internal politico-religious squabbles.

The measure of unity among practising Catholics accomplished by this papal intervention served to concentrate the energies of the Church on a solution to the newly-discovered dechristianization of France. The Church, forced to abandon politics as a means of support, suddenly discovered the massive extent to which France had, in effect, become a pagan country. Restricted by the state to its religious function and constrained to employ evangelical means to stay in business, the French Church became dramatically aware of its spiritual poverty. This consciousness was facilitated by the harnessing of sociology to religious concern and the use of survey techniques to establish the facts of Catholic commitment which were hidden behind the official statistics of religious affiliation. A new dynamism entered French Catholic life with the founding of the Jeunesse Ouvrière Chrétienne, a movement for the evangelization of youth which soon stimulated concern for recovering the allegiance of France's lost proletariat.

Three theologians—Fathers Chenu, Congar and de Lubac—who staked reputation and career on forging a theology of renewal in harmony with the new spirit of Catholic revival, merit particular attention both for the charismatic appeal of their writings and for the fact that their ideas survived considerable hostility from French conservatives (and hardly less from Pope Pius XII) to become the orthodoxy of the new Catholicism after Vatican II. A fourth and perhaps more famous innovator, Teilhard de Chardin, must be mentioned, not so much for the content of his theology or scientific work —his technical writings were quite inaccessible to the mass of radical clerics and laity who made him a cult figure of the *avant-garde*—but for the affinity of his language and metaphors with the radical spirit of the age.

Marie-Dominique Chenu, a Dominican, was one of the French theologians working for a renewal of dialogue between the Church and the world. For him and for others working within the tradition of Le Saulchoir, the theology centre in Paris of which he was the director, the fundamental theological problem since the modernist crisis was the relationship of faith and history, and this required the re-examination of the relationship between the Church and the world. For Chenu, who began his career as a medieval historian, the problems relevant to theological inquiry were raised in dialogue with the world outside Catholicism, and history provided the most fruitful method for such inquiry. Chenu's strategy of addressing the problems of the modernists in the idiom of St Thomas Aquinas, with the aim of a creative reinterpretation of scholasticism, disguised from his inquisitors his commitment to the historicity of faith and to the theological status of contemporary and worldly experience. The Church and the world were not enemies but partners in the unfolding of God's redemptive plan. Chenu did not escape without censure. His account of the theology of Le Saulchoir, *Une Ecole de Théologie*, which was privately circulated, was placed on the Index of prohibited books in 1942 and he was later condemned for his activities with the worker-priest movement.[7]

Chenu's colleague and fellow-Dominican, Yves Congar, was similarly committed to the historical method of theology and to the fact of contemporary experience as a source of theological inquiry. His intellectual and personal background placed him in intimate contact with Protestant theologians and laity and

[7] See Chenu (1969), pp.243–68 and Schoof (1970), pp.103–4.

stimulated in him a zeal for Christian unity and for the
development of an ecumenical theology which would entail the
reform of Catholic teaching and attitudes. His mission, in his
own words, was to 'rotate the Catholic Church through a few
degrees on its own axis'. In his most famous work, *Lay People in
the Church*, Congar criticized the historical development which
had reduced the laity to a position of passivity and resulted in
the identification of the hierarchy and the Church. Tracing a
theological history which helps to explain why the Church
required that the agent of sacramental validity be specified and
that it be specified as the priest, Congar shows that this
preciseness was achieved at the expense of lay participation,
not only in the liturgy but in the missionary, administrative and
teaching functions also. Clerics and laity shared in the priesthood of Christ, and while a division of functions between them
was fundamental to the structure of the Church, according to
Congar, a concentration of privilege or status in one or the
other could only result in damage to the Church's life and
mission.[8]

The third French theologian who achieved fame and notoriety for his pioneering work leading up to the Second Vatican
Council was Henri de Lubac. Born in 1896, de Lubac became a
Jesuit and published a number of early articles on the problem
of the supernatural. A colleague of Congar and friend of de
Chardin, he brought a personal and intellectual contact with
non-Catholic movements and sources to bear upon the
theological issues which he considered relevant to modern
conditions and inadequately treated within the neo-scholastic
perspective which dominated Catholic institutes of theology.
In his best-known and most controversial book, *Le Surnaturel*, de
Lubac provoked an intense debate about the role and nature of
the Church, stressing its expressive rather than its instrumental
function as an agent of salvation. Whether or not there exists a
natural desire for the Beatific Vision is rather a fine point of
scholastic theology and not a burning issue, one would think,
for a Church struggling to find a new role in the modern world.
But it gripped the theological world in the 1940s so intensely
that, as James Connolly notes, *Le Surnaturel* became a symbol of

[8] Congar (1965), pp.250ff. and 452ff.

all that was to be resisted or to be applauded in the new theology.[9] What aroused the passion of his critics was the fear that de Lubac's thesis, for which he claimed the support of St Thomas, would destroy the distinction between the natural and the supernatural, on which depended other distinctions fundamental to the structure of the Church.

De Lubac's interest in communism and atheism and his knowledge of Marxist and sociological literature informed his other writings in which he attempted to reconcile the religious and non-religious forces working towards humanistic goals. He was in complete sympathy with the search for a humanistic philosophy on which to base the social and political organization of society. The Marxist solution was incomplete, just as the Church, stressing the individualistic aspect of piety and salvation, was also defective: 'The happiest and most perfect form of social existence would be the most inhuman of conditions,' he wrote, 'if it were not ordered to the spiritual life, just as the latter would be, in a final analysis, only a mystification if it retired into itself in a sort of refined egoism.'[10]

It distorts the thinking of these three writers to summarize their views in terms of the categories in which popular opinion received and transmitted them. In the new theology which developed from their work there is much that all three—notably Congar—would repudiate. But the power of ideas to generate pressure for change derives not from their inherent logic but from their capacity to articulate confused hopes and aspirations and to function symbolically as the slogan of a social group or movement. The reduction of ideas to slogans seems to be a condition for their translation into action. If this is true of Marxism, nationalism, fascism—of reforming and revolutionary movements of all kinds in the secular world—it is no less true of the process of radical change in the Church.

The new theology was promoted by intellectuals who became the cult-figures of a mass movement of clerics and laity in France and Germany who, in turn, became the bearers of a simplified message for the Catholic world: to rid itself of its exclusiveness and its claims to privilege—and of the theological

[9] Connolly (1961), p.87.
[10] De Lubac (1946), pp.200–1.

distinctions on which that old mentality was based—and to embrace the world in recognition of its own spiritual dimension. The new theology became a new attitude.

This attitude was expressed most powerfully in the more popular writings of Pierre Teilhard de Chardin. Teilhard was the poet of the new theology. It was he who clothed its technical ideas in colourful language and captured, in phrases whose meaning is far from clear, the sense of optimism and openness to the world which was implicit in the scholarly work of the other theologians. By the end of the 1950s, the sales of his most abstruse work, *The Phenomenon of Man*, had reached almost half a million in hardback—an indicator, for those who have tried to read it, that its author was more revered for his stance and his style than for his scholarship. Teilhard had a vision of the inner cohesion of the universe growing towards its ultimate fulfilment in Christ. Through the cosmic Christ, the physical universe was in process of evolutionary struggle towards an 'Omega Centre', as he called it, towards the ultimate convergence of the created universe in God its creator.

Why this synthesis of science and theology should have had such a remarkable impact on the minds of French intellectuals and should have transformed Teilhard de Chardin into a cult-hero for millions of Catholics throughout the world is a problem to be discussed later in the context of a general explanation of change in the Church. It is appropriate here, however, to note the affinity of Chardinism with secular cultural trends which found their political expression in the 1960s, particularly in Great Britain and the United States. Teilhard provided an alternative cosmology to the Thomistic worldview which dominated Catholic thought. It was a thoroughly modern apologetic for Catholicism; it defended its reasonableness in terms of the aspirations and ideals of a secular faith in science and of a secular distrust of dogma and ideology. Teilhard's thoughts were perfectly attuned to the early sixties. John F. Kennedy, the exemplar of secular Catholicism, who intoxicated the youth of America and Western Europe with his rhetoric and cool optimism about 'uncharted areas of science and space, unsolved problems of peace and war, unconquered questions of poverty and surplus . . .' could not have found a more congenial apologist for his secular pragmatism than the

Jesuit, Teilhard de Chardin. 'Disease and hunger,' Teilhard had written, 'will be conquered by science and we will no longer need to fear them in any acute form. And, conquered by the sense of the earth and human sense, hatred and internecine struggles will have disappeared in the ever-warmer radiance of Omega.'[11] In such phrases Teilhard supplied a theological justification for the post-war optimism and faith in scientific progress which characterized the early sixties. We are all drawing closer together—this was the message both of Teilhard and of his great admirer Marshall McLuhan. In a world sickened by war, suspicious of ideologies and dogma, refreshed by the winds of change which promised a technological solution to age-old problems—in such a world it was comforting to believe in a scientific millenium and it was unimportant to understand the reasoning behind it. The writings of Teilhard, like those of McLuhan, have been admired by millions, read by few.

Young priests and lay intellectuals fashioned from the works of the new theologians, Congar, Chenu and de Lubac, the slogans of a new attitude to theology and to the mission of the Church and the promise of a new status *vis-à-vis* the non-Catholic world. The new theology had the merit of breaking the bonds of neo-scholasticism which constrained its adherents within a cultural tradition that was not only different, but, in the judgement of the world, outmoded and irrelevant. Ghetto Catholicism required for its legitimation and survival certain theological distinctions, the most fundamental of which was the distinction between God and nature. There is nothing in the writings of the three theologians mentioned to suggest a departure from this in the form of some kind of immanentism or pantheism. But by blurring the distinction between the Church and the world, Chenu's work was seen, both by the Roman authorities and by French intellectuals, as a threat to the justification and necessity of the Church; in rediscovering the priestly function of the laity Congar was interpreted as challenging the Catholic orthodoxy which viewed the hierarchic priesthood as radically distinct and separate from the laity; in

[11] Teilhard de Chardin (1959), p.287. I am indebted to Wills (1972) for noting the comparison with Kennedy.

encouraging doubts about the similarly radical distinction between the natural and the supernatural, de Lubac was lending his authority to a new immanentism which would affirm the existence of God but reject as primitive the attempt to locate or define him.

The blurring of these three distinctions comes together in the work of Teilhard. In combining a theology of hope with a scientific theory of evolution, he provided a new cosmology for Catholics. Instead of the old conflicts and dogmas dividing men, he stressed the underlying harmony uniting them, Christian and non-Christian, in a common purpose; instead of the old hopes and fears for the future, he stressed a new hope rooted in the present reality of God's kingdom on earth. In Teilhard de Chardin, old enemies were reconciled and old distinctions made redundant—Church and world, religion and science, body and soul, time and eternity. Even heaven, earth and hell were dislocated in the Chardinian perspective which viewed the cosmos, and the deity as its immanent principle of unity and progress, in a way which made the Church redundant as the instrument of salvation. In effect, the role of the Church became simply expressive or symbolic—somewhat similar to the role of the monarch in a parliamentary democracy. In its actions, and particularly in the Eucharist, the Church was the ritual and conscious expression of the cosmic process drawing all creation to its fulfilment. In the vision of Teilhard, it was difficult to retain any sense of the most basic distinction of all for the Catholic Church: the distinction between God and non-God.

In Catholic morality, as in doctrine, the search for an approach relevant to contemporary conditions took the form of a return to the sources of Christianity, and an examination of the scriptural and patristic literature provided moralists with a conception of Christian morality which contrasted sharply with Catholic orthodoxy. Gustave Thils and Emile Mersch pioneered the attack on the casuistry and negativeness of the theology manuals which formed clerical opinion in the 1930s and 1940s, and their work was followed up in 1949 by the influential and controversial book by Jacques Leclercq.[12]

[12] Thils (1940); Mersch (1939); Leclercq (1949).

Leclercq argued that a morality relevant to modern society required a stress on man's personal relationship to Christ and to his fellow-man in a positive framework of Christian love rather than the legalistic framework of the manuals. Traditional morality was obsessed with sin and obligation; a Christian morality must be oriented to the practice of virtue, which, like sin, cannot simply be defined in behavioural terms. Leclercq was not advocating situation ethics, but the affinity of his critique of moral absolutism with that of the existentialists in the 1950s made his work suspect in Rome. The relativism of Leclercq was derived from theological premises.

Another and more influential approach to moral relativism was based on scientific arguments. In the work of the French theologian, Marc Oraison, the attribution of guilt to persons whose actions are defined as materially sinful is a matter which cannot be decided without taking into account the findings of modern psychology. The discovery and exploration of the unconscious revealed a conditioning of the will which made it difficult, if not impossible, to attribute to any particular action the degree of freedom required for moral responsibility.[13] Not surprisingly, Oraison's work was placed on the Index. If the structure of the Church depended on clerical control of the supply of grace and access to the truth of revelation, it depended likewise on clerical control of the forgiveness of sin and on the legitimacy of the very concept of sin which Oraison's teaching seemed to threaten. The social scientists in the Church would later find stronger arguments and more favourable circumstances in which to press home Oraison's scientific approach to Christian ethics.

Movements of Reform

The search for relevance in the years preceding the Second Vatican Council was not confined to the sphere of ideas. The distinctions of the old Catholicism were also being challenged, albeit implicitly, in the reforming movements which were the products of the new theology and, at the same time, a stimulus

---

[13] Oraison (1952).

and encouragement to the new theologians. Chenu, Congar and de Lubac were all directly involved in the worker-priest movement in France. In part, their theology grew out of the pastoral experience of the priests engaged in that missionary experiment and was created by the demands of the worker-priests for a theology relevant to their work among the urban poor.

The worker-priest movement was an expression of the new relationship of the Church to the world urged by the new theologians. It was an unprecedented move on the part of a group of Catholic priests to extend beyond the bounds of mere strategy the Leonine policy of Catholic Action within secular institutions. Instead of trying to bring the world to the Church these priests chose to live as industrial workers in areas of heightened class consciousness and bitter anti-clericalism. They came to realize that mere physical proximity could not remove the clerical stigma; if they wanted to be identified with the workers they must share a commitment to the cause of the workers, to the labour movement with all its revolutionary implications. Rome intervened, and in January 1954 the priests were ordered to abandon their experiment. The movement failed to achieve its objective in France, but the questions it raised about the Church's relevance to the world in the minds of priests, theologians and bishops were asked repeatedly—not only in the Second Vatican Council, where Congar and Chenu were instrumental in gaining a commitment to social justice on the part of the Church, but, more dramatically, in the later revolutionary engagement of priests and laity in Latin America. The worker-priest movement was the new theology in action, mingling the Church and the world, the priesthood and the laity in a manner which, as the Roman authorities realized, endangered the integrity of the priesthood and its sacramental status *vis-à-vis* the laity.

Two other movements were of significance in providing new experiences to heighten the consciousness of those involved. In Germany, after the First World War, the beginning of an ecumenical dialogue between Catholics and Protestants took place in the context of universities with dual theological faculties. It is fair to say, however, that at least until the end of the Second World War, the notion that Christian unity meant anything to Catholics other than the submission of their 'separated brethren' to the authority of Rome was safely contained within the scholarly debates of academics and the private initiatives of a few theologians. The fact that in June 1948 the Holy Office found it necessary to forbid all meetings of clergy or laity with non-Catholics for the purpose of discussing matters of faith without express approval is a sign of the gathering pace of the move towards unity and the fears at Rome for its consequences. In the following year, cautious approval was given to ecumenical gatherings, provided they conformed to certain regulations and were strictly supervised by the local bishop. Fears were expressed in this latter document that Catholics, by taking the law into their own hands, would encourage indifference towards the historic claims and justification of the Roman Church.[14] In the decade following the Second World War, a wider, more inclusive definition of the Church was being tested, tentatively, for general approval and acceptance.

The third trend which was significant in exerting pressure for change on the Church authorities was the liturgical revival. There have been several liturgical revivals in the Church throughout its history. What distinguishes the modern movement from the monastic reforms of Dom Gueranger in the nineteenth century or the revival of eucharistic devotion encouraged by the encyclicals of Pope Pius X at the turn of the century is the stress on the reform of the liturgy itself as distinct from a concern with raising the level of lay devotion to it.

Over many centuries the Catholic Mass had become the preserve of the clergy, a property managed exclusively by priests, from which the laity could benefit under conditions controlled by priests. The historical process by which this clerical control was accomplished has been charted by historians during the past two decades and need not be summarized, except to draw attention to the two main features of the alienation of the liturgy from the community.[15] The liturgy in Catholic tradition has always been defined as the action of the Church and the worship of the whole community. But the lay section of that community became gradually separated from the liturgy by a process of symbolic detachment and privatized

[14] Instruction on the Ecumenical Movement, Vatican, 20 Dec 1949.
[15] See, for example, Jungmann (1959); Martimort (1961); Vogel (1972).

organization. Language was the first and the most important symbol to be appropriated by the clergy. The transition from Greek to Latin as the official language of the liturgy took place at the end of the fourth century. From that time until the Second Vatican Council, the laity was effectively excluded from understanding the action of the Mass and the rubrics and architectural setting of the liturgy were developed to further this incomprehension and separation. One consequence of this was the appearance of extra-liturgical devotions as a compensation for the loss of personal attachment to the Mass, an example of which was the growth of popular piety in the nineteenth century, discussed in Chapter 2. Whether or not the transformation of the Mass into an esoteric and quasi-magical cult reserved exclusively for priests had been the intention since legislation to that end began in the fourth century, there is fairly clear evidence that this has been the goal since the late Middle Ages. Pope Alexander VII forbade the translation of the Missal even for private reading, and in 1794 Pope Pius VI declared: 'The use of the vernacular in liturgical prayers is false and foolhardy.'[16] Paris de Grassis, writing to Pope Leo X in 1516—with charming frankness—pointed out the function of the symbolic detachment of the laity from the liturgy:

First of all I shall answer those who believe that religious ceremonies should be made accessible to all men. . . . Your Holiness is well aware that the authority and prestige of the Holy See depend on the attitude of princes and the powerful. They, in fact, believe that Popes are not mortal men but something like gods on earth; they submit to them, obey them, venerate and even worship them. . . . But if the secrets of the cult were revealed and ceremonies were made accessible [to all], the immediate result would be a loss of prestige.[17]

Vogel dates the origin of the private Mass, with one celebrant and no direct relevance to the pastoral needs of the community, at the sixth century. From then, the Eucharist became a pious devotion reserved to the celebrant priest and its function for the laity became progressively more individualistic—the Mass became a source of salvation for the individual Catholic. Given

---

[16] Denzinger-Rahner (1957), art.1566.
[17] Quoted in Vogel (1972), pp.13–14.

the laity's symbolic detachment from the liturgy and the belief that the Mass was the major source of the grace necessary for salvation, it is not surprising that the relationship between priest and laity came to resemble that of producer and consumer of a valued supernatural product. Votive Masses for the intentions of individuals multiplied and the need to procure the valued grace thus obtained led to the practice of the laity offering—and the clergy requiring—gifts of money to secure the privilege of Mass for one's own benefit. The Eucharist had become a commodity; it was not even necessary to be present at its celebration in order to profit from its ritual performance.

The first major act of modern liturgical reform came in 1951 with the restoration of the Easter Vigil to its primitive form. This decision by Pope Pius XII followed about thirty years of historical research and discreet pressure on the Vatican on the part of liturgists and theologians in Germany working to promote changes in the whole conception of the liturgy. The main figure in this German movement was Dom Odo Casel, a monk in the monastery of Maria Laach. His 'theology of mysteries', as it was called, drew from biblical and patristic sources an understanding of liturgy as the enactment of Christ's work in a sense which focused attention, not on particular gestures and formulae of the officiating priest, but on the sacramental action of the whole assembly of the faithful. It was followed by the more 'rationalistic' approach to reform which stressed the liturgy as a catechesis and urged radical changes, including the use of the vernacular, with a view to greater comprehension on the part of the laity; the pressures for change converged on the notion of making the congregation active participants in the worship of the Church. In a vague way, never quite explicit but not lost on a vigilant Roman Curia, the reforming liturgists were preparing the Catholic world for the acceptance of an active priestly role for the laity in the celebration of the Eucharist and a corresponding diminution of the sacramental power of the hierarchy.[18]

---

[18] 'The fact, however, that the faithful participate in the Eucharistic Sacrifice does not mean that they also are endowed with priestly power'—Pope Pius XII, encyclical *Mediator Dei*, November 1947.

The Implications of Reform

It is worth noting here that in all three movements discussed a constant and developing theme was the awareness of the irrelevance of the Church—its irrelevance not only to those outside it but even to the laity within who formed the bulk of its membership. What was meant by 'irrelevance' was never easy to discern, but the usual context of the term suggested that the irrelevance was demonstrated by evidence of declining commitment and membership. The change in theology emerging from this can be broadly characterized as humanistic, as distinct from transcendental. Theologians use the terms 'incarnational' and 'eschatological' to label the different theological attitudes which separate the new Catholicism from the old: the incarnationists emphasize the humanity of Christ as a basis for their favourable attitude to human values, human progress and humanistic movements in the world and, like Teilhard and de Lubac, they see the Church not so much as the instrument but as the expression and self-consciousness of the process of salvation. Eschatologists, or transcendentalists, on the other hand, stress the radical dissociation of this world and the next and are considerably less sympathetic to humanistic movements which are not consciously rooted in the Christian revelation. As Jean Danielou expresses it, 'no identification is permissible between the Christian hope and a belief in progress; they are radically different things.'[19] The newly emerging theology, therefore, marked a shift of emphasis from Christ's divinity to his humanity; from the Church as institution of salvation to the Church as community; from the objective to the subjective aspect of liturgy; from God's transcendence and otherness to his presence among men and in all creation; from the resurrection as a discrete event in the past and in the future to the kingdom already present in this world and in process of fulfilment; from a moral theology of sin to a moral theology of human development and interpersonal relationships.

The effect of this attempt to redress the balance of tradition was to create a sense of the openness of dogma reflecting the openness of the human experience from which the meaning of

---

[19] Danielou (1958), p.7. See also de Lubac (1946), p.69ff.

dogma must be derived. It was a method of doing theology backwards, as O. C. Thomas called it—starting from experience in order to discover the meaning of God's revelation rather than constraining experience within boundaries determined by theological speculation.[20] It was a method which demanded of its originators a level of rigorous historical research not always evident in the new theologians of the sixties. (Attracted by a rapidly expanding market for new theological literature during and after the Vatican Council, many popularizers dispensed with historical scholarship in favour of the more fashionable social sciences and new theology was to become something of an art-form on the fringe of social psychology.)

The official attitude of the Vatican to the new thinking in the Church was one of measured intransigence. For the first sixty years of the twentieth century, the Roman Curia was essentially Leonine in its approach to Catholic relations with the secular world, following a policy of encouraging Catholic leaders to work for the transformation of secular institutions according to the Catholic model. Some concessions to modernity were made, specifically in the ecumenical and liturgical movements, as we have seen, but on terms which gave no hint that the basic confidence in the Church's teaching and structure had diminished. During the investigations of the worker-priest movement in the early 1950s, it became clear to the Roman authorities that the new theology was gaining ground rapidly and winning wider support than was indicated by the low volume of its publications. During the period 1940–50, as Catholic historians have noted, mimeographed papers were widely circulated, particularly in France, disseminating the ideas of Teilhard de Chardin and other exponents of incarnationist theology among seminarians and younger clergy.[21] According to Vollert, the ideas current in this theological underworld included evolutionism, pantheism, and the symbolic interpretation of the doctrine of transubstantiation.

In 1950, Pope Pius XII published his encyclical *Humani Generis* in which, without naming individuals, he denounced what he called 'some false opinions which threaten to under-

---

[20] Thomas (1972), p.27ff.
[21] See Vollert (1951); Connolly (1961), p.189.

mine the foundations of Catholic doctrine'. With unmistakable
reference to Teilhard de Chardin and de Lubac, and with hints
at others which later resulted in disciplinary measures being
taken against Congar and Chenu, the Pope listed and condemned the errors of the new theology: false historicism,
dogmatic relativism, existentialism, the 'pantheistic notion
that the whole world is subject to continual evolution', the
neglect of traditional concepts in theology, the cult of fashionable trends in secular science and philosophy, the symbolic
interpretation of Christ's presence in the Eucharist . . . The
new theologians were 'lovers of novelty', bent on 'whittling
away the meaning of doctrines as much as possible in order to
free dogma from a terminology of long standing in the Church'.
The Pope indicated his awareness of the situation in France
and Germany: '. . . these ideas are spread not only among
members of the clergy, both secular and regular, and in seminaries and religious institutes, but also among the laity and
especially among those who are engaged in teaching youth.' He
predicted—rhetorically, one feels, but, in retrospect, accurately—that the qualified statements of the new theologians
'will tomorrow be proclaimed from the housetops and without
moderation by more venturesome spirits'. The remedy was the
strict enforcement of the regulation on the instruction of the
clergy in Thomistic doctrine and philosophy; the teaching of St
Thomas 'is in harmony with Divine Revelation and is most
effective for the safeguarding of the foundation of the faith and
for reaping, safely and usefully, the fruits of sound progress'.[22]

Humani Generis fell like a bomb on the Catholic world,
particularly in France. Gustave Weigel documents the extraordinary impact of the encyclical and the almost universal
consensus it achieved.[23] It was certainly effective in stifling the
publications and public pronouncements of the new
theologians who submitted, without exception, to the judgement of the Pope. Many feared a repetition of the heresy-hunts
which followed the condemnation of the modernists by Pope
Pius X and, given the obvious alarm with which Pius XII
viewed the new theology, this seemed a likely consequence.

[22] Denzinger-Rahner (1957), arts 2305–30.
[23] Weigel (1951).

Pius XII held as imperial a conception of the papal office as any of his predecessors and, as if to underline his antagonism towards a trend which he clearly viewed as modernistic, he followed his encyclical by proclaiming the beatification of Pope Pius X.

But there was no new inquisition. The option available to the Pope of mounting a campaign similar to that of anti-modernism was not as simple in the 1950s. In attacking the ideas of the modernists, Pius X employed the tactic of framing their ideas as a conspiracy against the Church and imposing on them a coherence they never possessed. In the work of Congar and Chenu, Rahner and de Lubac, Pope Pius XII was confronted with meticulous scholarship explicitly framed within the Catholic tradition—their principal method of demonstrating the inadequacy of conventional thinking in the Church was to show, not that it was unscriptural, but that it was untraditional. None of them could be accused of heresy, since that would be to condemn the tradition to which they appealed. The Pope sensed danger in the shift of focus advocated in the writings of these new theologians, but there was danger too in convicting them of error and censuring them personally in *Humani Generis*.

It is important to realize that, as recently as 1950, the Church, in the person of the Pope, could still command the submission of theologians and prevent the public display of actions and ideas which he judged contrary to Catholic teaching. Even if later events proved that he had not quenched the spirit of the new theology and if one must be sceptical about the nature of the 'universal consensus' which his encyclical achieved, the impact of *Humani Generis* was, nonetheless, a significant demonstration of the Church's continuing control of the beliefs of its members. In the 1950s, the Church was still unified. The basis of that unity—then, as in the nineteenth century—was still the teaching of the Church. The beliefs that united Catholics could still be specified, contrasted with heresy, and successfully defended against public challenge within the Church.

5

Interlude: A Runaway World

In the preceding chapters and in those which follow, the primary focus of attention is the Roman Catholic Church. We have been concerned with the structure of a particular organization—with the ideas, policies and internal politics of a particular Church and the way in which these were mediated to Catholics and influenced their attitudes and behaviour. But no institution or organization is so isolated from society that its change and development can be understood solely within its own terms, its own boundaries. Ideas, policies and struggles for power are never independently generated by individuals or institutions; changes in theology which are effective do not drop from heaven as the product of interior illumination. They are stimulated by social, cultural and economic changes in the wider society, the experience of which influences intellectuals and religious leaders to reflect again on the nature of their religious enterprise and conditions their members to receive and accept some proposals for change and to reject others.

This interplay between religion and society has been described in a discursive and unsystematic way throughout the book. In this chapter, I want—briefly and more abstractly—to focus on the secular world rather than the Church and to examine certain cultural and social changes which occurred up to the period of the Second Vatican Council. We shall look at features of modernity which came to fruition in the 1960s and which manifestly impinged on the consciousness of the pioneers of new theology in the early part of the twentieth century and on their successors at the time of the Second Vatican Council.

First, it is necessary to give a broad description of the cultural setting of medieval Catholicism by way of contrast with the modern secular culture which most of us experience today as the nature of things, the way the world really is.

The Medieval World

To survive, any culture must communicate ideals which demand some measure of self-sacrifice of its members and, at the same time, create some form of institutionalized release from the pressure this entails. To a degree, society must be so structured as to direct the attention of the individuals comprising it towards the collectivity, towards a communal ideal. The particular character of the ideal is what differentiates societies one from another. On the success of a nation's system of motivating its members and releasing them—on the balance between cultural control and cultural freedom, between collectivism and individualism—depends the survival of a society in any meaningful sense of the term. As Philip Rieff puts it, a culture survives 'by the power of its institutions to bind and loose men in the conduct of their affairs with reasons which sink so deep into the self that they become commonly and implicitly understood. . . .'[1]

Fundamental change occurs at the cultural level when the balance is upset—either when the collective moral demands are imposed to the exclusion of individual freedom, as in wartime for example, or when the individual's demand to be free of collective obligations and to be released from the pressure of conforming to communal ideals is successfully imposed upon the political establishment. This is true of any stable society, whether we are speaking of medieval catholicism or modern Western culture; the difference between them is not merely one of different character-ideals but of a different balance between social control and individual freedom.

Medieval Catholicism provided a culture for its adherents which, like modern Western society, imposed a communal character in a set of moral demands and provided a system of therapeutic release from those demands. But whereas in modern society the communal aspect is severely limited in its

[1] Rieff (1973), p.2ff.

potential for mobilizing collective thought and action, in medieval society the opposite was true. The dominant feature of modern culture is the individual's right to dissent and his moral obligation to seek self-fulfilment as a condition of successful participation in the various grades of community— family, profession, society. The dominant feature of medieval culture was the sacred character of the community and the individual's obligation to subordinate himself to it and to seek self-fulfilment by means of such subordination to the collectivity. Medieval culture defined the individual in terms of the social group and successfully communicated to him the moral obligation to seek therapeutic release from the strain of conformity through involvement with the community. Modern culture defines the community in terms of the individual and—equally successfully—communicates to him the obligation to seek self-fulfilment as a *prior condition* of communal involvement.

From a different perspective, we can look at the difference between the two types of culture by looking at the 'needs' fulfilled in each. As a social system, medieval Catholicism emphasized and fostered the need for community, for cognitive security and for emotional and moral justification. A strictly limited freedom for the individual was compensated for by what we would regard today as an oppressive integration into the collectivity. The relative lack of geographical and social mobility during the Middle Ages made such a level of integration both politically possible and emotionally tolerable. It was a static society and its stability facilitated authoritarian control and community participation.

The cognitive security provided for the individual Catholic has also disappeared in modern times. In the world of medieval Catholicism, questions about the existence of God, immortality and the pervasive influence of the supernatural did not impinge on the consciousness of most people. Ordinary men and women simply knew God and his works in their perception of the world about them, and questions about the nature of the sacred and the secular did not constitute a recurring topic of debate. The discussion which has dominated theology since the Second World War and which has culminated in the immersion of the supernatural in the natural, soul in body, church in world—or, to put it more accurately, in the acceptance that such distinctions can no longer be maintained—this was not a live issue for medieval Christians. Catholics and Protestants alike took for granted the existence of the supernatural realm and its interpenetration with the observable world. They disputed certain interpretations of God's revelation; that God had revealed himself, however, and that he continued to do so in the events which made up the history of each individual and society was a fact beyond contention. As Ernest Gellner remarks, following Weber, it is only to the degree that the sacred and the secular are interwoven in the fabric of consciousness that religious ideas and institutions are safe from the threat of secularization. What damages religion and undermines belief in God is not the denial of the transcendent as such but its separation as a distinct category from the rest of life. 'A society which is truly immersed in the transcendent does not see or recognize such orderly lines of demarcation.'[2]

Medieval Catholics were certain that God was in his heaven; if all was not right with this world, it would be put right in the world to come. And they enjoyed this certitude, not because of the compelling force of philosophical arguments; they enjoyed it, on the contrary, because the integration between Church and society prevented such arguments from being raised. (One can think of modern parallels—ideas and beliefs accepted without question today because they are similarly woven into the structure of our society: democracy, human rights, a taboo on incest . . . These are taken for granted. They are not topics for debate because they are structured into our institutions, our culture, the way we live.) The medieval Christian believed in God and the hereafter in a way that is impossible even for his most ardent counterpart today. Doubt is tolerable, if not virtuous, for the practising Catholic. In the Middle Ages, it was not an option.

The third function of medieval society which has disappeared in modern times in the justificatory role of religion. Much has already been said about the manner in which personal ills and social evils were transformed into the mysterious workings of providence and were made tolerable to believ-

[2] Gellner (1974), p.163.

ers. Social inequality, personal victimization, sickness and death were not seen as occasions for questioning the system or rebelling against it, but as inescapable accompaniments on life's journey. Today, by contrast, we have formal and informal institutions of resistance to injustice in welfare organizations, investigative journalism, human rights and an international network of terrorism. Society is not closed and self-justifying; in theory, at least, it is open to criticism and change.

Medieval Catholicism ensured the salvation of the individual by his incorporation into the religious and, therefore, the societal community. The publicly available solution to social and personal ills was provided by the individual's conversion to the community and its moral ideals. Salvation was collective, guaranteed by membership and participation in the community. In modern terms, one's sense of identity and self-fulfilment were social achievements, not personal accomplishments. By contrast with contemporary Western societies, individuals in medieval society were sheltered from crises of identity; they were guaranteed self-fulfilment in so far as they were integrated into the religious community. The meaning of life became problematic only when modern social conditions encouraged the fragmentation of community and the privatization of the individual. Medieval culture was effective in preventing the question from being publicly debated or privately experienced.

Modern culture invites and constrains individuals to save themselves. It is no longer the community and one's participation in it which cures the pains of being human, but the detached individual, equipped with reliable information and trained to exercise self-control in place of the collective controls which functioned under the old system. Life has only that significance given to it by the individual; the need for some meaning which transcends the individual—objective, authoritative, discernible—is a sickness cultivated by ideological communities, notably religious. The task for the modern individual is to empty his consciousness of grandiose cosmological designs and to cure himself of the disease of metaphysics. We are individuals, according to Freud, moulded by our own biographies, yet forced by society into the communal mould of the Christian ideal. Cosmological designs only exist within saving communities; we cannot have one without the other. But saving communities tend to be authoritarian, and such groups function efficiently and without resort to physical force only through the mechanism of guilt. Conversely, the removal of guilt, of fantasies about moral responsibility, can only be achieved by the destruction of the community which contains the mechanism and the desacralization of the authority which controls it. We gain freedom from our sense of guilt at the cost of our sense of community. We throw off the ethical burden of the Christian plan of salvation, which encouraged the community to scrutinize our behaviour and to impose its penalties for our transgressions, at the cost of detachment and some degree of isolation. Medieval society depended for its operation on faith in the need for salvation outside oneself and on faith in the means of salvation supplied by a Church which demanded the renunciation of self in favour of a communal ideal. As Rieff sees it, modern culture has put an end to this tyranny of the community as the dynamic of social order. 'Crowded more and more together, we are learning to live more distantly from one another, in strategically varied and numerous contacts, rather than in the oppressive warmth of family and a few friends.'[3]

The Context of Modern Catholicism

It is a commonplace to observe that the conflict between capitalism and socialism in the nineteenth and early twentieth centuries transformed the character of Western society. In theory, capitalism should have brought immense benefits for the common good. The zeal for scientific discovery was motivated by Christian principles and the enterprise of commerce was inspired in part by the Puritan ideal of industry as virtue and worldly work as a supernatural calling. The disruption of traditional values in Western society, which was inescapable if the material benefits of the new technology were to be available, should, ideally, have been accompanied by a new social order extending these benefits to the greatest number according to the humane principles of the liberal ideology which

---

[3] Rieff (1973), p.208.

inspired the Industrial Revolution. Economists and philosophers who preached economic liberalism as a form of applied Christianity probably did sincerely believe that the welfare and happiness of mankind would result. But in practice it was the welfare of the strong and the exploitation of the weak which their policy promoted. The economic and industrial revolution, which spread from England in the eighteenth century to the rest of Europe and North America, institutionalized greed and selfishness in a new way and on a scale hitherto undreamed of. Since 1871, when European socialism finally broke with liberalism, the character of Western society has been fashioned by the struggle and compromise between the opposed ideologies of capitalism and socialism.

Nineteenth-century socialism and capitalism each provided contrasting models of freedom and control of the individual, and our society is the product of the conflict between them. The bourgeois ideal of capitalism envisaged the freedom of the individual as the removal of constraints, particularly those of an economic kind, imposed by the state. The individual, in return for such freedom, must submit to the control exercised by the free play of market forces: only the economically strong should survive and the weak must pay the price exacted in the economic as in the biological order. Only thus can individuals be motivated to work for their own wealth and for society's good; any interference with the nature of things—that is, with the free-market economy—will in the long term be injurious to society and counterproductive for the welfare of its individual members.

In the socialist model, the individual's liberty can only be gained through a system of centralized planning which allocates scarce resources to each according to his need in order to counter the inequality of hereditary wealth and privilege. Socialism envisages freedom, not as the absence of governmental controls inhibiting individual initiative, but as the removal by the state of inbuilt inequality which militates against the exercise of such initiative. It is the freedom to be equal rather than the freedom from state intervention which distinguishes the socialist ideal from the capitalist.

From this fundamental difference and the struggle for power to which, historically, it gave rise, we owe the major features of modern industrial society. The welfare state, the growth of bureaucracy, institutionalized individualism and cultural fragmentation can all be interpreted as characteristics of the 'mixed economy'; they are the result of a failure of each of the two major ideologies to dominate Western society to the exclusion of the other. Depending on one's basic assumption about the nature of man, one will approve or disapprove of the consequences of this historic development for the individual. There can be no dispute about the effect of modernity on the organization of the Church; modern culture is unambiguously the enemy of Catholicism in a form recognizably continuous with the traditional Church.

It would be an over-simplification to attribute the growth of the welfare state in Western societies to the threat of socialism alone. In nineteenth-century Europe, the free-market system functioned perilously without the checks and balances which most countries instituted in order to predict and control events and to prevent an unprofitable exploitation of labour. It was the increasing complexity of modern urban life, not simply fear or concern for the plight of the masses, which influenced European governments to regulate the market and intervene in the lives of their people. They discovered that the efficient operation of a *laissez-faire* economy required, paradoxically, constant vigilance and intervention by the state, and this intervention included legislation dealing with public health, safety standards in factories and mines, and compulsory education. The regulation of child labour in Prussia and England in the early nineteenth century was an accomplishment of army officers and Tory politicians motivated by criteria of efficiency and productivity, rather than of socialist reformers.

But in the latter half of the century, the organization of workers to protect their interests against bourgeois politicians and entrepreneurs forced governments throughout Europe to initiate social reforms in order to prevent revolutionary action. By the end of the century, the industrial nations of Europe had already created the basis for a state-administered system of welfare. 'From this point on,' writes Henry Jacoby, 'state concern for conditions of life resulted in official intervention in all areas of human existence, and ultimately mushroomed into the all-enveloping social security systems of the second half of the twentieth century.'[4]

Tocqueville's prophecy of 'a sort of despotism democratic nations have to fear', uttered over a century ago, appears to have been fulfilled in a way he had not anticipated. Western society has exchanged the unpredictable despotism of monarchs and aristocrats for the all-too-predictable dictatorship of bureaucrats, and there has been a growing awareness of the frightening erosion of personal freedom under the guise of democracy. It is not the centralization of authority which is the root cause of this fear and of the consequent distrust of authority endemic in the West, but the bureaucratic nature of government itself, whether local or centralized. Our society is characterized by contradictory developments: the decline of loyalty to any form of authority and the expansion of bureaucratic control over the lives of individuals. Today, as a consequence, the state is less potent than it was a hundred years ago, though its intervention by bureaucratic means in the lives of its people is greater than ever before.[5] There appears to be no resolution of this contradiction, no end to the withdrawal of personal commitment to institutional and governmental authority on the one hand and the growth of bureaucracy at all levels on the other. It seems that we have only one strategy for coping with the insatiable demands for freedom: the extension of state bureaucracy which erodes it.

Local movements of self-determination are an expression of the demand for individual freedom from centralized government. In the twentieth century, and particularly in the period after the Second World War, nationalist movements have sprung up in most of the old regions of Europe, seeking the devolution of government to the local level or the complete secession of local communities from the nation which rules them. Here again a contradiction is at work: at a time when national political and economic structures are yielding power to new international groupings—both formal, like the EEC or the United Nations, and informal, through the control of multinational agencies and corporations—communities within

[4] Jacoby (1976), p. 57.
[5] Lukacs (1970), p.50.

nations themselves are finding their own government intoler-
able and are seeking to establish the economic and cultural
conditions for becoming a nation in their own right. The
political consensus which makes centralized government
workable and efficient and which implies a general subscrip-
tion among the population to a common set of beliefs and
values seems to be a thing of the past. At the same time, our
eagerness for self-determination and the growth of nationalist
feeling throughout Europe, Africa and South America create
an imperative to institutionalize international relations as a
safeguard against the explosion of nationalism into wars and
terrorism.

The efficiency of international structures of power, like the
EEC, is limited by the absence of ideological consensus which
would add considerably to their bureaucratic control over the
individuals and institutions they govern. But they are powerful
structures nonetheless and their capacity for increasing the
degree and scope of their intervention into the affairs of
member-states is all too obvious. The same does not hold for an
international Church, the efficiency of whose bureaucracy
depends on its ideological control over the minds of its members to a far greater extent than an economic institution like the
EEC. The structural changes of modern industrial society—the
expansion of governmental authority through bureaucracy and
welfare and its erosion through movements of nationalism and
devolution—have undermined the Church at two levels. On
the one hand, the state is increasingly pushing back the area of
competence traditionally claimed by religion and taking over
the educative, welfare and leisure functions which previously
bound the individual and the family to the Church. At another
level, Catholics are increasingly exposed to the anti-
bureaucratic ideology of individualism, freedom of thought,
self-determination. The task of maintaining control of thought
and action, fundamental to the sacerdotal Roman Church, has
become insuperable unless the Church can again isolate its
membership within the confines of a ghetto.

The Prestige of Social Science

Certain cultural developments, as distinct from the structural changes outlined, have further contributed to the destruction of the conditions in which the Church can best function and survive. The prestige of science—particularly social science —has not only popularized freedom of thought as a moral ideal but it has done so in a peculiarly destructive way for Catholicism. It has removed moral responsibility from the individual to the environment and, at the same time, it has cultivated an inquiring, investigative attitude towards all authority, especially of a traditional kind. A third and related consequence of the legitimation of the scientific approach to society has been the establishment of social change as a norm.

Paul Halmos documents the dominance of social science in the training of educators, managers, nurses, teachers, social workers—the functionaries of what he calls the 'personal service society'.[6] The experts of applied social science, he argues, have forced the more technological world to accept that there is such a discipline as a science of society, and its impact is in evidence in all sectors, not only in the personal services where a formal training in the theory and method of sociology and psychology are a normal requirement for entry into a career. Since the Second World War, society has abandoned the clergy as its moral experts and theology as its moral expertise and set up social workers and social science in their place. Rather than resist the redundancy of their theology, the clergy have joined the queues in colleges of higher education for the qualifications necessary to continue in employment and to maintain their status.

The fact that social workers have taken over the moral role of clerics is not immediately evident from the literature of social administration, nor is it an obvious and acceptable interpretation of their role to social workers themselves. Many feel that they are solving society's problems according to the canons of science. But the abandonment of theology in favour of Freudian and Marxist theories of personality and society represents only an apparent shift from the normative to the descriptive and scientific. These theories are based on no less moral assumptions about the nature of man and society than the theology which they have replaced.

The individual thus converted to modern social science is

[6] Halmos (1970).

relieved—by both Freud and Marx—from the burden of personal guilt which linked him for centuries in a relationship of dependence on the Church. The source of thoughts and actions previously attributed to the free will of the individual—who was thereby made morally responsible for them—is now located in the family or social environment. Feelings of personal guilt were an inadequate and unhealthy response to conditions for which the individual could not bear responsibility, according to the experts of social science. The correct and healthy treatment for such private troubles as poverty, theft, masturbation, pious scruples and so forth, is to engage in a therapeutic and scientific analysis of one's biography or one's society. Information and political action replaces meditation and ritual.

In his account of cultural change in Britain, Christie Davies has charted the development outlined.[7] He is not concerned so much with the social conditions which brought about the state of affairs in Britain commonly described as 'permissiveness' as with the cultural changes which facilitated it. Notably in the field of law, there was a shift from what Davies calls 'moralistic' thinking to 'causalistic'. That is to say, the debates and arguments as a preliminary to new legislation changed from dependence on the notion of the moral good or evil of an action in itself to that of the usefulness of an action in terms of its practical consequences for the individual or for society. Taking public issues like capital punishment, Davies documents the change in the rhetoric of debate from the 1940s—when an action was praised or condemned by politicians and the media in so far as it was acceptable within a moral theological framework—to the present day when theology has lost its rhetorical force. Today, the retentionists in the capital punishment debate are compelled to use a weak deterrence argument to support their case rather than risk the charge of moralism by relying on the old-fashioned retributionist argument.[8] (As

---

[7] Davies (1975).

[8] The same 'causalistic' thinking dominated the debate to amend legislation on abortion in the British House of Commons (March, 1980). The deep-rooted moralism which clearly inspired the anti-abortionist campaign was suppressed in favour of the more fashionable—and, as it proved, unsuccessful—scientific approach.

we shall see, permissiveness in the theological world was accompanied by a similar change from moralism to causalism. Modern Catholic theologians are sometimes late but seldom apathetic in adapting secular cultural forms to the task of modernizing the Church.)

Social science is not intrinsically radical and destructive of conservative ideas and institutions, as many sociologists have repeatedly pointed out, urging their fellow-academics to a more balanced political outlook. But historically, the language and concepts fashioned by social theorists into the academic discipline of today lent themselves more readily to the investigation and critical analysis of established institutions and stable, developed societies. That less attention is paid to the investigation and criticism of left-wing revolutionary movements and post-revolutionary societies is not a necessary consequence of the discipline but an accident of its history. Nonetheless, the accident has occurred and its effect has been to highlight the precariousness of authority and of the social forms in which it is embodied.

Since the beginning of this century, there has been a growing popular awareness of the contingent nature of political power and social structures to the point where, it has been rightly said, we are all Marxists. Even those who passionately disavow theoretical Marxism—like those who oppose theoretical Freudianism—find themselves thinking and discoursing in a framework impregnated with the ideas and concepts of Marx and Freud. They are the mentors of our age, as Aquinas and Aristotle were the mentors of the later Middle Ages, even for those who had never read a word of their writings or who found them morally objectionable or intellectually trivial. They fashioned the culture which conditioned the attitudes and coloured the language of that age, just as Marx and Freud have bequeathed to us a basic set of attitudes towards the structure of society and personality which transcends the particularities of national or political allegiance. It was Karl Marx, more than any other thinker, who successfully challenged the medieval cosmology which held men in thrall to Church and state for centuries and which led to the desacralizing of authority which is today a chronic problem for political and industrial leaders in the West. Marx made traditional authority transparent, a proper object of investigation, and in so doing he created the cultural conditions for the emergence of popular democracy.

The third accompaniment of the development and popularization of social science was the awareness of social change as a normal, healthy feature of society rather than an unusual and disturbing occurrence. The social sciences were born of the experience of social change in the nineteenth century—an experience which required analysis and definition because of its novel and frightening character. But the explanations given by social theorists not only account for particular incidents of social change; they also condition the recipients to regard such phenomena as normal. Given the persistence of the social conditions which brought about a change under question, the function of the theorists explaining it is to make change of the same order more tolerable, more legitimate. Similarly, in the practice of Freudianism the explanation of the psychoanalyst is not only consequent upon the problems of the individual patient; it also makes the symptoms more normal, acceptable, and their future occurrence in this patient and in others familiar with popular Freudianism more likely. In this sense, the social sciences established change as a social norm and made deviants of traditional institutions which found no occasion to amend their charters and to alter their structures.

Individualism

The term 'individualism' refers to a complex phenomenon impossible to define precisely, even to the satisfaction of most thinkers who recognize certain features of modern thought and behaviour that can only be described in that way. Industrial society is a cluster of contradictory trends, as we have seen, some of which appear to the liberal mind as an unprecedented restriction of the liberty of the individual. Even those features which are, by general consensus, individualist in the sense of abolishing restrictions on liberty of thought and action, do not turn out, on closer examination, to be sufficiently diffuse or significant to justify the use of the term as a general description of modern culture.

Nonetheless, 'individualism' has been attached by popular

usage to modern culture and it seems practical to conform to that usage provided we understand the difficulties involved. The characteristics of modernity outlined in this chapter refer to certain observable changes in society which reached a climax in the period following the Second World War. They are changes in the conditions which affect people's lives and which are reflected in politics, education, the economy, industrial relations and all the major institutions which link the individual to the social structure. It remains to be seen how these conditions are mediated to the individuals who experience them and who, in turn, contribute to their growth and development.

A central theme of modern culture is the substitution of personal satisfaction for politics. Since the sixties, there has been a growing despair among intellectuals, socialist groups and the young middle class of changing society. In place of the ideals which, a short time ago, could still mobilize collective action and generate a community consciousness among those committed to them, there is now the option of cultivating self-improvement or joining the latest in the parade of cultic or sectarian religions. In a society which offers less and less hope of effective political participation by the individual and in which the power of the ordinary man and woman is increasingly eroded by bureaucratic controls imposed ostensibly for their own good, we have turned to the self as the only worthy object of analysis, the only effective theatre of action. What was once a trivial pursuit for the well-to-do and the idle has been raised to the status of a creed for the masses as we encourage one another to resist permanent involvement, sexual repression and collective responsibility and to embrace ourselves in the cosy world of the individual consciousness.[9] The therapeutic man described by Rieff uses the metaphysical language of another age, but his understanding has emptied the key terms

[9] The shift from politics to narcissism is reflected neatly in the fashionable *What's Wrong* books listed in the British and American catalogues. From the mid-fifties, we had *What's Wrong with* . . . the Hospitals, the Charter, the Unconscious, British Industry, Parliament, the Church, General Practice . . . and others in similar iconoclastic vein. By the end of the sixties, all had gone from the lists except a sad title which appeared in 1970: *What's Wrong with Me? A Guide to Symptoms.*

of their distinctive meaning: 'meaning' no longer refers to a character-ideal which distinguishes the aspirations of one particular community from another but to a purely subjective sense of well-being. 'Love' is a word which has become indistinguishable, in the therapeutic society, from egotism; since the personal relationships which are the proper context of love must not be carried to the point of self-denial and sacrifice, it is clear that the term is merely descriptive of a particular strategy for the fulfilment of self.

The irony of modern culture is that the energy expended on the search for self and for the cultivation of right feelings towards others—a search which has been massively exploited by the media and the purveyors of popular art—has resulted in the impoverishment, not the enrichment, of personal life. The more we seek our selves, it seems, the more the culture industry sees an opportunity for quick profit and turns our search into a commodity for mass—and, if possible, endless—consumption. We have built personal defences against the restrictiveness of community involvement and the submersion of identity and individuality suffered by our forefathers. The effect has been to create a collective crisis of identity and a withering of our capacity for stable social relations to the point that our encounters with others, from the most intimate to the most casual, all share the characteristic of being brittle, problematic and the proper object of advice and guidance by experts who never agree. We live for the present; we have rejected as unhealthy and oppressive the sense of historical continuity with our fathers and children, our past and our future. As a consequence, ageing and death exercise a special terror over our minds, adding force to the sense of emptiness and meaninglessness which have become the fashionable and self-fulfilling descriptions of middle-class experience.[10]

Since the sixties, every aspect of popular culture has been democratized and transformed by the prevailing mood of self-discovery and celebration. The worlds of fashion, art, music, journalism, literature, education have become permissive in the sense that law and public morality are permissive. In place of the old elitism by which our cultural artefacts were

[10] Kernberg (1976).

created by a small and visible group of powerful men and distributed to us for our edification, if not enjoyment, we now have equal access, not only to the consumption of art but to its production. The old boundaries between classical music and pop, between *haute couture* and clothes, between literature and graffiti have been shattered and we are all experts now in the classless world of popular culture. The ideological bondage which enabled the powerful few to control our minds and to dictate standards of excellence in schools and in the media has been broken by the force of individualism.[11] That a new form of elitism lurked behind the illusion of cultural democracy; that many of the most strident voices in the protest against cultural authoritarianism were economic predators in disguise only began to dawn on popular consciousness at the end of the seventies. In our disillusionment, however, we are left with the knowledge of how the system works but without the power to improve it or the language to tolerate it. We *know* there is no basis for discrimination on intellectual or aesthetic grounds. Someone is ripping us off, but we can do nothing about it except retreat to the one arena of life where we can be sure of an honest and appreciative audience: the self.

Identity is a moral concept, not a bureaucratic one. The sense of identity refers, not to the possession of information detailed on one's passport and isolating the individual in his uniqueness and particularity, but to an awareness of the fact of belonging to an historic past and future, exemplified in the social relationships which constitute our present community and which determine our goals and set limits to our aspirations. Once the self is isolated as a category separate from community there can be no end and no solution to the problem of identity. Who we are and where we are going are questions which only others can answer for us; they can only be resolved, in other words, in the context of supportive and constraining social relationships. To withdraw from social involvement in order to settle these questions first is to create the conditions in which

[11] Centuries earlier, Luther accomplished a similar transformation of consciousness which enabled the man in the street in Northern Europe to realize that he was as much an expert in communicating with God as the ordained priest.

they will become insuperable personal problems. The dis-
illusioned radicals of the sixties thought that the self must be
perfected before political involvement could be effective. They
were mistaken. But our culture left them—and us—with little
choice but self-indulgence as an antidote to crises of identity.
Our society differs from the medieval in that the identity of the
individual is no longer underwritten by the language and
symbols of everyday life; in Rieff's terminology, we rely on
information, not the community, for salvation.

A word, finally, on the ambiguity of the term 'individualism'
applied to modern culture and on the illusions it encourages.
Individualism in the secular sphere—and the same is true for
individualism in religion—is not a description of the reality of
autonomous thought and behaviour. The term refers—paradoxically—to a change in the way our lives are *structured*,
making the individual responsible in some areas previously
under social control and compensating by a shift of control to
others. (The twin growth of individualism and bureaucracy in
the political arena is a striking example.) The fact that the
release occurs in an area which has been successfully defined as
significant—sexual morality, for example—permits individualism to acquire the mythical properties of a moral ideal determining the character of society as a whole.[12] Like the related
concept 'democracy', individualism is double-edged: it focuses
attention on a particular change or arrangement which is
defined as the 'reality' of social life and deflects it from
others.

The myth of individualism implies the changed attitude to
authority described here as 'desacralization'. Authority can no
longer command allegiance on the basis of the sacred character
of public office, but must be accountable—in theory—for every
detail of the exercise of power. Desacralization of secular

---

[12] 'Do your own thing' was a slogan characteristic of the 1960s and it
typifies the rhetoric of individualism. One's own thing in the organization of
domestic life—or religion—usually looked so remarkably like the thing others
were doing that it seems more apt to describe it as a change of fashion than a
new and authentic expression of self. It is revealing that another usage of the
sixties—'into' as a description of cultural involvement, as 'into self-
sufficiency', 'into sex therapy', 'into Buddhism'—gave at least a verbal nod in
a more realistic direction.

authority creates problems of management which are severe but not insuperable. The growth of trade unionism since the fifties can be interpreted as a consequence of desacralization which, in turn, has become a new medium for the exercise of power and control rather than an instrument of accountability. The unions which once challenged the state now serve as agents of state power; the system functions less efficiently but, in the context of our individualist culture and given the need for authority to appear to be accountable, it works effectively. Individualism in the sphere of theology cannot be managed so easily, as we shall see.

6

The Second Vatican Council

Pope John XXIII announced his intention to hold an ecumenical Council of the Catholic Church on 25 January 1959. When he died, four-and-a-half years later, the Council had only just begun and none of its findings had been promulgated. Under his successor, Pope Paul VI, the Roman Church was to carry forward the most fundamental reappraisal of its doctrine, liturgy and relationship to the world in its 2000-year history. Whether the published proceedings of the Council would have met with John's approval is impossible to say; if one must judge from his writings and statements during his pontificate, it is quite likely. Whether he would have approved of the Church which emerged in the years following the Council is less clear.

The response of the Catholic world to the announcement of the Second Vatican Council varied from curiosity to alarm. No group had cause for enthusiasm. Conservative circles could find evidence from his past to support a suspicion that Pope John intended to subvert the structure of traditional Catholicism along the lines attempted by the modernists. The right-wing *Corriere della Sera,* for example, claimed that he had been a modernist in his youth and that the purpose of calling a Council was to establish a modernist Church.[1] Equally, one could interpret his life and his writings as evidence of unimaginative piety and run-of-the-mill clericalism; there was certainly not much excitement among progressive theologians at the news of the Council, and some of the Pope's actions— notably the ban on worker-priests and his encyclical on the use of Latin in seminaries—placed him firmly in the papal tradition of conservatism. The Pope himself seemed taken aback by the boldness

[1] Lindbeck (1965), p.45.

of his plan and, until the start of the Council in 1962, he gave little indication of having any clear idea of what the Council should or could achieve—other than expressing enthusiasm for the idea of *aggiornamento* and the feeling that this modernization or renewal should lead in the direction of Christian unity. He saw the Council as a significant event in the life of the Church and he described his own pontificate as being 'on the point of occupying a more or less important place in history', but that judgement does not appear to have been based on any realistic attempt to weigh the problems facing the Church. He was an optimist and a man of simple faith.

In this chapter, I shall not attempt to summarize the vast documentation on the Council nor to analyse the theological content of its decrees and constitutions. That work has been done elsewhere and it would serve no useful purpose to repeat it.[2] The problem faced here is, rather, to provide an interpretation of the Council in the wider context of religious and secular history and I shall try to abstract from the documents those issues which seem relevant to that purpose and which constitute the major points of the Church's departure from traditional Catholicism.

The Relativity of Belief

In the mind of Pope John, the crisis facing the Church in the twentieth century was not an attack on its structure and faith but a crisis of inertia. The Church was out of date; it was failing to fulfil its divine mission to evangelize the world because of its resistance to change and its insistence that the world must adapt itself to the Church. What is new and, indeed, revolutionary about John XXIII is that he was the first Pope in history to accept the world as in some sense setting the standard for the Church. The message he gave to the Council Fathers in his opening address was that their task was to make the Church relevant to the world, not to condemn that world for its manifest rejection of the gospel. The bishops and theologians were not called to Rome 'to repeat in greater detail the teaching

[2] Laurentin (1962); Rynne (1966); Berkouwer (1965).

handed down by the Fathers of the Church and by early and more recent theologians'.

. . . There was no need to convoke an ecumenical council to hold discussions of that kind. . . . What has to be done is . . . to investigate and explain this certain and unchangeable doctrine . . . in such a way that it is adapted to our own times. For the substance of the deposit of faith or body of truths which are contained in our revered doctrine is not identical with the manner in which these truths are expressed, though the same sense and the same meaning must be preserved. If necessary, a great deal of time must be devoted to this manner of expression, and patience to elaborating it.[3]

The problem of relevance, which had first emerged in the early years of the nineteenth century and which had been consistently defined as a problem for the world and, later, as offering a strategic opportunity to the Roman authorities, was finally and formally accepted as the responsibility of the Church. The Council was called to change the Church in recognition of this responsibility and to remedy the defects in Church teaching and practice which had contributed to its declining credibility in the world and within the fellowship of Christians. This led one commentator to liken the Council to 'a trial which is taking place in our midst, in which we shall see the Church making frequent admissions of guilt'.[4] And it led the Council Fathers, in their Decree on Ecumenism, to teach that the Church has need of continual reformation. 'Therefore, if the influence of events or of the times has led to deficiencies in conduct, in Church discipline, or even in the formulation of doctrine,' they declared, '. . . these should be appropriately rectified at the proper moment.'[5]

Pope John's distinction between the truths of faith and their mode of expression seems, in retrospect, rather obvious and conventional. He was not allowing that the Church's teaching was erroneous; merely that its formulation could not enjoy the

[3] Opening Speech of Pope John XXIII at the Second Vatican Council. Text in Abbot (1966), p.710ff.; above translation from Schoof (1970), pp.232–3.
[4] Nierman (1968), p.viii.
[5] Decree on Ecumenism, art.6.

same status of infallibility as its content. As we shall see, this seemingly innocuous distinction would be pressed to its limits by theologians and bishops both during and after the Council and would have the most far-reaching consequences on the structure of the Church. It was this distinction between content and form of expression which Pope Pius XII rejected in the encyclical *Humani Generis,* and which conservatives and progressives alike heard his successor preach at the Vatican Council with some astonishment.

As we saw in Chapter 4, the new theology which had been checked by *Humani Generis* but which was still making considerable headway in France and Germany and other countries of Northern Europe, tended to blur the sharp distinctions traditionally made between God and man, Church and world, clergy and laity. The guardian of these distinctions was the Holy Office of the Roman Curia, and it was from Curial officials that the attack was launched on the attempt by new theologians to have relativist ideas adopted by the bishops of the Council and embodied in the official documents.

The dilemma which faced the Council Fathers was that few of them—least of all Pope John—were prepared to acknowledge the possibility that the Church might have erred on matters of doctrinal or moral substance. Yet the task before them was to renew the Church in terms relevant to the world, that is to say, to formulate Church teaching in a manner which would encourage dialogue and communion with Christians and non-Christians, with groups and institutions hitherto regarded as heretical, erroneous and reprobate. Since the Church could not be seen to have erred in its past understanding, and since there was no likelihood that those who held 'erroneous' ideas would recant, the new dialogue and communion could scarcely proceed. The dilemma could only be solved by a new theory of knowledge which would allow for theological statements to be valid but revisable. The Church required a new epistemology, rooted in the contextuality of language and the relativity of thought.

Clearly, we shall not find in the Council documents an explicit statement of the new epistemology or a systematic account of the perspective in the social sciences from which it is drawn. The documents are a monument to ambiguity; considered as a whole, they offer support for diverging and, at times, incompatible theologies. This ambiguity reflects the wide difference of opinion between the conservative and progressive bishops and the degree of stubborn resistance to compromise which the Council procedure facilitated. Other councils in the past were far from unanimous in their decisions, as Hubert Jedin makes clear.[6] What distinguishes the Second Vatican Council and makes it unique in the history of the Church is that the disagreement of its participants—who form the highest teaching authority, or *magisterium*, of the Roman Church—is incorporated into the Council documents themselves and made manifest in the official teaching which that *magisterium* is believed infallibly to express. In the First Vatican Council, the document on infallibility approved by the bishops was the outcome of considerable disagreement which is inadequately reflected in the voting figures. But those who dissented from the ultra-conservative position finally adopted either submitted to the will of the majority or broke away from the Church. The view of Pope Pius IX and his Curia prevailed and those who did not believe it before its proclamation had a choice of clear and historically-legitimated options when the teaching was solemnly defined. Then, as in previous conciliar disputes, a specific teaching was victorious and other views were seen to be excluded by the final statement of belief, leaving the vanquished with the choice of submission or schism. The all-important consensus was achieved and the *magisterium* of the Church was seen to be unanimous, even if, as in the First Vatican Council, some bishops refused to submit. As long as they were in a small minority, their rejection by the Church and their departure into a schismatic group could be used to strengthen the control of beliefs and the ideological cohesion of the Church by displaying the force of the sanctions which inhibited dissent. The achievement of consensus and the display of unity were greatly facilitated, of course, by the fact that conciliar proceeding never took place publicly, under the daily scrutiny of the media. Council participants were not subjected to the pressure of public opinion to advance or sustain a particular viewpoint nor, conversely, were the Councils under

[6] Jedin (1960).

the influence of the constant feedback of public reaction to the proceedings.

The Second Vatican Council was extraordinary in that the consensus of the Council Fathers was reached, not on a number of specific propositions which excluded others as erroneous, but on general statements of attitude whose precise meaning is obscure and, in many cases, allowed to stand with other statements which are either inconsistent or contradictory. With some exaggeration, it might be said that the Fathers of the Council agreed to differ. This expression of doctrinal tolerance represents a victory for the progressives, since the traditional view is seen to be neither correct nor erroneous but simply traditional—one perspective among many equally valid. The fact that conservative bishops and theologians seldom appeal to the documents of the Second Vatican Council to authenticate the traditional viewpoint is an indicator of this victory for the progressives. Since the Council, in fact, the wells of conservative theology appear to have dried up while those of their opponents are amply supplied by a constant stream of conciliar insights and ideas. There is still a market for conservative literature but it focuses more on the excesses of the progressive school of theology than on the conservative aspects of the conciliar teaching.[7]

The relativity of faith and morality is a basic principle of the new theology, authorized and endorsed by the Second Vatican Council. It is nowhere explicitly stated and analysed, rather implied. What is meant by the relativity of faith is that the meaning of any statement of doctrine is always open to interpretation, never finally captured in any particular form of expression for all times and for all cultures. The fact that only some questions of faith were disputed at the Council and others, such as the divinity of Christ and the historical reality of his death and resurrection, were unambiguously reaffirmed by both sides to the dispute does not mean that these latter questions were rendered immune from reinterpretation and relativization. Although it would have been unthinkable at the time that any Catholic bishops should argue for a symbolic interpretation of such basic tenets of Christianity, the same

[7] See, for example, Hitchcock (1971); Bouyer (1969).

principle of relativity of faith which allowed the Council to sanction a new interpretation of biblical innerancy and of the relationship of Scripture to Tradition could be consistently applied to Christ's divinity and resurrection.

It was the fear of the Curia that relativity was a trojan horse that would scatter the whole structure of Church teaching which led to the bitter disputes and backroom politics which characterized the Council, particularly in its earlier stages. As Thomas O'Dea writes:

> The Catholic Church is afraid that giving up its fundamentalism in these respects would mean giving up its authority; it fears further that a weakening of its authority would mean a loss of that sense of God's reality and of his relation to men through Christ which has been the core of its strength and very existence. For this reason this scriptural area will remain a difficult one in the postconciliar period. It will also prove a strategic one. Within the Church two rival models are in subtle conflict. One clings to the old Church—authority, submission, verbal deposit, closedness; the other seeks to renew the Church and fulfil its present promise in leadership, cooperation, living faith, and openness.[8]

On the innerancy of Scripture, the Syllabus of Errors in 1864 stated that it was a grave error to hold that 'divine revelation is imperfect, and therefore subject to continual and indefinite progress which corresponds with the progress of human reason'. This teaching was reaffirmed by the First Vatican Council in 1870 and, again, by the encyclical *Pascendi Gregis* of Pope Pius X in 1907. Vatican II's view of the matter appears at first sight to be substantially in line with this tradition:

> Since everything asserted by the inspired authors or sacred writers must be held to be asserted by the Holy Spirit, it follows that the books of Scripture must be acknowledged as teaching firmly, faithfully, and without error that truth which God wanted put into the sacred writings for the sake of our salvation.[9]

As David Wells shows, however, a careful scrutiny of the statement reveals a new and, to conservative minds, alarming

---

[8] O'Dea (1968), p.234.
[9] Constitution on Revelation, art.11.

possibility. The Bible teaches 'without error', but what it teaches depends upon what we consider to be necessary for the sake of our salvation. To put it the other way round, we do not have to believe that Scripture is infallible in matters which are not necessary for our salvation. But who can say what is necessary for our salvation? If we needed to know much to be saved it would put a premium on the acquisition of knowledge and give intellectuals a considerable advantage in the pursuit of salvation and in the exercise of piety—an implausible hypothesis, particularly in the light of the Church's discovery in the nineteenth century of a divine bias towards ignorance.

Bishop Butler, the English Benedictine theologian, holds that 'the date of the appearance of the human species in natural history is not formally relevant to our salvation; the reality of Christ's death and resurrection is formally relevant'.[10] If it were so easy to set limits to the application of relativism to Catholic doctrine conservative participants at the Council might have made concessions more often and more graciously to the new theology. Butler's implicit judgement that certain relevant facts such as Christ's death and resurrection are manifestly true and unproblematic while others are not cannot be supported. Christ's death is attested by history. But in what sense his resurrection is a 'reality' is a question as much open to relativization and reinterpretation as the Syllabus of Errors or the teaching of the First Vatican Council. Pope John's distinction between the content of faith and its mode of expression was to prove more revolutionary than even the most liberal and progressive theologians anticipated. It was this distinction which was at the root of the opposition between the Curia and its conservative supporters on the one hand and the new theologians and bishops on the other. The final version of the Dogmatic Constitution on Revelation is a good illustration of the ambiguity of Vatican II and of the manner in which that ambiguity undermined the conservative position in the Church. Given the critical impetus and initial support of Pope John, the Council legitimated the new theology by legitimating a relativist principle which destroyed the sense of doctrinal clarity and conceptual precision which was the basis of tradi-

---

[10] Butler (1967), p.56. See also Wells (1973), pp.26ff.

tional Catholicism. The section on the innerancy of Scripture is probably the clearest application of John's relativist distinction to a basic point of traditional teaching.

In the section on the relationship of Scripture and Tradition, the old controversy about the sources of revelation—Scripture alone or Scripture *and* Tradition?—was resolved with characteristic ambiguity. In the sixteenth century the Council of Trent, reacting against the Protestant insistence on Scripture alone as the source of divine revelation, held that Scripture and Tradition were two sources from either of which, independently, elements of faith might be drawn. In the Second Vatican Council these two sources are said to form 'one sacred deposit of the Word of God'. Both of them, 'flowing from the same divine wellspring, in a certain way merge into a unity and tend toward the same end'. However—'both sacred tradition and sacred Scripture are to be accepted and venerated with the same sense of devotion and reverence', since 'it is not from sacred Scripture alone that the Church draws her certainty about everything which has been revealed.' On the other hand . . .

It is clear, therefore, that sacred tradition, sacred Scripture, and the teaching authority of the Church, in accord with God's most wise design, are so linked and joined together that one cannot stand without the others, and that all together and each in its own way under the action of the one Holy Spirit contribute effectively to the salvation of souls.[11]

It is clear from these, as from many passages in the Council documents, that the Fathers opted for ambiguity if the only alternative was a clear statement of old or new theology.

To the alarm of many bishops, the Council came as near as the most optimistic new theologian could wish to defining the historical relativity of the Church's teaching. Dealing with the development of tradition, the document on Revelation states:

This tradition which comes from the apostles develops in the Church with the help of the Holy Spirit. For there is a growth in the understanding of the realities and the words which have been handed

[11] Constitution on Revelation, arts 9, 10.

down. This happens through the contemplation and study made by believers, who treasure these things in their hearts, through the intimate understanding of spiritual things they experience, and through the preaching of those who have received through episcopal succession the sure gift of truth. For, as the centuries succeed one another, the Church constantly moves forward toward the fullness of divine truth until the words of God reach their complete fulfilment in her.[12]

The discussions which preceded the acceptance of this statement underline the degree of polarization within the Council and the fundamental issue of the relativity of faith on which the two sides were divided.[13] The bishops of the Church, who collectively form the *magisterium*, and who, in *Humani Generis*, were accorded the decisive role with the Pope in the development of dogma, are here given third place after the laity and theologians in this development. In articles 2, 5 and 6 of this document, there is a re-emphasis of faith as a personal commitment rather than intellectual assent to verbal propositions. In this way the new theologians' stress on the intuitive aspect of faith was given some prominence, much to the alarm of some Cardinals and bishops who found this as threatening to the unity and structure of the Church as the similar progressive views of the modernists at the turn of the century. The new approach is explained by George Tavard:

Revelation is neither essentially a doctrine, although it implies one; nor a set of propositions and formulations to be believed, although it may be partially expressed in such propositions; nor the promulgation of an ethical law of prescriptions, although it also implies judgment of the morality of human behaviour. Essentially revelation is a life. It is the very life of God imparted to man through the incarnation of the Son; it is the communication of God's Word understood by man in the Holy Spirit.[14]

The acceptance of faith as an experience rather than a submission to the verbal formulations of an ecclesiastical authority

[12] *Ibid.*, art.8.
[13] See Schoof (1970), p.251.
[14] Tavard (1966), p.17.

would have repercussions beyond those envisaged during the Council deliberations. Together with relativism, of which it is an aspect, the subjectivism of faith could not be as easily contained and limited in its application as was first envisaged.

The relativity of dogma was a precondition of a positive approach to Christian unity which avoided the conventional denunciation of non-Catholic Churches as heretical and reprobate. Similarly, the debate on the two sources of revelation was marked by concern for the effect of neo-scholastic teaching on the Church's relations with Protestants who rejected tradition as a separate or independent source and who emphasized Scripture alone as the basis of faith. Pope John's initial statement setting out the terms of reference of the Council continued throughout the discussions to strengthen progressive resistance to the Curia. His commitment to ecumenism and his instinctive openness to the positive values of the non-Catholic world were remarkable in an Italian prelate, less so in those bishops and theologians of France, Germany and the Netherlands whose backgrounds were less traditional and for whom the Pope's intuition was a professional theological position. In the Decree on Ecumenism, the acceptance of the relativity of faith, of the divine inspiration of non-Catholic Churches and of the fact that the Roman Church itself must share the sin of Christian division is a remarkable testimony to the charisma of Pope John and to the influence of the North European bishops who shared his attitude and ideals.

The Catholic Church's teaching on morality was intended to be the subject of a specific document at the Council, and three traditionalist authors, Fathers Hurth, a Jesuit, Gillon, a Dominican, and Lio, a Franciscan, were instructed to prepare the *Schema de Ordine Morali*. Their intention was to reiterate the traditional casuistic morality of the manuals according to which the objective and absolute nature of the moral order is communicated through the commandments of the natural law and through the evangelical counsels. Such a morality has little place for charity, and the draft version of *De Ordine Morali* cautioned against a moral theology of charity, which the authors understood as mere sentimentalism and likely to result in the error of situation ethics. Against the danger inherent in the precept 'Love and do what you will', they counterposed the admonition in Matthew's gospel: 'If you wish to enter into life, keep the commandments.'[15]

The draft schema was rejected by a majority of the Council and the whole idea of a document specifically on moral theology was abandoned. Instead, we must look to other documents, notably the Dogmatic Constitution on the Church in the Modern World, to find the Church's new teaching on morality. The striking feature of the Council documents is a shift from the objective to the subjective in defining morality and from the level of the individual to that of the community in locating the conditions for moral behaviour. A legalistic system of morality and a casuistic approach to it are replaced by a conception of the law as a framework within which 'every man has the duty, and therefore the right, to seek the truth in matters religious, in order that he may with prudence form for himself right and true judgments of conscience, with the use of all suitable means.' In Chapter 5 of the Constitution on the Church, the pre-eminence of charity as 'the first and most necessary gift . . . by which we love God' marks the gap between the Council's teaching and the Curia-inspired schema on morality which was originally presented. Man's response to God cannot be constrained: morality, like faith, is a free response of the individual acting according to his conscience.[16]

Concern for improving the material conditions and working 'with all men in constructing a more human world' is a Christian obligation and a preliminary to full acceptance of the gospel message. Human development, including material, is part of the divine plan.[17] Whereas previously the Church tended to refer all moral obligation to the attainment of happiness after death and to regard secular values as 'merely human', the Council stressed the unity of nature and the supernatural order, the dignity of man and the goodness of creation. In the second section of the Constitution on the Church in the Modern World—parts of which read like a sociology text—there is an emphasis on the relation of social

[15] See Delhaye (1972).
[16] Declaration on Religious Freedom, arts 3 and 10; Constitution on the Church, art.9; Church in the Modern World, art.22; Constitution on Revelation, art.5.
[17] Church in the Modern World, art.57.

structure to moral commitment and an appeal for the greater development of the human sciences and a collaboration between them and theology. Social circumstances are acknowledged as an important factor in conditioning the moral response of the individual. To be a Christian it is not sufficient to adopt the individualistic ethic of traditional piety. Human development requires social development and the elimination of inequality between races, classes and sexes.[18] There is therefore a strong resistance among the Council Fathers to the framework of individualistic piety which encouraged the traditional obsession with the definition of sins and the calculation of sinfulness. Sin is a rejection of God's grace, and the majority of the bishops did not consider it their business to specify the objective conditions of individual responsibility for such an action, but rather to indicate the social conditions which might facilitate or inhibit it.

The Reform of the Liturgy

From its deliberations on the liturgy, the Council produced the remarkable and revolutionary Constitution on the Sacred Liturgy, which was to have the most visible and dramatic effect on the life of the Church. Though it, too, is marked by the same ambiguity reflecting the stubbornness of conflicting opinion among the bishops, its practical directives for the reform of the liturgy are sufficiently precise to leave little room for conservative interpretation. After 400 years of liturgical rigidity which had become one of the marks of the Church and a proud boast of its apologists, the bishops at the Council cast off the burden of history with a speed and enthusiasm which, in retrospect, seems staggering. Since Pope Pius V laid down in 1570 the liturgical norms for the Latin Church in perpetuity, and added severe warnings against any deviations from them, Catholics have enjoyed the security of a ritual unchanging through time and space. With few exceptions, the Mass, like the Church, was everywhere the same, and if its participants understood little of its language or symbols, they were offered the sense of a deeper

[18] See especially arts 224, 229–30.

significance in a ritual which symbolized the presence of a transcendent God and the stability and universality of his Church. The miracle of the consecration was an event performed by the priest for the people. The idea that the congregation should have the power to participate in its accomplishment and to share in the celebration of the Catholic Eucharist was unthinkable, except by a minority of theologians and lay reformers who, even as late as the 1950s, were widely regarded as cranks and harmless eccentrics.

The changes in liturgical attitude and practice brought about by the Council can be summarized. Firstly, the Constitution stresses active participation by the laity in order to realize the communal achievement which makes the liturgy possible. It is not a clerical preserve but the work of the whole people of God 'whose full, conscious and active participation in liturgical celebrations . . . is demanded by the very nature of the liturgy. Such participation by the Christian people as "a chosen race, a royal priesthood, a holy nation, a purchased people" is their right and duty by reason of their baptism'.[19] The priesthood of all believers, a Scriptural teaching whose implications was for centuries ignored by the Church, was not here being pressed with all its Lutheran force, but the exaggerations of the division between hierarchy and laity at the liturgical level were modified. The laity is now said to offer the Mass 'not only through the hands of the priest but also with him'.[20] This emphasis on lay participation is further elaborated in article 11 of the document, where the conventional understanding of the liturgy as an achievement of priests independent of lay cooperation is significantly modified: '. . . in order that the sacred liturgy may produce its full effect, it is necessary that the faithful come to it with proper dispositions, that their thoughts match their words . . .' Later changes in liturgical practice would follow from this concern to make the liturgy a saving experience for the laity and would in turn emphasize the importance of the subjective and therapeutic aspect of worship.

Secondly, the significance of the consecration of the bread and wine into the body and blood of Christ—the action attri-

[19] Constitution on Liturgy, art.14.
[20] *Ibid.*, art.48.

buted to the power of priests exclusive of the laity and on which, above all, clerical prestige traditionally depended—was effectively diminished. In articles 50 and 56 of the Constitution, greater emphasis is required on the unity of the whole Mass and on the significance of its several parts which form a single act of worship.[21] Thirdly, the traditional conception of the Mass as sacrifice is here complemented by the new theological notion of the Mass as meal, and the moral implications of this change are drawn. The Eucharist is described as a memorial of Christ's death and resurrection, a sacrament of love, a sign of unity, a bond of charity, a paschal banquet, which 'inspires the faithful to become of one heart in love when they have tasted to their full of the paschal mysteries'.[22] The old vertical relationship between God and man, mediated through the hierarchic priesthood, is no longer exclusively the framework of eucharistic theology. The conception of the Mass as a meal does not entirely replace that of sacrifice in the Council documents but it serves to add a horizontal dimension to the meaning of the Eucharist which later official and unofficial experiments in liturgical reform would emphasize.

The fourth factor to note in the Constitution on the Sacred Liturgy is the introduction of the vernacular as part of the process of adapting the liturgy 'to the genius and traditions of peoples'. Much scorn had been poured on the argument for the universal retention of Latin as the language of the liturgy—the unity achieved by having a dead language was not worth the price of incomprehension, it was claimed. This rationalist argument was given weight by the new importance attached to the reading and study of the Scriptures and the need to restore the Bible to a central place in the spiritual lives of all members of the Church. (The argument is not as compelling, nor was its effective implementation as simple as first appeared, however. For all the respect of the bishops for the social sciences, manifest throughout the documents, they showed little aware-

---

[21] For an account of the exaggerated focus of attention on the consecration and the relative insignificance of other parts of the Mass in the traditional liturgy, see Jungmann (1959), p.91: 'To look at the sacred Host at the elevation became for many in the later Middle Ages the be-all and end-all of Mass devotion.'

[22] Constitution on Liturgy, arts 47, 10.

ness that the loss of a common language, even a dead one, could have symbolic consequences of a different and unanticipated kind; the loss of a sense of mystery in ritual might prove to be a greater sociological obstacle to Christian commitment than the intellectual deprivation of not understanding the words.)

Finally, the document is notable for the very fact of the reformability of the Mass, whose irreformability had become part of its meaning, linked in a vague sense to its objectivity and validity. While the first changes introduced left intact the words of the central part—the Canon of the Mass, as it is called—it would not be long before that too was adapted to the 'genius and traditions of peoples'. The pressure to be relevant was shifting the Church rapidly from a position of historical stagnation, in which the past was sacrosanct and an obstacle to change, to one of historical relativity in which the past was contingent and an obstacle to be overcome. Time would tell whether the weight of history was being too rapidly cast off to preserve the identity of the community which carried it.

The Break with Traditional Catholicism

With the Second Vatican Council, 'the Catholic Church', as O'Dea has noted with evident approval, 'has returned to relevance'.[23] The resistance to dogma and to hierarchy and the pressure to embody ideas of individualism and social equality in the institutions of secular society—these post-war changes in Western Europe, together with increasing economic prosperity and intolerance of traditional resistance to change encouraged the Catholic Church to re-think its attitude to the world and to modify its teaching in accordance with society's values. This modification, contained within the Council documents, does not by any means uncritically adopt the standards of the non-Christian—or even the non-Catholic—world. But it does constitute a change in doctrine and attitude at the level of the Church's *magisterium* sufficient to stimulate the continued search for relevance and to justify a more extensive adaptation of teaching and practice to contemporary ideas and values.

[23] O'Dea (1968), p.250.

What the Council achieved was to legitimate the search for relevance of the Church to the world as an ideal and to authorize the relativization of doctrine as a principle to be applied in its pursuit. 'The substance of the ancient doctrine of the deposit of faith is one thing, and the way in which it is presented is another,' said Pope John. The Decree on Ecumenism would go as far as the conservative bishops would allow in extending that teaching and endorsing theological pluralism as an expression of doctrinal relativity. The new epistemology is nowhere more prominent than in this document in which the bishops faced the problem of Christian unity under the constraint of not being allowed to condemn or to retract. (At the Roman Catholic–Protestant Colloquium at Harvard in 1963, Cardinal Bea, Head of the Secretariat for Christian Unity, faced the same problem, but his different emphasis underlines the importance of nuance in the study of Catholic teaching: 'First and foremost the fundamental teaching of the Catholic Church will not be changed. Compromise on points of faith which have already been defined is impossible . . . Again it would be simply dishonest to suggest that there is any likelihood that the dogmas of the primacy or the infallibility of the Pope will be revised. The Church has solemnly proclaimed all these doctrines to be of faith, that is to say, truths revealed by God himself and necessary for salvation.'[24] In the new Catholicism, one theologian's revision is another theologian's reformulation.)

The Council was concerned to defend religion against typical secular charges of magic and superstitution and to encourage the elimination of those practices which might lend substance to such criticism. The argument in the Constitution on the Church in the Modern World is that the elimination of these practices, condemned by the world, would purify religion and foster 'a more vivid sense of God'.[25] It is a moot point whether the rationalization of religion in accordance with the standards of secular science is the best way of fostering a vivid sense of God, particularly in a Church which, for centuries, had encouraged its members to see signs and omens of the super-

[24] Quoted in Dulles (1973), p.156.
[25] Church in the Modern World, art.7.

natural in the world of nature and was now abruptly switching to a more empirical outlook. In the Vatican Council, the Church, which hitherto claimed to judge the world, was now preparing to acknowledge the authenticity of secular society and to submit itself to its judgement in the critical question of faith and the knowledge of God. The extent to which the legitimation of religious truth has shifted from ecclesiastical authority to secular science is indicated by the matter-of-factness of O'Dea's comment: '. . . Catholicism cannot continue to develop in a condition completely askew with respect to the important advances in human knowledge and the transformations of human outlook taking place in our day.' Somewhat innocently, O'Dea accepts the historical victory of science over religious authority as the victory of truth over error, not, as most modern philosophers and sociologists of science hold, as the victory of one form of knowledge, with associated political implications, over another.[26]

The Curia's control of doctrine and discipline throughout the Church appeared to be secured even at the beginning of the Council, when Curial officials placed themselves in key positions to influence the formulation and content of the Council proceedings. Curial influence was by no means eliminated, but its reduction was decisive in bringing about a victory for the bishops and theologians of France, Germany, Holland and Belgium and for their new theology. It was a victory of an intellectual elite whose peculiar history and social circumstances greatly strengthened its position in the politics and debates in Rome. This point will be discussed further in trying to locate the Council historically and to explain its occurrence in the 1960s. For the moment it should be noted that circumstances in the Council itself favoured intellectuals whose skills and background gave them an advantage over the Roman prelates in a Council called to address the world and harmonize Church teaching with it. Without the support of Pope John, both tacitly throughout his period of the Council and explicitly in resisting attempts to silence the new theologians or to leave them at a disadvantage in the Preparatory Commissions, the Curia would undoubtedly have triumphed.

[26] O'Dea (1968), p.31.

On Pope John's death and after the election of Pope Paul VI, the influence of new theology and theologians was checked, but it was too late to eradicate it as the new Pope might have wished. The presence of non-Catholic observers at the Council, for whom the new theology in the Catholic Church represented a welcome, if belated, acceptance of many of the principles of Reformation doctrine, also contributed to the influence of intellectuals. Finally, the presence of the media, for the first time in history reporting the formal debates and conflicts as they occurred in the Council chamber and the lobbying and political manoeuvres behind the scenes, made it difficult, if not impossible, for the Curia to stifle the opinion of the new theologians, who had already gained international repute and prestige. Through the media, the world was effectively present at a Council called to determine its status and to improve its relations with the Church, and was made daily aware of the sharp polarization of opinion at the level of the *magisterium* on fundamental questions of doctrine and morality. Those best equipped and practised in communicating through the world's press, radio and television were, of course, those whose ideas and values were finely tuned to the media, and among them the intellectuals of Northern Europe predominated. There is evidence to substantiate the view that the effective leadership of the Council was largely in the hands of the bishops of a small number of North European countries, which had already been notable for the contribution of their theologians to the new theology. An analysis of Council leadership by Rocco Caporale shows that the top four positions in a table of nationwide distribution of leaders according to other bishops' assessment of influence were occupied by Belgium, Germany, Austria and Holland.[27] Among European countries, the lowest positions were occupied by the most traditional Catholic countries, Spain and Italy.

A relatively low score in this table for France, despite the widespread opinion that France shared with Germany the highest place in the origin and development of the new theology, can be explained by the fact that in France a traditionalist

[27] See table: Nationwide Distribution of Leaders According to the Bishops' Own Indication, in Caporale (1964), p.157.

episcopacy co-existed with a progressive clerical movement. The social and religious circumstances in France generated a movement for change from below, from among the lower ranks of the clergy whose work placed them in daily contact with anti-Catholic and anti-clerical masses in urban areas. Unlike Germany, the religious divisions in France were not institutionalized in large Catholic and non-Catholic religious organizations with their respective faculties of higher education providing the basis for dialogue and cooperation. The divisions in France were between practising and non-practising Catholics and between clerics whose work-status forced them to re-think their theology and those whose geographical or hierarchic position gave them less cause to question the traditional methods and teaching.

The response and attitude of the Council Fathers to the new theology in terms of the three distinctions which mark the break with the old Catholicism—the distinction between clergy and laity, between Church and world and between God and nature—can now be considered. We have seen that traditional Catholicism defended these distinctions in their absolute form: the clergy, by virtue of the grace of order conferred upon priests at ordination, enjóyed power as agents of the supernatural which was not given to the laity; the Church was the visible institution, divinely ordained to proclaim the revelation and to mediate the saving grace of Christ, and God's truth and salvation were not available to those outside the Church except in special circumstances and conditions of inculpable ignorance; and the supernatural and the natural were radically distinct and separate realms, natural man requiring for salvation a transformation from his state of fallen nature in a sense which excluded humanism and human development as an evolutionary substitute or equivalent of the realization of God's plan. These three distinctions are aspects of the general distinction between nature and grace which informs traditional Catholic theology, and they are closely related: the distinction between God and nature has its visible expression in the distinction between Church and world and its organizational embodiment in the distinction between clergy and laity. To these may be added a fourth distinction between body and soul, rooted in traditional Catholic psychology, which expressed the duality of man in harmony with the duality of nature and grace. This separation of body and soul was significant in determining questions of morality with regard to the autonomy of the will, considered as a faculty of the soul in Aristotelian and Thomistic psychology. The body, as an element of the physical and social environment—relevant, in modern terms, to moral behaviour—could, in Thomistic terms, be regarded as having only relatively minor influence on the freedom of the will.

In Chapter 4, the tendency of the early new theologians to dissolve these distinctions was noted. In the documents of the Second Vatican Council the same questioning can be discerned alongside the traditional reiteration of the distinct and objective realities of God, church, hierarchy and soul. The division between God and nature and between the Church and the world are blurred in several passages which adopt the incarnationist perspective of the new theology against the old eschatological view. In the Constitution on the Church in the World, the Council accepts the view that the entire universe of created things is contained in the plan of redemption. Endorsing the work of Teilhard de Chardin, de Lubac and Rahner, which fuses the natural and the supernatural in an evolutionary conception of redemption, the Church teaches:

For after we have obeyed the Lord, and in his Spirit nurtured on earth the values of human dignity, brotherhood and freedom, and indeed all the good fruits of our nature and enterprise, we will find them again . . . On this earth [Christ's] kingdom is already present in mystery. When the Lord returns, it will be brought into full flower . . . While charity and its fruits endure, *all that creation which God made on man's account will be unchained from the bondage of vanity* . . . Then the human race *as well as the entire world* . . . will be perfectly re-established in Christ.[28]

In article 11 if the same document, the Council underlines the reorientation of Catholic thought on the distinctions between God and man, Church and world. The Church's task is to interpret the signs of the times and to assess 'those values which are most highly prized today' in order to respond to them. From

[28] Church in the Modern World, art.39; Constitution on the Church, art.48 (my italics).

the answers given by the Council, 'it will be increasingly clear that the People of God and the human race in whose midst it lives render service to each other. Thus the mission of the Church will show its religious, and by that very fact, its supremely human character.'

The fact of stressing the presence of God in the world and the interpenetration of the Church with secular values hitherto conceived as providing the contrast by which the Church was defined—this endorsement by the Council of widely-held religious attitudes of the 1960s can lead to difficulties. Chardinian theology, with its buoyant hopes for the future and its enthusiasm for technological progress, is a revelation for the young and the healthy living in conditions conducive to optimism. It is not so helpful for others in other circumstances. As Wells notes:

> When the being of God is identified with secularity and even with trees, river, grass, streets, buildings and atomic bombs, the idea of his personality becomes difficult to maintain. When this occurs, the personality of man also becomes doubtful. He may be nothing more than a chance collation of atoms, in which case the search for meaning in human life will probably end in failure.[29]

Keeping in mind, once again, that these passages from the Council documents are balanced and, at times, contradicted by others which repeat the older viewpoint, one is nontheless impressed by a fundamental shift in apologetics. It is no longer simply faith in the revelation of a personal God, unique and distinct from his creatures, which informs and judges experience. The Constitution on the Church in the World stressed the authenticity of human experience and the manner in which modern man bears witness in his life and aspirations to the truths of faith and to his need for God. Unlike the more traditional approach to apologetics, which raised problems for man from the content of revelation in Scripture and Catholic tradition and which invited men to submit to the Church's judgement of their experience, the Council Fathers seek to show the solidarity of the Church 'with the entire human family with which it is bound up, as well as its respect and love for that

[29] Wells (1973), p.53.

family . . . by engaging with it in conversation about [its own] various problems'. The Fathers do not come to sit in judgement on the world; their task is one of 'scrutinizing the signs of the times and of interpreting them in the light of the gospel'. 'Hence the pivotal point of our total presentation will be man himself, whole and entire, body and soul, heart and conscience, mind and will.'[30] This anthropocentric theology, which sees the nature of man as pervaded by the supernatural and, hence, as the starting-point of Christian apologetics, inspires the Council's efforts 'to decipher authentic signs of God's presence and purpose in the happenings, needs, and desires in which this People has a part along with other men of our age' and to direct their minds 'to solutions which are fully human'. In a passage which has shocked conservatives during and since the Council, the bishops proclaimed: '. . . we are witnesses of the birth of a new humanism, one in which man is defined first of all by his responsibility toward his brothers and toward history.'[31]

The organizational strength of traditional Catholicism depended, ideologically, upon the acceptance of two beliefs about the Church as separated and distinguished from the world. Salvation is attainable only within the Church; and salvation is attainable within the Church only through the medium of sacramental grace made available through the objective actions of priests. The Church and the sacraments are necessary for salvation. Thus, to put it crudely, Catholics were rewarded for their membership of the Church and compensated for the sacrifices this entailed by the visible and infallible guarantee of Christ's presence in the sacraments and of the pledge of heaven which it offered.

Both these beliefs were the subjects of lengthy discussion and varying interpretations among traditional theologians themselves, long before the Second Vatican Council. But the common understanding of them within traditional Catholicism never went beyond extending salvation to non-Catholics in exceptional cases or questioned the objective sacramental power—*ex opere operato*, as it is termed in scholastic manuals—given exclusively to priests. This power of order, which

---

[30] Church in the Modern World, arts 3–4.
[31] *Ibid.*, arts 11 and 55.

separated priests from laity, and which, being attached to the office of the priest rather than to his person, guaranteed the continuity of the Church's saving work by protecting it from the vagaries of the personal dispositions of individual priests, had as its concomitant the power of objectively valid knowledge of revelation. Infallibility in matters of faith and morals was believed to be attached to the office of the Pope—though a collegial interpretation of infallibility rivalled the papal version until the dogmatic statement on the question at the First Vatican Council. In practice, however, a degree of infallibility rubbed off on the whole clergy. The popular attribution to the priest of a superior access to the truths of revelation cannot be explained simply in terms of clerical expertise acquired during seminary training. Priests not only performed actions imposs-ible for the laity but they had the gift of preaching and counselling which derived similarly from the character bestowed upon them at ordination. The rite for the ordination of the clergy explicitly linked the teaching function of the priest to his power of order in a way that supports this popular conception. The clerical power to make grace available carried with it the clerical power—personified in the Pope—to under-stand the Word of God whose grace was mediated. If infallibil-ity was not to be regarded as a clerical prerogative—whether it was understood to be expressed by the Pope alone or by the hierarchy as a collegial body—then it would be difficult to sustain the belief that the clergy had exclusive control over the mediation of grace.

The Second Vatican Council, while not denying either of these two traditional beliefs, performed the necessary task—from the progressive point of view—of authoritatively undermining their clarity by shifting their meaning sufficiently to make it problematic and thereby to permit a wide divergence of opinion. As in so many other matters addressed by the Council Fathers, the *raison d'être* of Church and priesthood was presented in the final documents as a teaching whose meaning could not be finally and unambiguously decided by the bishops.

The distinction, firstly, between clerical and lay functions in the liturgy is stated in its traditional form in article 10 of the Constitution on the Church; here, as elsewhere, the authority of the clergy over the laity in matters concerning the mission and apostolate of the Church is affirmed.[32] The clergy is stated to differ from the laity 'in essence and not only in degree . . . the ministerial priest, by the sacred power he enjoys, moulds and rules the priestly people. Acting in the person of Christ, he brings about the Eucharistic Sacrifice, and offers it to God in the name of all the people.' The laity is required to collaborate with the priest in every missionary undertaking. Lay people have 'very important roles to play', but the missionary work of the Church is entrusted 'in a special way to the clergy'. But in the document on the liturgy, the emphasis on lay participation offers the contrasting view of the new theology which is more in line with the Protestant interpretation of the priesthood of all believers. There, as elsewhere, we are taught that 'the faithful join in the offering of the Eucharist by virtue of their royal priesthood'.[33]

The conflict at the Council between papal infallibility and collegiality almost gave to the progressives a clear victory over their opponents and allowed them to neutralize the stark individualism of the teaching of Vatican I, which stated that 'definitions of the Roman Pontiff of themselves, and not by virtue of the consent of the Church, are irreformable'. The Constitution on the Church emphasizes the infallibility of the whole Church—hierarchy and laity—and the *sensus fidei* expressed through the collegial infallibility of the Pope and bishops acting in concert. This is fully in line with a proposition *rejected* at the First Vatican Council—'the Pope . . . using the counsel and seeking the help of the universal Church . . . cannot err.' Such was the alarm of Pope Paul VI at this redefinition of infallibility, as he saw it, that he personally intervened without permitting a discussion or vote on the matter and explained the Church's teaching along traditional lines in an appendix to the Constitution. The effect was to deny the statement already made by the Council Fathers that infallibility was vested in the Church and expressed by Pope and bishops equally. Nonetheless, the Council succeeded in casting some doubt on the clarity of the distinction between hierarchy

---

[32] Apostolate of the Laity, arts 6 and 10.
[33] Constitution on the Church, art.10.

and laity, between the power of the ministerial priest and the power of the priest who remains a layman. In future years, this fact would be exploited to question the need for priests and the significance of their function in the Eucharist.

The point of being a Catholic is reaffirmed, though in a weaker form than traditionalists would wish, in articles 8 and 14 of the Constitution on the Church. The Catholic Church was divinely ordained as a necessary means of salvation and only Catholics are fully incorporated into the Church of Christ. This doctrine was first formally defined in the sixth century, and it has been repeated and defended throughout the ages, though specific directives from Rome have gradually modified its medieval harshness. Up to the Second Vatican Council, there is no evidence in the theological or pastoral literature of the Church to suggest that the commonly held view of clergy and laity throughout the Catholic world allowed for *equal* access to salvation both outside and inside the Church. However, the immediate context of the Council's affirmation of the traditional doctrine raises considerable doubt as to its meaning. It is clear from article 13 of the Constitution that the term 'church' does not refer exclusively to the Roman Church, and the frequent interchanging of 'church' and the new theological term 'people of God' suggests that membership of the Church, outside which there is no salvation, cannot be determined by counting heads or baptism certificates. The language of the Council's references to non-Catholic Christians, to non-Christians, and to atheists, indicates that the Fathers of the Council had no wish to exclude any of them from salvation but to suggest that the visible structure of their moral lives was less than perfect for accomplishing this.[34] Since membership of the Roman Church is not a sufficient condition for salvation, and since all men of good will can possess charity which is the necessary condition for it, then it is not completely clear what advantage accrues to being a Roman Catholic as distinct from an atheist. As Butler says in his commentary on the documents, the teaching of the Council 'may be taken as a shift in emphasis from objective to subjective. Salvation is, for the individual,

---

[34] *Ibid.*, arts 15–16; Church in the Modern World, art.22; Declaration on non-Christian Religions, arts 2, 3, 4.

radically dependent on subjective good intention [rather] than on external ecclesiastical allegiance.'[35] The point of believing in the Catholic faith and the traditional rewards for a moral life lived by Catholic standards seem to have disappeared between the lines of the vague and ambiguous Conciliar decrees.

One can readily understand the political reasons for the traditional interpretation of *extra ecclesiam nulla salus*. Like any other religious organization which imposes a fairly rigorous discipline on its members, the Roman Church needs to offer some compensation for compliance. If, following the Council, it becomes clear to Catholics that Protestants, Jews, Buddhists and atheists are in no clear way disadvantaged by not belonging to the Roman Church, then a more fundamental upheaval of the Church's structure than was dreamed of in the Vatican is likely to follow as a consequence.[36] We shall look later at the changing perception of the Church which can be inferred from the writings of theologians and from the behaviour of Catholic clergy and laity in the years following the Council.

The Authority to Dissent

What was achieved by the Second Vatican Council? The answer usually given varies, depending on the progressive or conservative inclinations of the respondent. As we have seen in the preceding chapters, it makes some sense to regard the Church as a unity in the period of the nineteenth century and, to a lesser degree, in the first half of the twentieth century. Curial decrees on matters of faith or discipline enjoyed the respect and won the acceptance of most bishops and were effective in commanding the obedience of most of the clergy and laity. By contrast with the Church of England, for example, or with contemporary Roman Catholicism, the Church may not have been exceptionally holy or indisputably apostolic but it was certainly one and catholic. The *magisterium* spoke fre-

---

[35] Butler (1967), p.167.
[36] Intellectuals may survive for a time in such a 'mystical' church. But if the mobilization of its adherents into collective action is of the essence, it would be unwise to rely upon them.

quently, unambiguously and authoritatively and Catholics responded positively—at least in public.

If one is to judge the effect of the Second Vatican Council from a non-evaluative point of view, terms such as 'relevance', 'humanization', 'Protestantization', are clearly inappropriate. By not speaking with authority on issues that matter to traditionalists, the Council has made the Church irrelevant for them. By not seriously tackling the important questions of social injustice and inequality, the Church continues to be irrelevant for many others. The Council documents cannot be said to hold any particular message for the Church as a whole. The effect of the Second Vatican Council is negative rather than positive and it is thoroughly modern: the authority to dissent. The principle of the relativity of doctrine, sanctioned by Pope John in his Opening Speech, could have no other consequence than to weaken commitment to the validity of particular traditional beliefs and to the very notion of validity with respect to religious belief in general. The simple candour of John's trust in 'the methods of research' and 'the literary forms of modern thought' as an aid to 'doctrinal penetration . . . in faithful and perfect conformity to the authentic doctrine' was not enough to ensure that the authentic doctrine would survive. As a means of demonstrating the validity of the traditional teaching of the Church in contrast with the 'fallacious teaching, opinions and dangerous concepts to be guarded against and dissipated', a relativist epistemology is not the best tool. After the Vatican Council, who can say what is valid or fallacious, and whether it is true or false or simply meaningless to hold that God became man or that outside the Church there is no salvation?

The appropriateness of modern methods of historical research to the social sciences is widely acknowledged by academics who are more interested in interpreting cultural phenomena than in making valid statements about them, and for whom the authority to dissent is the only dogma in their creed. It is unlikely that Pope John, encouraging his bishops to display their own dissent before the world, anticipated that a similar creed might soon replace that of the outdated catechism.

PART THREE

THE TRIUMPH OF
RELEVANCE

7

The Victory of Progressive Theology

In the last chapter, it was seen that the documents of the Second Vatican Council offer support for two different theologies, at times conflicting and incompatible. This makes it difficult, and sometimes impossible, to make an objective assessment of what the Church teaches on any particular point according to these documents. The Protestant theologian, David Wells, underlines the dilemma with particular reference to the question of papal authority:

How do we interpret the Constitution on the Church? Do we side with the progressive majority, accepting their position in its wholeness, ignoring that which contradicts it from the conservative side? Or do we take our cue from the legal head of the Church and, on his authority, ignore the major part of the document? There is no easy way out of this impasse.[1]

In general, progressive theologians have less difficulty than their conservative opponents in resolving the dilemma. They treat the documents as a coherent and consistent body of teaching and tend to ignore the parts which do not fit the picture. As we have seen, there is some justification for this. The very fact of ambiguity in the Council documents—the fact that the teaching of the Vatican Fathers is expressed in terms of conflicting theological positions—can itself be interpreted as a particular conciliar position on a major issue raised in the new theology: the absolute or relative character of revealed truth. The presence of conflicting opinion in the Council documents can be seen as an expression by the *magisterium*—albeit an

[1] Wells (1973), p.33.

unwitting one on the part of most bishops—of the principle of doctrinal relativism. The near-monopoly of Catholic publishing by progressive commentators and theologians since the Vatican Council and the failure of conservative writers to develop a less radical theology of the Council are indicators of this. The relativity of doctrine, sanctioned by Pope John, was seized upon by theologians anxious to grasp and exploit the new freedom of conscience and scholarship which was denied to them in the old Catholicism.

Theological Pluralism

Doctrinal relativism is not simply a question of reinterpreting a doctrine enjoined on the whole Church in one period of history—the definition of papal infallibility in 1870, for example—in terms uniformly applicable to the whole Church in the present day, but of accepting also that the Church in any one period is culturally diverse and different areas interpret differently the same article of faith. Doctrinal relativism, in other words, is not only temporal but spatial; and theological pluralism, which is a corollary of relativism, involves a readiness to discern cultural differences and to respect local customs and expressions.

What do we mean by 'pluralism' and what is implied by the claim that a society or movement is pluralist rather than uniform or homogeneous? Pluralism presupposes unity. The concept of a plural society is applicable where there is a degree of consensus, socially controlled by, and manifested in, common political and economic institutions. The stability of the political and economic unity achieved functions as a guide to the extent of social and cultural diversity which can be permitted as a counterpoint to it. Pluralism is the characteristically modern alternative to the uniformity typically ascribed to primitive societies. Through the mechanism of political and economic unity, plural societies can ensure the minimal consensus necessary for social order—the minimum necessary for them to be referred to meaningfully as a 'society'. The danger in a society which has developed in a pluralist direction is that the new awareness of internal solidarity experienced by the various ethnic, linguistic, religious or racial groups which pluralism draws into relief will stimulate demands for separate political and economic institutions. If such demands are met then clearly the successful group has ceased to form part of a plural society. A central issue in the debate about devolution in the United Kingdom is precisely the question of whether the conditions of unity can be maintained or whether Scotland and Wales will secede and become new societies.

It is obvious in the political sphere that these conditions of unity do not occur mysteriously, simply as an outflow of individuals' good will. Unity is first and foremost a political accomplishment, not a moral consensus. (Whether it also reflects a moral consensus is an important ethical issue, but that is another matter.) The existence of a plural society, therefore, depends upon the existence and adequate functioning of a social mechanism which can ensure cohesion and prevent fragmentation. And the fact that the provision of such a mechanism is a necessary condition for the achievement of unity in a plural society is a consequence of the *complexity* of large-scale human groups. It reflects the sociological reality of the group, not the moral degeneracy of modern man. To ignore it, to seek to dispense with it, is to be naive, not optimistic.

There is no hint in the progressive theology of the periods before or after the Council that individual Catholics should become the arbiters of their own beliefs. Theological individualism was not on the agenda. On the contrary, it was argued that a greater measure of diversity was demanded by the need to preserve the unity of faith—the survival of dogma could only be assured if the rigidity of its imposition by the *magisterium* was relaxed. The political and moral ethos of the 1960s and an antagonism towards all forms of cultural imperialism exposed the Catholic Church to theological criticism for its insensitivity to the diversity of cultures within its own boundaries. The theologians made frequent reference to the pluralism of society and to the need for the Church to be relevant to it. Borrowed from secular culture, the term 'pluralism' implied that the relaxation of doctrinal rigidity throughout the Church would result in the same unity-through-diversity manifested by so-called plural societies.

Once the concept of theological pluralism was accepted in

the Second Vatican Council and pressed home in the later progressive literature, both Church and theologians were faced with the problem which seldom arose during the debates at the Council: in what sense and by what means could the unity of faith be established and maintained? The rhetoric employed by the advocates of pluralism was about unity, but their real concern was to establish a tolerance of diversity in a Church which, over the centuries, had grown increasingly centralized and imperialistic. A basic unity of beliefs was essential, it was accepted. But the conditions for providing it and the sanctions for sustaining it were not considered. The practical problem of promoting and maintaining unity-through-diversity was left, it seems, to the Holy Spirit. Theological pluralists rested their arguments about cultural diversity on the evidence of sociologists and anthropologists; they felt no need to create the sociological conditions which are necessary for consensus and without which any large group must divide and fragment.

Theological pluralism, which, in a very restricted sense, has always been tolerated within the Church, became after the Council a theological norm. It became a slogan of progressive theologians, counterposed in their literature to 'theological uniformity', which rapidly acquired the pejorative connotations of authoritarianism and intolerance. Different cultures interpret differently the same article of faith according to their cultural background, it was argued, relying for support on the expertise of social scientists. The interpretation of belief and the resolution of disputes about its validity have become problematic in modern societies. Religious belief is filtered through cultural experience; its meaning is determined by the world in which people live and through which, inescapably, they acquire their faculties of perception, cognition and interpretation. If that world could be assumed to be homogeneous then the problem of resolving disputes about religious belief would be purely intellectual. It could be tackled adequately by theologians and philosophers at the level of theology and logic.

But in a pluralistic world, a dispute about the meaning of a particular belief requires an adequate description of the cultures in which the belief is held and through which it is filtered. A theologian, therefore, can say what a belief means only if he is provided with an adequate sociological description of the culture in which it is held. It follows that in plural societies a belief will have as many different meanings as there are cultures, and the valid interpretation of a belief will depend on the availability of adequate descriptions of the cultures. The adage 'when in Rome do as Rome does' expresses this pluralism at the behavioural level and underlines the obvious fact that one needs first to know what the Romans do in order to know how to behave in a way that will not be misinterpreted.[2]

It underlines also the assumption behind cultural and theological pluralism. Although societies are not culturally uniform but diverse, nonetheless *particular cultures* within a society can be treated as uniform and homogeneous, can be identified by an observer and adequately described in order to facilitate the resolution of disputes about behaviour or beliefs. The Church is multiform; societies and even groups within societies differ culturally and that difference affects their interpretation of religious beliefs. But there must be some limit to diversity if theologians are to discuss and evaluate beliefs. There must be some point at which cultural homogeneity is assumed if theological pluralism is to make sense and if theology is to be possible. It is not of great consequence to a tourist if a Tourist Guide's description of Roman behaviour and symbolism is inadequate—tourists are not likely to attribute any gaucheness or embarrassing misunderstandings to the sociological poverty of the description given in their Guide. It clearly does matter that theologians, who reject theological uniformity on the grounds of cultural pluralism, should be in a position to say what a belief means in different cultures. Otherwise they are implicitly adopting the position of theological *individualism* and abandoning as impossible the task of distinguishing truth from falsity in the matter of religious belief—a position which they all emphatically reject.

While the advocates of pluralism reject the extension of doctrinal relativity to the experience of each *individual* and regard such a development as doctrinal anarchy, it is clear that the case for pluralism cannot be limited to localities, races, classes or any such conventional settings. If the deposit of faith is one thing and the manner in which it is expressed is another,

---

[2] On cultural relativism see Gellner(1974), especially pp.47ff.

who is to say what counts as a true or false expression of faith even within a particular group? If the meaning of a doctrine is relative to cultural experience, who is to arbitrate between competing formulations of doctrine within the same culture—surely it can be claimed that cultural differences, giving rise to conflicting interpretations of belief, exist within races, classes, even families? The vagueness of the term 'culture' makes it impossible to set a limit to the application of the principle that doctrine is relative to cultural experience. Once adopted, and not limited by a social mechanism ensuring unity, the principle cannot but have the consequence of encouraging diversity of faith to the point that unity becomes meaningless—at any stage in a dispute about a particular belief, cultural relativism can be invoked to demand tolerance of each and every interpretation.

The social sciences provide no adequate descriptions of cultures for theological purposes. The sociological evidence is negative, not positive: it demonstrates that societies are not culturally uniform and, although some sociologists make certain assumptions about the unity of groups, there is no compelling evidence offered in support.[3] The same process of reasoning which breaks up the homogeneity of larger groups and collectivities can be applied just as plausibly to the smaller. In modern society and with modern methods of research at our disposal, we cannot assume homogeneity in any groups, small, medium or large. All are more or less cosmopolitan, the smaller being simply microcosms of the larger. Culturally, Rome is a fiction of the Tourist Guides. Like Italy, it is a geographical location, not a cultural unity.[4]

As we shall see, the doctrinal relativity advanced by Pope John and the Second Vatican Council was taken up by theologians and developed in a manner which stressed diversity rather than unity and had the effect of making *individual* experience rather than cultural experience the touchstone of

[3] The division in modern sociology between those who accept and those who reject such assumptions has been institutionalized by the emergence of the school of ethnomethodology, which focuses on the absence of stable structure in social groups.

[4] Metternich was correct but for the wrong reason. The Roman analogy is drawn from Gellner (1974).

authenticity. In the literature since the Council, the term 'theological pluralism' is seldom used except in the context of negating a traditional interpretation of doctrine. One does not encounter it in the positive context of stating what the underlying unity of faith means and what it excludes as erroneous. 'Theological pluralism' seems to be a euphemism adopted by theologians to disguise the extent of doctrinal tolerance as a consequence of the Council's acceptance of the principle of relativity. From this principle followed an emphasis on the autonomy of individual experience and a *de facto* liberation of the individual from all formal, objective constraints on belief. In the sphere of belief, and increasingly in the sphere of morality also, the old collectivism began to disappear and the old compulsion to conform one's thought and behaviour to a pattern determined by ecclesiastical authority began to give way to the new freedom to be an individual.

The old certainty of pre-conciliar Catholicism and the awareness that faith was supported by a world-wide community which looked for guidance to an infallible teaching authority has disappeared in modern theology. Doubt is now a virtue. Papal infallibility is a formula which must be retained and respected if the continuity of belief is not to be flagrantly destroyed, but its meaning is so problematic and contentious that it can no longer fulfil its old function of aiding the unity of faith. While it is clear that those with a non-intellectual commitment to Catholicism—the mass of ordinary laity—will continue for a time to experience their faith in the old way until the new theology has filtered through the ranks of Church membership, their religion is no longer being buttressed by the old authority. As the Church discipline affecting the laity becomes increasingly modified by the new theology, which now enjoys virtually unchallenged status in Catholicism, so it will become increasingly difficult to define a Catholic in terms either of faith or morality. As Wells remarks, Catholics will be recognized, not because they adhere to the same objective teaching but because they appear to share the same subjective experience.[5]

The American theologian, Avery Dulles, is one of the more

[5] Wells (1973), p.102.

moderate exponents of new theology whose views are widely respected throughout the English-speaking world. Unlike the more radical Hans Küng, he enjoys the trust and respect of his ecclesiastical superiors, both in the United States and in Rome. Dulles states the relativity principle thus:

... the truth of revelation is never known in its naked absoluteness, but is always grasped with the perspectives of a sociocultural situation. ... The fact that men in the past expressed the Christian revelation in a manner suited to their own times does not mean that we should reject what they said; nor does it mean that we ought to speak the same way. Our task is to 'appropriate' what they said ...[6]

Consciousness of the relativity of all human utterances is, for Dulles, a precondition of discovering 'in and behind the faulty words of men the divine truth that is coming to expression through, and partly in spite of, its human witness'. Dulles is clearly committed to the survival of the unity of faith through the diversity of its expression. He rejects extreme relativism—the denial of the possibility of validating statements of belief by reference to criteria of validity outside the consciousness of the believer. For Leslie Dewart, he notes, the substance of Christianity is the Christian consciousness of its adherents and propositions about the faith are only valid as expressions of this consciousness. Dulles emphatically opposes this and holds that there are some beliefs which cannot be denied without loss of substance to the faith. He is not a relativist, he claims; his intention is not simply to negate the truths of Catholic tradition but 'to clear the way for a more positive appreciation of the tradition.'[7]

When we examine Dulles's treatment of particular doctrines of Catholic tradition, however, it is hard to avoid the conclusion that the substance of faith, the fundamentals of Catholic belief, disappear. The dilemma posed for Catholic orthodoxy by the principle of relativity is that no verbal proposition can capture the meaning of a religious truth in an absolute sense valid for all time. Thus, a statement which was valid in one period may be invalid in another without contradiction. Dulles's readers are

[6] Dulles (1973), p.178.
[7] Dewart (1969); Dulles (1973), pp.200ff. and 188ff.

easily persuaded by this argument since he restricts his illustrations to different historical periods. It is easy to accept that there may be no contradiction involved in holding today that faith alone is sufficient for salvation while at the same time recognizing that the Church taught the opposite in the sixteenth century.[8] But the relativity principle applies spatially as well as temporally; it applies to different cultures of the same period, not only to different periods. If the meaning of 'faith alone' is problematically tied to the cultural context of the sixteenth century, it is no less problematically tied to the indeterminable social and cultural contexts which comprise the Church of the twentieth century. What the Dutch understand by 'faith alone' may be quite different from the meaning given to it in Spain or in Ireland. And, as I have argued, there is no reason to limit the exploration of context to the boundaries of societies, or even groups within societies. Ultimately, the principle of relativity makes the individual autonomous as a measure of truth. The 'conceptual agnosticism' of Dewart, which Dulles rejects, is a valid extension of the argument which Dulles advances.

To press home the point, we may look at two particular doctrines of Catholic tradition which Dulles accepts as fundamental to Catholic faith and for which he claims validity, but not in the verbal form in which the Church has expressed them. Regarding the teaching on the necessity of the Church for salvation, Dulles acknowledges that there can be no doubt about the literal sense in which it was held, in the Middle Ages, to exclude from salvation all those who were not members of the visible institution of the Church. But this ancient understanding is repugnant to most Catholics in the modern world, whose 'mental and social structure' leaves no room for an exclusivist concept of the Church as a community of the saved. Dulles will not concede that the old teaching was wrong, however. 'It was based on a valid insight into the ecclesial character of all Christian salvation; it called attention to the inseparability of

---

[8] This is not to say that there is *not* a contradiction. By careful theological management, Catholics are easily encouraged to tolerate doctrinal or moral peculiarities in the Church's past, provided they are not too recent or too frequent. For the Church, as for any ideological movement, the management of history is a critical task of leadership.

the grace of God from the church of Christ.'[9] There is no evidence that the teaching authorities of the Middle Ages really meant the Church of Christ when they referred to the Roman Church in defining the dogma in question.[10] On this kind of mystical reasoning, there is no proposition which could not be defended as true in some sense since the criteria of truth are locked away in the inaccessible regions of 'mental and social structure'.

If Dulles consistently applied this relativistic argument to all beliefs, one might agree that there was some justification for his position, though it would still raise considerable problems for his thesis about the survival of dogma. But he insists, against Dewart, that certain events are fundamental to Christian faith and their meaning is not optional. He would, therefore, reject an allegorical interpretation of Christ's divinity and resurrection. But there are today many who affirm their faith in both while emphatically denying their reality as real historical events, and they support this symbolic interpretation of dogma on the same relativistic grounds that Dulles advances against the teaching discussed above: that the doctrines were defined within a cultural context which is not that of our modern world-view. Dulles, in response, would be left with the task either of defining 'our modern world-view' in terms which would support a literal interpretation of the doctrines—an impossible task—or of dogmatically asserting his own literal position on these beliefs, while insisting that one's world-view inescapably coloured other, more dispensable articles of faith.

Again, on the doctrine of transubstantiation—the change believed to be effected in the bread and wine at the Eucharist—Dulles implies that the medieval scholastics held it in some form not adequately expressed by the term traditionally employed, and states that there is need for a new term which

[9] Dulles (1973), p.165.
[10] The practice of shifting between 'Catholic' and 'Christian' is a strategy of many modern theologians who interchange the terms according to personal choice. It is a strategy which relies for its success on a general moral preference for the Christian over the denominational and on the ambiguity of an overlap between the two concepts. The exploitation of such ambiguity stands in a long tradition of equivocation in the Church, which new theologians are usually anxious to condemn.

expresses the mysterious and non-magical character of the change. One must ask, in this regard, why difficulties about the precise meaning of 'substance' should make theologians like Dulles confident that the Church did not intend the popular 'magical' understanding of the Eucharistic change, while terms like 'incarnation', 'redemption' and 'atonement' are not equally mysterious, problematic and open to symbolic interpretation. One may disapprove of Leslie Dewart or disagree with some points of his argument. But symbolic reductionism, if unacceptable as yet to most Catholics, at least has the merit of consistency. The more 'orthodox' progressives like Dulles are trapped in the dilemma: either they assert that the Church was wrong in the past and accept that all beliefs are matters of opinion—and risk the charge of breaking the continuity of faith—or they must adopt a fundamentalist attitude on some truths while at the same time relativizing the others.

It is notable that the reinterpretation of dogma on the grounds of changed cultural context is invariably pursued in a negative fashion. The negation of the conventional understanding of old formulae appears to be the only effect of applying the relativity principle in progressive theology. Dulles denies that this is his intention, but his theological method is underwritten with doubt to the point that no statement of faith emerges from it which could possibly be denied. The burden of his theology is not to make positive statements which can be refuted but to negate a selection of such statements drawn from traditional Catholicism. It is not difficult to infer that the basis of selection is not the manifest inadequacy of the traditional interpretations—as is claimed—but the pressure to accommodate Catholic teaching to the non-Catholic world without entirely lapsing into agnosticism. Dulles claims to write as a Catholic, in line with the historical tradition of Catholicism, but he holds a theological position which effectively empties that tradition of its content.

Hans Küng is less reluctant to acknowledge the past errors of the teaching authority of the Church. His is the faith of a liberal Protestant, as his colleague Karl Rahner once described him. He argues, not for a commitment to the validity of verbal propositions, fundamental or otherwise, but to the indefectibility of the Church, to the truth of its life and mission. Küng's rejection of papal infallibility, and his writings on the priest-hood which deny to priests the indelible character of ordination separating them from the laity and giving them the exclusive power to consecrate the Eucharist, have been condemned by the Sacred Congregation of the Faith. Like Dulles, Küng bases his arguments on the relativity principle. But he is one of the few Catholic theologians who refuse to equivocate when it is clearly no longer a question merely of reinterpretation but of fundamental change involving the denial of previous Church teaching.[11] Küng's views were condemned in the document *Mysterium Ecclesiae* issued from Rome in July 1973. While upholding the traditional position on matters contended by Küng, the document is remarkable for what it concedes to the relativism of new theology—to the principle which, as I have argued, logically leads to the kind of reinterpretation of beliefs which the Sacred Congregation finds unacceptable.

The relativizing of doctrine by the progressive theologians since the Council employs arguments which appeal to the unreasonableness of doctrinal rigidity on the one hand, and which, on the other, reassure Catholics that beliefs will not disappear into the mists of relativism if the old absolutism is abandoned. The truth will prevail; the fundamental beliefs of the Catholic tradition are not being abandoned but reinter-preted; far from destroying the unity and continuity of faith, the new theology will protect and strengthen them. Dogma 'can and will survive', as Dulles puts it, because 'dogma has an in-built elasticity'.[12]

While Dulles and others cling to the notion of fundamen-tals—of some basic propositions of faith which distinguish the Catholic from the non-Catholic, the Christian from the non-Christian and which unite members of the Church in their faith—their relativism systematically undermines the possibil-ity of such propositions. They fear the revolutionary conse-quences of abandoning fundamentals entirely. They have a vague notion of orthodoxy, but since they cannot tolerate the idea of heresy—which is a necessary condition for claiming that a belief is orthodox—their catalogue of orthodox beliefs is

[11] Küng (1971), p.142ff.; (1972), p.66ff.; (1967), p.419.
[12] Dulles (1973), p.212.

meaningless. One must conclude, therefore, that the doctrinal relativists who want truth without error, orthodoxy without heresy, are attached, not to beliefs, but to formulae—statements whose historic importance in the Catholic Church gives them special significance but whose meaning for modern Catholics is entirely optional. This would be in line with Dulles's claim that belief in the historical reality of the redemption is essential to Christianity '. . . however variously it may be conceptualized'.[13] With this Alice-in-Wonderland qualification, even belief in God can be understood in a way that atheists would find perfectly acceptable, and belief in Christ's resurrection could be made consistent with disbelief in the possibility of life after death. It is clear how such a theology facilitates diversity; it is not clear in what sense it can be described as pluralist.

What seems to have happened in the short period since the Second Vatican Council is that beliefs have ceased to function as a mark of unity and common identity. There is no dogma, from the most peripheral to the most fundamental, which cannot be denied by Catholics with relative impunity, and there is increasing evidence that this authority to dissent is rapidly changing the structure of the Church. The direction of change is certainly towards diversity; a more precise characterization of modern Catholicism must await the evidence of the next chapter.

The declining capacity of beliefs to function as a mark of catholic unity does not imply that Catholics *in fact* express wildly diverging beliefs and do not still enjoy a greater measure of consensus than, for example, the Church of England.[14] The structural conditions for dissent have been created, but time is needed for the new structure to become established and to transform the practices and beliefs of the laity. The effect, when

---

[13] *Ibid.*, p.201.

[14] Until the beginning of this century, the bishops of the Anglican Church, too, were attached to the concept of pluralism and much given to proclaiming the fundamental unity of beliefs which that implies. A *de facto* consensus among their laity on certain fundamentals lent substance to their claims. The decline of this consensus has forced a tacit agreement on the bishops not to be specific about the grounds of unity and to employ formulae to cover the range of beliefs instead of more precise language which might be exclusive.

it comes, will be to make the Church simply a mirror of society's values and to remove all possibility of mobilizing its members for the missionary task of changing society which is still believed to be the *raison d'être* of the Church. Theological dissent is still subject to certain limitations in the Catholic Church. Emphatic rejection of traditional formulae still requires more courage or audacity than professional theologians can usually afford. Their strategy is to acknowledge and defend the formula but to alter its meaning and to appeal to the Vatican Council's teaching in support. Thus Thomas Corbishley, the English Jesuit and a popularizer of progressive theology, explained in a Catholic journal not renowned for its radical views: '. . . one theologian's account of ultimate reality is not necessarily truer than another's, except in so far as one may contradict flatly an official statement. But, granted that a theologian does not explicitly deny a traditional formulation . . . he should be given the benefit of the doubt.'[15]

The trend among theologians towards a symbolic interpretation of traditional dogma caused some unease before the Second Vatican Council, but it seemed unproblematic at that time to allow such intepretations to be disseminated as long as they were restricted to the books of the Old Testament. After the Council, the doctrines of infallibility, the virgin birth, transubstantiation, were freely reinterpreted as symbols of a mysterious truth in terms which had the important property of not being specific enough to stand contradiction. *A New Catechism*, commissioned by the hierarchy of the Netherlands and compiled by the Higher Catechetical Institute in Nijmegen, is a manual of progressive theology for the modern world. 'The whole message, the whole of the faith remains the same,' wrote the bishops in their Foreword. But the traditional interpretation of the virgin birth, which stressed the physical reality of the virginal conception of Jesus, becomes, in the Dutch Catechism, a parable of the uniqueness of Jesus and of his status as Messiah. Similarly, the doctrines of transubstantiation and infallibility are expressed in their traditional forms but explained and emphasized in a way which diminishes the importance of their literal interpretation.[16]

[15] Corbishley (1976).
[16] *The New Catechism* (1970).

These reinterpretations may be correct according to the findings of biblical and historical research. The point here is not to question their validity but to consider their function and the social implications of these views for a Church which is effectively unable to prevent similar symbolic interpretations of each and every other dogma of Catholic tradition. It is difficult to understand what is meant by the claim of the Dutch catechists that the doctrine of the virgin birth is the same, that they are proclaiming the same faith because the same formula is employed—only the meaning is different. It is difficult to make sense of the claim that Catholics are—or should be—united on fundamental truths if the meaning of those truths is so symbolic that it would be meaningless to dissent. What would it mean to contradict, say, Dulles's version of transubstantiation, Küng's interpretation of infallibility, the Dutch bishops' view of the virgin birth?

If the relativization of faith has been undertaken with a view to facilitating the catechetical and missionary role of the Church then it has been brilliantly—if ironically—successful. Whereas Catholics and potential Catholics once anguished over their beliefs and tried to resolve their doubts by recourse to prayer and spiritual guidance, they can now be assured that such anguish is redundant. To be a Catholic may still involve, for social reasons, the adoption of a particular style of behaviour and a particular set of moral values. But the articles of the Creed, to which one is theoretically committed, and which formerly divided people as radically as the tenets of Marxism are opposed to those of capitalism or fascism, are now publicly available in the form of truisms that could not be denied without suspicion of irrationality. In the new theology there are no compelling theological grounds for becoming a Catholic. On the other hand, there are no particular reasons for not becoming one—it is no longer a matter of great consequence one way or the other.

The concern of Pope Paul VI with the erosion of Catholic unity as a result of the desire to implement the theological pluralism of Vatican II has frequently been expressed. He describes as 'pathological' the situation of those who promote 'dogmatic relativism', seeking 'formulas deceptively easy to understand but which dissolve the real content of mystery.

. . . While making use of the words of the gospel, they change their meaning'.[17] Nine years previously, the same Pope denounced the tendency of theologians to stress the symbolism while playing down the physical reality of Christ's presence in the bread and wine of the Eucharist, using terms like 'transignification' or 'transfinalization' in preference to the traditional concept.[18] But the Pope and his Curia are in a position of more visible powerlessness today than during the Vatican Council. Whatever the authorities in Rome may say and wish to the contrary, belief, it appears, is now optional for Catholics. The Vatican Council sanctioned dissent and the principle of the relativity of faith is now the overriding dogma of the Church which neither the Pope nor any of his bishops can delete from the documents, even if they deplore its consequences. The dilemma for the Pope and for all Catholics is how to understand the rationale of membership and commitment if faith has evaporated into truisms and Catholics are no longer distinguished from non-Catholics by the beliefs they hold. If there is no one with the authority to interpret the faith in a manner which distinguishes it from the beliefs already held by any rational human being then the Church's mission to convert the world is not a very credible ideal.

The Primacy of Experience

One finds in the new Catholic theology the same tendency to dogmatize about the human condition that characterized the writings of the French and German existentialists since the Second World War. On the basis of certain elementary and inescapable facts of life and death, an elaborate psychology is constructed and offered as a science of man which reveals the transcendent in the facts of human struggles for life and fulfilment. The early writings of Karl Rahner helped to legitimate this kind of 'theological anthropology'.[19] In its popular version, man and God are defined in terms of each other and theological labels are indiscriminately attached to generaliza-

[17] Pope Paul VI, Apostolic Exhortation, 8 Dec 1974.
[18] Pope Paul VI, encyclical *Mysterium Fidei*, 1965.
[19] Rahner (1966).

tions about humanity and its condition. Whereas Karl Marx claimed to perceive in theology the projection of purely human ideals and described as false consciousness the condition which produced this illusion of another world, the new theologians stand Marx on his head and claim to see in man's struggles for survival convincing evidence of the existence of that other world.

The attractiveness of this approach is obvious: there is no more eloquent demonstration of the relevance of religion in a rapidly changing world where religious values and commitment are declining than to anchor theology in the data of human psychology. It is a modern variant of Aquinas's proofs for the existence of God. Whereas St Thomas pointed to a stable social and political order as proof of God's existence and benign concern for the works of his creation, his successors point to change, conflict, human *angst,* as evidence for the supernatural. With this theology, the search for relevance has ended in triumph: to live in the world and to experience its limitations—we have little choice in the matter—is to bear witness to the reality which theologians call 'ultimate', 'divine', 'transcendent'. There is a significant difference between this theology and that of St Thomas, however. For Aquinas, it was the natural order, not human experience, which bore the burden of proving God's existence. Given the medieval expectation of stability in that order, individuals' beliefs and behaviour could be set under the control of a particular stable conception of God's revelation, namely, the Scriptures interpreted by the visible institution of the Church. Experience was not autonomous, for St Thomas, but was subject to the judgement of revealed truth, and the individual must conform to the requirements of a stable and objective body of Church law and teaching if his life was to be authentically Christian.

Modern theological anthropology, on the other hand, sees no such stable order within which the visible institution of the Church can be located as God-given and God-directed; the Church and the Scriptures are both human products which cannot make *definitive* judgements of contemporary human experience since the meaning of any such objective judgement is as problematic as the meaning of human experience itself. Theologians, once again, are caught in a dilemma: they cannot specify what are Christian beliefs and behaviour except in terms so general and elastic as to exclude no one from the definition; on the other hand, they still wish—as they must—to see the Church as something more than simply a mirror of experience. It must be the leaven in the mass, whose function is to judge the world of human values and experience and to transform that world into conformity with God's plan as revealed in Scripture. Their solution is to inject into the language of tradition a measure of elasticity which allows it to expand and contract to fit all possible situations.

Gregory Baum is another theologian of influence in the English-speaking world whose prolific writing has helped to popularize the works of the new theological scholarship and to interpret the Council documents in the light of the social sciences. Baum is an enthusiastic advocate of the anthropological approach. 'The contemporary theologian will ask the question . . . whether a careful description of human life might not reveal that man is open to the supernatural. . . . Is it possible, the theologian will ask, to discern the supernatural or the divine in the finite actions of man?' Like Feuerbach and Marx, Baum denies that there is a God prior to and independent of man. But this does not mean that God is a mere projection of man's highest ideals—'this, obviously, is not our position.' In seeing the task of the theologian to investigate empirically the condition and experience of modern man, Baum believes that he is merely restating traditional doctrine and justifying Christianity to a modern age. 'God is the Good News that humanity is possible', he writes, quoting the Dutch theologian Schillebeeckx. 'For divine revelation . . . is not information about God, nor, therefore, an explanation of the universe and its origin, but self-revelation and hence the initiation of man into a new self-consciousness.' Theological method, for Baum, consists of constructing 'a careful description of human life' in order 'to discern the supernatural or the divine in the finite actions of man'.[20] He claims that his is an empirical approach to theology, but there is no evidence to support what he describes, and his descriptions of human life are such that it is difficult to imagine what state of affairs could conceivably invalidate them.

[20] Baum (1971), p.39, 181, 218.

In the light of these writings, one is forced to the conclusion that the problem for the Catholic and for the Christian is not *what* to believe or *how* to behave, but what to claim for one's beliefs and behaviour. And the problem for the theologian is not to employ clear language to sharpen the blurred images of the Scriptures and to spell out the content of faith and the ethical obligations that follow from it, but to use the right metaphor for human existence, to attribute self-awareness and self-realization to the right source. On this reasoning, Christians differ from atheists, not in terms of the content of their beliefs or the specification of their ethics, but in terms of the different claims they make and the different accounts they provide of their common participation in the human condition. This theological anthropology offers an amnesty to the world by making anyone a believer who dares to assent to the proposition that 'man is always more than man and . . . he is on his way to a destiny that transcends him'.[21]

An earlier writer who shared Baum's concern to derive the supernatural from a description of human psychology was Rosemary Haughton, whose work *On Trying to be Human* was an influential text for the English catechetical movement after the Council. Though Haughton's style is exploratory and her tone less dogmatic than that of Gregory Baum, one finds here also a tendency to reduce the Catholic to what is personally relevant for the individual, here and now. 'Ultimately,' as Charles Davis writes in criticism, 'this makes one a prisoner of a limited experience.' The tendency to subordinate the meaning of Christian beliefs to personal experience, while laudable in its intent, is destructive of the tradition it purports to interpret and preserve. For that teaching only survives as a tradition because it has been handed down 'by generations faithful to authority when much in what they passed on was not to them personally very meaningful'.[22]

Clearly, if it were possible to generalize about human experience, to provide the 'careful description of human life' which Baum desires, then theological anthropology would be on firmer ground. If one could offer an adequate account of how

---

[21] *Ibid.,* p.234.
[22] Haughton (1966). See foreword by Charles Davis, pp.11–12.

people actually feel and of what their innate needs and unconscious motives actually are, then one would be in a stronger position to draw general theological conclusions. But the defect of theological anthropology is precisely its implicit dogmatism in imposing upon humanity descriptions of experience based on evidence no less trivial and no less culture-bound than the fashionable slogans of existential psychology.

Theologians are not happy to accept religious authority as the judge of the validity of Christian beliefs and behaviour. They seem equally unhappy to abandon all objective standards of validity; some criteria of truth and falsehood are required. Therefore, they construct an image of social science as an authoritative and consensual body of knowledge from which the nature of man can be more objectively deduced than from Catholic tradition. Scientifically, however, there is no reason to prefer one account of man's nature to the other. There are no *empirical* grounds, in other words, for claiming that Catholic tradition is any better or worse guide to the human condition than the work of Freud, Marx or Durkheim. The nature of man is not an object of scientific investigation but of moral decision. The writings of social scientists contain certain assumptions about human nature; they contain no revelations. It is the implicit claim of theological anthropology that science—social science—has discovered the facts of human nature in some objective, culture-free sense which can function as the arbiter of religious belief in place of the old-fashioned authority of tradition. Most sociologists would agree with the theologians that religious belief is culture-bound. There are few who would dare to exclude their own discipline from the same cultural conditioning.

Ethical Relativism

It may be argued, however, that doctrinal beliefs are not the only dimension of unity in the life of the Church. Other religions, for example Islam, place less emphasis on beliefs and stress more the place of ethics in the construction of religious identity. If Catholicism after the Council is undergoing a shift in religious consciousness from beliefs to ethics, from the identification of Catholics in terms of what they believe to their moral identity as practising Christians, then clearly there would be an important sense in which the transformation of the world was still a meaningful and credible ideal.

The old Catholicism imposed a moral life on its subjects which was certainly distinctive in its application to behaviour—Mass on Sundays, no meat on Fridays, sex on specified conditions—and precise in its sanctions of venial sin, mortal sin, excommunication, etc. There is no doubt that it was an ethical system relevant to a particular conception of the Church and the world, though its relation to the Scriptures and its relevance to the social and economic conditions of the mid-twentieth century were far from clear. Under such conditions, the Catholic catalogue of sins was becoming less tolerable. People of apparent goodwill and high status in the secular world, with no particular antagonism towards religious authority, were finding divorce, sex outside marriage, contraception and other areas of forbidden conduct more attractive, more tolerable and more functional in conditions of high social and geographical mobility, of changed economic status of women, etc. The moral rules which were functional for the traditional Church were not particularly suited to an economic system developed independently of it and, at times, in opposition to it.

The prestige of the social sciences—of sociology and the various schools of psychology, in particular—provided a scientific legitimation for a new morality in a paradoxical way. Whereas the new theology emphasized the individual at the expense of the collectivity, as we have seen, the new morality tended to shift responsibility for particular actions from the individual to his social and physical environment. While the old morality always included an element of subjective intention as a defining characteristic of sin, the general awareness among traditional Catholics placed so much emphasis on the ethical character of objective, individual *actions* that one's intentions and one's environment could function as little more than excusing factors. In the new morality, the individual's intention is given primacy in the determination of the morality of action. But that intention cannot be inferred from any particular action; our behaviour is conditioned by genetic and environmental factors which make it impossible to make any *a priori* judgement attaching motives to actions. The proper response to any behaviour considered to be undesirable is not to impute moral responsibility to the actor but to locate the cause of action by empirical investigation of the social, physiological and psychological circumstances of the individual. The world, the flesh and the devil are no longer considered to be independent of the individual—encouraging sin but leaving intact the free will which can choose between good and evil. They are now within the individual, around him and overlapping with his faculties; they reside within the human personality which they have created, chronically limiting if not destroying the freedom without which the individual cannot be held responsible for his actions.

We have seen in Chapter 5 how the shift from moralistic to causalistic or scientific attitudes towards behaviour was accomplished, particularly in the legal sphere. An accompaniment of this trend in secular society was the expansion of the social services to provide a remedy for the conditions which were considered to cause anti-social behaviour. Within the Church, the new morality stimulated a parallel movement of social concern, which was soon translated at the diocesan and parochial levels into organizations of social welfare which altered the traditional role and status of the priest. (In a sense, the Church was becoming a microcosm of the state, with similar ideals and concerns, similar ideas and functionaries. Catholic parishes began to take on the colour of a welfare agency, their clergy acting as supervisors of a range of services by voluntary workers which resembled as much the work of a Social Services unit as the Catholic Action of old. This new relevance brought with it a change of role and status for the clergy which was welcomed by those who were embarrassed or disenchanted with their liturgical role. But although the new role was generally more acceptable, the new status was hardly likely to match the aspirations of educated men of the world. The world had enough professional social workers to make clerical amateurs feel less than secure.)

In the writings of Bernard Häring, Catholic morality received the same thorough criticism and reinterpretation as Catholic doctrine in the hands of the new theologians. The same fundamental principle of relativity informed both enterprises—beliefs could be understood only within the context of a particular culture and the morality of an action could only be determined in the context of an individual's environment. Since the environmental factor cannot be measured in any way that would permit a general judgement of its effect on individuals, it follows that the decision to accept the social scientific evidence entailed the abandonment of the old legalistic morality. In the pre-Vatican II era, moralists concentrated on the objectivity of individual sinful actions, writes Häring:

... the manuals and the whole background of ecclesiastical life favoured a certain concentration on discrete acts. Now depth psychology, and the developmental psychology in particular, make it easier for us to understand the biblical morality that is, above all, a call to radical conversion of heart. ... We see much more clearly today how the individual act is conditioned by a person's whole earlier development.[23]

Häring's work is a useful guide to the new Catholic morality, not simply because he is one of the few remaining specialists in the subject of moral theology but because, like Dulles, he is respected as a moderate interpreter of the Vatican Council documents. For Häring, the individual's intention is not merely an excusing factor to be weighted in consultation with one's spiritual adviser. Intention determines moral responsibility. Like many other contemporary moralists, however, Häring reveals an old-fashioned Catholic mind behind new ideas when it comes to discussing particular actions repugnant to the traditional morality. Masturbation and abortion, for example, are evil—not in themselves, but by virtue of an unloving intention. But Häring appears to build into these actions in a dogmatic and *a priori* manner the unloving intention he imputes to them, thereby smuggling back, in practice, the objectivity he was at pains to eliminate in principle.[24] (In yielding to the pressure to conform to the traditional attitude, Häring exemplifies the characteristic Catholic approach to ethics depicted by Max Weber: the channelling of grace through the institution of a church makes it 'particularly important that sins remain

[23] Häring (1974), p.10.
[24] Häring (1971), p.130ff.

discrete actions against which other discrete deeds may be set up as compensations or penances'. A consequence of this is that the individual feels no pressure to attain the certitude of salvation by his own powers. This fact has significant social implications which Weber explored in his study of the relation between Calvinism and the development of capitalism.[25])

The merging of the sacred and the secular, which originated—for modern theologians—in the theological anthropology of Teilhard de Chardin, de Lubac and Rahner and which can be supported from the documents of Vatican II, is a key element in the new morality. The intention which defines the moral status of an action is itself defined as good in so far as it promotes the common good and the good of the individual:

There is no room for sacred biological and other impersonal laws that can oppose the truly sacred rights of persons to development. Any imposition of abstract principles, untested against the historical context as to whether they really serve the good of persons and of the community, is considered a sin against man who is made in the image and likeness of God.[26]

Enda McDonagh is another respected moral theologian of the new Catholicism for whom morality begins as a human phenomenon and only in that light can it be considered theological. Any action—sexual, political, whatever—can only be justified if its consequences can be judged to promote universal harmony: '. . . the Christian summons is now to a fuller realization of the community of all men.'[27] All virtues reside in the intention of the subject. Chastity is not an ideal of abstinence, for example, but 'a continuing call to recognize, develop and integrate one's sexuality in the love and service of others'.[28] Since love and service are also subjective, chastity loses all objective character and, as a generalized moral ideal, becomes ethically impotent. The new morality offers no clearer identity to Catholics than the new theology. Ethical prescriptions, like doctrinal formulations, have acquired the virtue of impreci-

[25] Weber (1966), pp.188–9.
[26] Häring (1974), p.11.
[27] McDonagh (1975), p.137.
[28] *Ibid.*, p.118.

sion. A Catholic's ethical obligations, like his beliefs, must conform to a Christian ideal so broadly interpreted as to exclude no one. As Steinbeck comments in *The Grapes of Wrath:* there ain't no sin and there ain't no virtue; there's just stuff people do.

Like Häring, McDonagh feels the traditional constraint to label some actions as immoral, notwithstanding the subjectivity of his general argument. His choice of nationalism in developed countries as sinful, inadequate, outmoded, is difficult to understand, given his acknowledgement of the complexity of modern society as the reason for abandoning the simplistic labelling of behaviour as moral or immoral. One can understand how, by a different reasoning, some theologians were led to attribute sin to particular kinds of social institutions rather than to individuals. But this is not McDonagh's point. Like Häring, he is willing to leave moral judgements to the individual—in principle. In practice, there are some exceptions where, he claims, the universal good and the fuller realization of the community of all men are objectively hindered or promoted by certain courses of action.

One can appreciate the reluctance of Catholic moralists to appear to lend support to 'situation ethics', which has been frequently condemned by Rome. If it is not objective behaviour but subjective intention alone which defines moral responsibility, then Catholics are liberated from all objective constraints on their behaviour. The Ten Commandments and the laws of the Church are simply guidelines which are useful only to the degree that the social circumstances in which they were formulated can be assumed to remain constant. Since this assumption is plainly absurd, Catholics may adopt the principles of Joseph Fletcher, whose book, *Situation Ethics: The New Morality,* published in 1966, became the gospel of do-it-yourself morality. 'We cannot dogmatize,' according to Fletcher. 'Any sexual act (hetero-auto-homo) engaged in, in or out of marriage, will sometimes be good and sometimes be bad depending on the situation.'[29] The dilemma of Catholic moralists is usually resolved, as already described, by asserting the general principle which makes the individual's intention the criterion of

[29] Fletcher (1966); see (1965), p.409 for quotation.

morality but then condemning certain actions by describing them in evaluative terms. McDonagh's definition of nationalism would not satisfy a sociologist, nor would it be acceptable to a nationalist who might consider that the common good required self-determination and justified the means necessary to obtain it. If social life is complex enough to warrant the general principle of the new morality, it would seem to be complex enough to rule out dogmatism on the practical obstacles to promoting the common good.

The New Catechism faithfully transmits to the Catholic laity the teaching of the theologians on the new morality, offering a blend of old formulae and new interpretations which disguise the extent of change. The traditional teaching of the Church is to be respected, but the old moralism which condemned actions because they were wrong and regarded the demonstration of their injurious consequences in scientific terms as a bonus, an additional reason for avoiding them, is replaced here by the new causalism. God's will, manifested in the natural law, which traditionally determined the morality of an action and to which the hierarchy, through the *magisterium*, had privileged access, is revealed in *The New Catechism* through the findings of social science. It is a metaphor for human well-being. Thus, for example, the reasons why a couple should not live together before marriage are primarily scientific; cohabitation 'brings with it on the one hand the sense of being married, and on the other the conflict of knowing that they are not married . . .' and the result is 'profound inner tensions'. This is not a compelling scientific argument, but it is clear at any rate that the Catechism regards social science as a vehicle of God's revelation. 'From all these human reasons, we can deduce God's will and law—that only married people should live together.'[30] Other classic moral dilemmas are treated in similar fashion—homosexuality, contraception, masturbation.

The publication of *The New Catechism* in 1967 and its rapid translation into English and other European languages gave cause for alarm at Rome that a version of Catholic doctrine and morality, based on a progressive reading of the Council documents, was being disseminated with the approval of the Dutch

[30] *The New Catechism* (1970), p.387.

hierarchy, lending credibility to it as an authoritative and official account of the Church's teaching. Accordingly, a Commission of Cardinals was set up in 1968, charged with examining the Catechism and publishing a 'modification' of its contentious passages.[31] With regard to the moral teaching of the Catechism, the Commission's general comment speaks for itself:

It should be made quite clear that there are moral laws which can be so clearly known and expressed by us that they bind our conscience at all times and in all circumstances. . . . It is quite right that much importance should be attached to the person's fundamental moral attitude, but care must be taken to ensure that this attitude is not made too independent of deeds.[32]

The unprecedented step for the Church of publicly acknowledging dissent within the episcopal college and of doing so in a publication intended for lay readers underlines the extent and character of the change in the Church since the Second Vatican Council. To see in *The New Catechism* a healthy expression of theological pluralism, as some would wish, is too simple. The commission was not established by Rome to present an alternative view to that given in the main text, but to correct that text and to defend the truth of the Church's teaching against alternative views. The Catechism underlines the powerlessness of the Church's teaching authority to prevent dissent on questions so fundamental as to warrant open conflict with a national hierarchy. The Dutch hierarchy shares with the *magisterium* the belief in the unity and continuity of the Catholic faith. But, in practice, the two parties exemplify only diversity; they agree, not on fundamentals, as they would wish to believe, but on formulae.

The Catechism is a demonstration at the highest level of the effect of the Vatican Council: the legitimation of dissent. For two reasons, the Commission of Cardinals found it necessary to temper criticism of it with praise for the 'worthy intention of the authors' and its 'admirable pastoral, liturgical and biblical

---

[31] *Acta Apostolicae Sedis*, 60, 1968. The modification appears as a Supplement to the English translation of the Catechism.

[32] *The New Catechism* (1970), Supplement.

character'. First, there is nothing in the Catechism which could be flatly denied without appearing to deny also the teaching of the Vatican Council. It is not what the authors said, but what they did not say on the Eucharist, Infallibility, Marriage and Sexuality that the Commission found objectionable. Second, a vigorous denunciation by the Commission in the language used by conservative theologians to describe progressive contributions to the Vatican Council debates would have created an even worse situation for the Pope and the Curia than the fact that the Catholic faith was being presented in a manner which distorted the whole truth, as they saw it. By careful management, it still seemed possible to project the image of a unified Church and to marry the requirements of teaching the truth of Catholic doctrine to the demands of expediency. (As we shall see in a different context in the next chapter, these problems of management would become insuperable; the strains of marriage would increase.)

Pluralism in the Liturgy

In the Eucharistic liturgy, discontinuity and diversity were more visibly accomplished in the decade following the end of the Second Vatican Council. The central act of Catholic worship, whose stability and universality both expressed and reinforced the belief in the unchanging nature of the Church, of its teaching and of its hierarchic structure, was transformed by a series of official decrees and unofficial actions into an experimental theatre. The attempt to create a liturgical pluralism, under the unifying guidance of Rome, by granting authority for national and diocesan variations in the ritual form was unevenly successful in the first years of the new liturgy. National hierarchies of conservative temper made minimal concessions to the cause of pluralism, while Dutch, French and German Catholics enjoyed all the novelties of a national liturgy with indeterminable local variations. Commenting on the relatively sober state of affairs in England, the editor of the *Clergy Review* wrote:

Liturgy has become a matter of thumbing through a bewildering variety of fat tomes, ring-files and flimsy leaflets, none of which appears to know its own mind. Priests and people have been turned into objects of a never-ending series of experiments carried out by committees of nameless faddists who have never acquired any sort of pastoral or scholarly standing and who are now betraying the work of the great liturgists.[33]

By the mid-seventies, it was clear that the multiplication of forms and tongues and structural changes had failed to promote the renewal desired by the Council. Reformers has assumed that language was the main component of meaning and that the translation of the liturgy into everyday terms and its restructuring to give greater prominence to the verbal elements of the Mass would automatically make it more meaningful. If the volume of literature is an indication of the interest of intellectuals in a topic, then liturgists had lost interest in the liturgy by the mid-seventies. There is now nothing more to be said, apparently, and little that can be done by Church authorities to remedy a liturgical situation which, by general consent, has failed to promote a sense of unity in worship except to continue with the experiments. It should come as no surprise that the liturgical renewal failed to materialize, given the dependence of liturgy on theology. Rearranging the parts of the Mass to give prominence to the proclamation of the Word is, in a sense, more meaningful if the language of that proclamation is comprehensible. But it is more profoundly meaningless if the Word is believed to be authoritative yet its meaning is permitted to be optional for the different cultures, groups and individuals who comprise the worshipping community of the Church. Then the Eucharist, intended to manifest and create the underlying unity of the Church, becomes a sign of its division; it becomes a stand on which the Church displays its fragmentation.

Liturgy, like dogma, has acquired a degree of elasticity which threatens its survival. The old belief in its objective character as an efficacious rite to which the members of the

---

[33] *The Clergy Review*, April 1975. For a comparative account of legislation on liturgical reform in Europe and the United States see the documentation in *Concilium*, Vol. 2, No. 8, 1972. Peter Hebblethwaite has described the chaotic state of the modern liturgy in his interesting account of the new Catholicism, *The Runaway Church* (1975), ch.2.

Church had to submit if they were to obtain the benefits made available to them depended upon a common understanding of the meaning of the Word of God of which the Mass was the ritual expression. That belief is threatened by the multiplication of ritual forms at the behest of ever-smaller groups of people, whose need to participate is argued as a reason for adapting the rite to the demands of the occasion. In the old Catholicism, the Mass was believed to be the sacramental sign of the Church, the highest point of its activity, the expression of its supernatural power. For this reason, Catholics were obliged regularly to kneel in submission to its authority and to the power of its unchanging ritual to evoke the sense of continuity with the past and of divine intervention in human affairs. In the new Catholicism, the Mass tends to become a therapy for the individual, its efficacy discussed and evaluated in terms of its success in stimulating right feeling towards one's fellows.

But what are one's *right* feelings towards one's fellows? The question falls within the competence of psychoanalysts and their response is tailored to the personality and needs of the individual patient. Most theologians and moralists would reject individualism to that extent and would claim that theology can make some objective and meaningful response to such a question. But there is little agreement among them and, from the structural change in the Church since Vatican II, there is every reason to expect that their disagreements will multiply. Their responses are as diverse as the groups and the movements which have replaced the monolith of the Church and which will form the topic of the following chapter.

The content of new theological writing has been critically examined here not simply to point out certain fallacies and inconsistencies. Such defects need not necessarily inhibit the translation into action of the values and ideals embodied in the new theology. Whether the ideas of intellectuals are transformed into action and generate social or religious change is not entirely dependent on their depth and internal consistency. The new theology has been examined here in order to show at work the process by which one view of an essentially ambiguous teaching in the Second Vatican Council was victorious over its rival. In demonstrating this, the new theology was revealed as an inadequate instrument to accomplish the renewal desired by the new theologians themselves. What it did accomplish can only be described by moving to a more concrete level of analysis.

8

Profile of a Relevant Catholicism

The task of renewing the Church without dismantling its
structure and destroying its basic unity was not viewed by
progressive theologians—as it was by their conservative opponents—as a problem fraught with risks, bristling with difficulties which required detailed and exhaustive study of the complex issues involved. One could say that the new theology was
packaged and sold to the bishops in a spirit of almost irresponsible optimism; God would find a workable social framework to
embody the new ideas. It is clear that theological pluralism was
an ideal consciously promoted, not in order to destroy the basis
of doctrinal unity, but simply to weaken the source and mitigate the effects of the old uniformity. The analysis of the new
theology in the last chapter makes it equally clear, however,
that the ideas and the ideal were not adequately matched.

We now turn to an examination of the current state of
Catholic practice and commitment and try to assess the degree
to which the Church in the concrete conforms to the model of
pluralism. In that model, a diversity of expression within the
framework of a common faith and a common moral commitment was proposed and envisaged as the Church's response to
the social and political reality of modern society. The rhetoric
of Catholic bishops and theologians stresses the reality of
pluralism and its continuity with historic Catholicism.

Even to the casual observer, the facts do not fit the model; the
actual development of Catholicism since the Council does not
lend itself to an interpretation which fits the unity-through-
diversity ideal to which Pope John XXIII committed the
bishops of the Church at the opening of the Second Vatican
Council. The Church today is not dissimilar in its organization
to traditional Catholicism; it is not unrecognizably Catholic in

its services and rituals; a case might be made to establish a formal continuity between the new theology and some variants of the old. But as a community of faith holding specific and recognizably similar beliefs, pursuing specific and recognizably compatible goals, the members of the Roman Church do not express themselves articulately and persuasively. 'They have virtually no common principle of coexistence,' wrote Rosemary Ruether as early as three years after Vatican II:

> . . . even when they use the same symbols, they mean very different things by these symbols. It is not unfair to say that probably never in the history of Christianity has there existed, within the formal boundaries of a single ecclesiastical institution, poles of opinion which share so little of what we might call 'a common faith'.[1]

Ruether sees Catholicism as the expression of a 'Free Church Movement', whose notable characteristic lies in the willingness and ability of dissidents to remain within the Church and to find there, or to create, a community compatible with their 'heretical' beliefs and attitudes. 'Spiritually we are already in schism,' she notes, and if that break has not yet been formally ratified she attributes the fact more to 'cultural lag' than to any underlying unity.

It should be noted that Ruether was commenting on a major split between old and new Catholicism in 1968. The situation as she interpreted it was one of incompatibility between two poles of opinion, two churches locked in combat, each claiming allegiance to the same tradition. Implicit in her article is the view that this polarization of the Church, while it breached the unity of faith, was a prelude to a renewal of faith and to a new consensus among Catholics on the fundamentals of doctrine and morality. The unity which was lacking in the whole Church could be found, strengthened and more intensive, in each of its divisions.

Over a decade later, there are not two combatants but several; there are not two conflicting theologies but a multitude, making it difficult to reduce the level of dissent to manageable and analysable proportions. The major conflicts of

[1] Ruether (1968).

theology and morality which characterize contemporary Catholicism can be grouped into four categories.[2] I shall argue that the Roman Church today constitutes a type of voluntary association in which the variety of beliefs and ethics, publicly available and acceptable, far exceeds anything that could plausibly be labelled 'theological pluralism' In the awareness of most Catholics, the Roman Church may not yet have achieved the level of religious tolerance institutionalized in the Unitarian Church, for example, or even the Society of Friends. One would not expect a world-wide community, trained in passive submission to authority, to shake off so rapidly the moral constraints of a centuries-old tradition. It will be argued, however, that the conditions facilitating this achievement are already present.

Political Catholicism

The first of the four groups under consideration is that body of opinion and action within the Church which seeks to transform Catholicism into a movement for the elimination of social and political injustice and thereby to effect a change in the structure of society along more or less socialist lines. Various terms have been used to describe this orientation to the Church. I use the term 'Political Catholicism' for want of a more neutral and accurate label. This does not imply, it should be emphasized, that any of the other groups after the Council, or Catholicism as a whole before it, are apolitical in the sense that their beliefs and practices are not movitivated by political considerations and do not have political implications. Nineteenth-century Catholicism was politically implicated to a high degree and the same could be said for the Traditionalist movement in the present day. The difference is that Political Catholicism tends towards an overtly political theology—it identifies the transformation of society as the necessary condition, if not the realization, of salvation. The more traditional approach is covert, implicit; in

---

[2] It must be emphasized that these are analytical categories. The real concrete situation is more complex than the impression here conveyed of a tidy division into four competing groups.

the jargon of sociology, the political function of traditional theology is latent rather than manifest.

Latin America has provided a training-ground for political activists in the Church as well as the main laboratory for testing the ideas of European intellectuals. There is still only a small minority of bishops, priests and laity in Latin America committed to some form of Political Catholicism; their work has been influential beyond the boundaries of their Catholic countries and the tendency to exaggerate their numbers is understandable.[3]

Catholicism in Latin America, for almost its entire history, has been a reactionary political force upholding conservative values and government and resisting attempts to alleviate the condition of the poor and to derive an egalitarian social policy from the teaching of the Church and the Scriptures. In Brazil, where the Catholic population is the highest in the world and where the Catholic Left is numerically strong and militant relative to the rest of Latin America, Political Catholicism had its origins in the revival of Catholic Action in the 1920s.[4] The rapid modernization and the accompanying multiplication of social problems in the decade following the Second World War created a situation of continuous crisis and alerted the Roman authorities to the condition of the Church in Brazil. A more liberal episcopacy was encouraged, whose individual members increasingly pressed for reforms to alleviate the conditions of the poor. A militant branch of Catholic Action based in the Universities, the Juventude Universitária Católica, broke its ties with the Church and formed an organization committed to revolutionary socialism. It retained its Catholic orientation, however, and constituted an attractive alternative to main-

[3] This exaggeration occurs primarily outside Latin America, where the media in secularized liberal democracies tend to regard the overthrow of authoritarian regimes as desirable and where Catholic intellectuals, with access to the media, view the situation as an opportunity for demonstrating the relevance of the Church. A comparison of the media coverage of the papal address at the Puebla Conference of Latin American Bishops, 1979, with the actual text of that address by Pope John Paul II is instructive in this regard. See *Tablet*, 3 Feb 1979.

[4] For the historical material which follows see de Kadt (1970); Lewy (1974), p.504ff.; Vallier (1970).

stream religion for militant Catholics of the Left in the early 1960s. Its appeal and its legitimacy was helped, writes Guenther Lewy, by the fact that Pope John XXIII avoided the wholesale condemnation of Marxism in his social encyclicals, *Mater et Magistra* (1961) and *Pacem in Terris* (1963), and gave special attention to the problems of underdevelopment which concerned the Latin American students.[5]

The Brazilian bishops helped in the establishment of a Movement for Basic Education in 1961 and, following the guidance of educationist Paolo Freire, this organization rapidly expanded its work of raising the consciousness and the level of literacy of the masses. A radical socialist ideology motivated both movements and gave cause for concern to many of the bishops, who found elements of the education programme unpalatable:

The whole people must participate in government. Some men have more than enough, while many have nothing at all. Some make too much. Many work and their work is exploited by others. A lot of things are wrong in Brazil. A complete change is needed in Brazil.[6]

With the military coup in 1964 and the removal of President Goulart, whose liberal policies had encouraged radicals working within the Church and on its fringe, the more conservative majority of the bishops began to recover their voice and their more traditional political role. They discerned the hand of God in the counter-revolution of the Brazilian army: '. . . Divine Protection made itself felt in a tangible and straightforward manner . . . the Armed Forces came to the rescue in time to avoid the implantation of bolshevism in our country'.[7] Emanuel de Kadt documents the increasing tension towards the end of the 1960s between a numerically small but militant and articulate Catholic movement for radical change and the military government which enjoyed the support of the majority of Catholics and Church leaders. State censorship, which stifled the expression of views critical of the government's social and economic programme, allied to state aid to combat poverty

[5] Lewy (1974), p.514.
[6] Cited in de Kadt (1970), p.159.
[7] *Ibid.*, p.191.

and illiteracy in the most deprived regions, provided a response to the movement which blunted its radical edge and led many of its revolutionary clerics and laity to the belief that the Church was not an adequate instrument for the realization of their ideals. A reformist policy to alleviate the condition of the poor and the deprived may be the only means of ensuring the stability of an unjust social order, as Marxists would claim. In conditions of mass awareness of injustice and pressure for change, the presence of a powerful Roman Church can be a critical factor in making such reformism possible and in deflecting revolution from its course.

It is to counter this resistance within the Church to revolutionary change that the movement of Christians for Socialism continues to work for the education and greater political awareness of Catholics and others and provides the most visible expression of Political Catholicism in the contemporary Church. Founded in Chile in 1972, this movement has spread throughout Latin America and in most of the Catholic countries of Europe, including great Britain, Spain, France and Italy. Its aim is to spread a political awareness among the Christians through the theology of liberation and the struggle to overthrow the capitalist system—by violence, if necessary—as the major source of human exploitation. This purpose was expressed by Gonzalo Arroyo, a Jesuit priest and one of the movement's founders, who emphasized the intention of working within the Church: 'We aim at a Church in solidarity with the interests and struggles of the workers,' he said, 'but without breaking with the present Church.' The Church cannot be renewed independently of a radical social transformation:

. . . a renewed Church will be able to grow to the precise extent that growing numbers of Christians will identify themselves with liberation movements to destroy the old society and bring about a new one which will more fully allow men to have hearts which beat for others.[8]

There is little evidence that Christians for Socialism—or any other organized expression of Political Catholicism—will continue to pose a serious challenge to the conventionally individualistic piety of Catholics and their leaders. The world-wide

[8] Arroyo (1974).

economic depression of the early and mid-seventies was not accompanied by any visible growth of activity or membership on the part of Political Catholicism. On the contrary, the swing to the left which radicals hoped for and which many observers of the Church in Latin America anticipated at the beginning of the decade appears today as remote a possibility as ever. This is not to say that the concerns of Political Catholicism have not made an impact on Catholic consciousness and leadership. In most European countries as well as in Latin America the leadership of the Catholic Church is more sensitive to the political dimension of religion and expresses a more liberal attitude on a variety of social questions than has ever been the case in Catholic history. Since the pontificate of Pope John XXIII, official policy in the Vatican has extended Catholic tolerance to include even Communism, and the election of the Polish Cardinal Wojtyla to the papacy was widely interpreted as a significant step towards better relations with the Communist world. But in this respect the Church is merely reflecting the attitude of most secular states in the developed world. Whether the new liberalism expresses a fundamental moral change which will move the Church to the offensive on behalf of the poor and deprived and will result in the Church taking the initiative even when the initiative is unfashionable and costly in organizational terms—the acid test of moral leadership—is not clear. One may argue on historical evidence, like the French philosopher Jacques Ellul, that Christian participation in liberation movements owes more to the success of secular propaganda than to leadership in the Church—but one does not thereby destroy the moral justification of such participation.[9] 'If the cause is right,' the politicized Catholic might respond, 'better late than never.' If the bandwagon is moving in the right direction one should not refrain from jumping on it simply because one is not in the driving-seat.

It is not the intention here to evaluate the theology of Political Catholicism nor to attempt to judge the motives of those who work for the conversion of the Church to its theory and practice. From the social and political perspective of this

[9] Ellul (1969).

book the more pertinent question concerns the relation of Political Catholicism to other groups in the Church and to its official leadership and the potential for survival of a Catholic movement explicitly committed to political ends. To continue the metaphor, what is the likelihood that Catholics will jump off the bandwagon when there are no longer spectators to applaud its course?

If one confines attention to historical precedents in the Catholic Church there is little light to be thrown on the matter. Political Catholicism in the nineteenth century was taken over and managed by the Vatican under the leadership of Pope Leo XIII. In the process, the movement was transformed into Catholic Action—a movement for the restoration of papal power through the religious integration of secularized aspects of urban political and economic life. But the Vatican today lacks either the will or the authority to exercise that degree of control over those who claim to be practising Catholics. Less militant groups than Christians for Socialism have resisted attempts to force them to conform to official policy and there is no likelihood that the Vatican authorities, even if they so wished, would risk a public rebuff by threatening politicized Catholics with the traditional penalties for non-conformity. Within Protestantism, however, there is a longer history of dissent which it may be helpful to consult in order to gauge the viability of a politico-religious movement within the contemporary Catholic Church.

One can distinguish three broad tendencies in Protestantism, deriving from Reformation theology, in response to the social and political conditions of the modern world: Evangelicalism, Social Reformism, and Fundamentalism. The last-named is more widely represented and institutionalized in the Protestantism of North America; the origins of Social Reformism can be traced to Northern Europe, where it has been a powerful force within the mainline Protestant churches; Evangelicalism has its distinctive English and American types which, for the purpose of crudely mapping the development of Reformation theology, can be ignored without undue distortion. Evangelicalism and Fundamentalism once formed scarcely distinguishable tendencies within the same movement of Revivalism. Fundamentalism acquired its distinctive shape only in the 1920s and predominantly in the United States.[10]

The revivalist origin of Evangelicalism and Fundamentalism was essentially an expression of religious individualism; it emphasized the freedom and autonomy of the individual in relation to the state and to God. Its chief characteristics were the belief in the radical transcendence of God, the commitment to personal conversion and the emphasis on salvation as a religious experience. Fundamentalism resulted from a split between liberal and conservative forces on social and scientific issues—a split which had its counterpart among the English Evangelicals of the 1920s but did not result in an institutionalized separation of the two attitudes.[11] Modern Fundamentalism retains the essential traits of the revivalist tradition, but adds to them a militant resistance to liberal theology; against the modernist tendencies of the Evangelicals, Fundamentalists hold to the verbal inerrancy of Scripture, divine creation as opposed to evolution, and the imminence of Christ's return to establish his kingdom.

If Reformation theology manifested a major concern with the freedom and autonomy of the individual, a compensating tendency developed concerned with the organization of secular society and the resolution of social problems. The Protestant response to the increasing visibility of poverty and deprivation during the nineteenth century took the form of social reform movements, variously institutionalized in Europe and in North America, which had in common a commitment to some degree of Christian socialism. Social Reformism can be distinguished from Evangelicalism in terms of its chief characteristics: God is conceived, not in his transcendence, but in his immanence—in his presence in nature, in history, and in human beings and their institutions; the religious impulse is not to convert individuals but to transform society into a structure facilitating Christian living. It is a consequence of these two characteristics that Social Reformism tends to blur the distinction between the supernatural and the natural, between God and man, and to focus attention, not so much on the kingdom to come after this

[10] Marsden (1977).
[11] *Ibid.*

life but on the fuller expression of it in the kingdom of this life. Sin and grace tend to become institutional categories rather than personal and individual. Furthermore, in so far as the goal to be achieved is the reform of this world—a goal which Christians share with others of no religious persuasion—the task of achieving it establishes ideological links with secular bodies which diminish the visibility of Christians in the world and relativizes the source of their inspiration. The end and the means of attaining it are not so clearly drawn from Christian revelation and distinguishable from secular ends and means as is the case with either Evangelicalism or Fundamentalism.

To the extent that a Christian church shifts its attention from traditional religious attitudes and practices towards social activism of the kind described, one would expect certain consequences: firstly, the leaders of such a movement—almost always the clergy—must appropriate some secular idea-system to buttress their new theological ideas in order to provide an adequate framework for addressing the problems of the social order in their own right; secondly, one would expect considerable resistance on the part of a middle-class laity to anything more than a token shift to social activism; thirdly, the fellowship with secular groups resulting from the adoption of a secular ideology of social reform is likely to strengthen those groups but to weaken the Christians' attachment to their religious institutions.

Research into social activism in the 1960s confirms these predictions and highlights the organizational dilemmas of Christian socialism. In the movement studied by Harold Quinley, the resistance of church authorities to the shift of resources and fundamental change of attitude called for by activist leaders had the effect, not only of splitting the church between social reformers and traditionalists, but also of isolating the clerical leaders of the new movement. The laity who gave their support tended to lose interest in religion and, as their attachment to the church declined with their increasing commitment to social reform, the clergy—with careers at stake—were left with an increasingly conservative church membership.[12] The major factor weakening the commitment of

---

[12] Quinley (1974). See also Hadden (1969); Garrett (1973).

political radicals to remain within their church and to work for the transformation of their religious institution into an agency of social reform appears to be the necessity for an ideological alliance between religious and non-religious radicals and the increasing redundancy of religion—the other-worldly dimension—as this alliance develops into personal sympathy and community.

There is no *logical* reason why political radicals should be irreligious or why Christians should not interpret the Scriptures along socialist lines and organize their churches accordingly. A perfectly respectable theological argument in support of Christian socialism can be advanced.[13] It is not the weight of theology which militates against a Catholic conversion to socialism but the weight of history—of church history and of socialist history. The Church, on the one hand, carries the burden of a centuries-old tradition of other-worldliness and supernaturalism which is woven into the fabric of its organization, making the socialist conceptions of good and evil repugnant to the Catholic mind. Socialism, on the other hand, has already been pre-empted by Marxism, which not only successfully presents itself as the organization best equipped to achieve that ideal but, for historical reasons already discussed, ideologically excludes Catholicism as a competent ally. One could as easily imagine a conversion of Catholicism to socialism as one could envisage a similar conversion of the Gaullists in France, the Republicans in the United States or the Tory Party in Britain. The concept of Christianity which Christian socialists preach may be theologically sound but it is sociologically unthinkable within the tradition they have inherited. Their success in converting Catholics to Marxism has established an escape route from conservative religion; it has not given a Christian dimension to radical politics.

No political movement can survive without organization. Political Catholicism can only survive to the extent that it acquires an organization capable of sustaining and synthesizing its religious and its political elements. Hitherto the movement has turned—perforce—to Marxism to furnish the intellectual framework for a new orientation to the social order.

[13] See Gutierrez (1974).

Whether the Catholic Church will swing leftward and lend its organizational and ideological resources to the movement or whether its support will be limited to token gestures whenever these are considered strategically necessary is hardly difficult to predict. An alliance with socialism of the kind envisaged in Political Catholicism is not an option for any religious organization with a strong commitment to survive as a church. Unless there is a catastrophic collapse of authority—and that is not the present condition of the Roman Church—there is no reason to suppose that the arguments of Political Catholicism will impress themselves on the hierarchy. Within the predictable future, the Roman Church will use the socialist question as, in the Leonine period, it used the social question—an issue to be exploited for its propaganda value and for its usefulness as a means of control. Meanwhile, of course, the benefits gained in terms of improved social conditions, particularly in Latin America and South Africa, may be considerable. But the conversion to socialism will be strategic; the commitment to structural reform as a precondition—if not the realization—of salvation will be conditional upon the continuing *decline* of the Church's moral authority and the continuing secular support in Europe and North America for socialist reform in safe, far-off places.

The fact that the Third World countries represent a numerical majority in the Church and that Political Catholicism is today seen as the voice of the Third World is not in itself relevant to the question. This is the logic of German Guzman, the biographer of the revolutionary priest Camilo Torres, and it reflects the opinion of most apologists for Political Catholicism: 'If charity is the service of men,' he writes, 'if the majority of men is seen to be mired in subhuman conditions, the Christian must be a revolutionary.'[14] Some Church leaders might agree with the sentiment. They might even agree that economic conditions constitute the most critical dimension of human suffering. But they belong to a religious tradition which gives primacy to the toleration of suffering for a supernatural end, not to its alleviation as an end in itself. And it is in that worldly mould that history has cast socialism and continues to cast liberation theology.

[14] Cited in Lewy (1974), p.533.

What has been described as the incarnationist tradition of theology, which was successfully reinstated in Catholic doctrine by the new theologians, certainly draws attention to the structures and institutions of this world as a theological problem requiring a pastoral solution. Indeed, one section of the Vatican Council documents might be interpreted as a justification of Political Catholicism:

By its very nature, private property has a social quality deriving from the law of the communal purpose of earthly goods. If this social quality is overlooked, property often becomes an occasion of greed and of serious disturbances. Thus, to those who attack the concept of private property a pretext is given for calling the right itself into question. In many underdeveloped areas there are large or even gigantic rural estates which are only moderately cultivated or lie completely idle for the sake of profit. At the same time the majority of the people are either without land or have only very small holdings, and there is evident and urgent need to increase land productivity. . . . Depending on circumstances, therefore, reforms must be instituted . . . insufficiently cultivated estates should be distributed to those who can make these lands fruitful.[15]

The documents, however, do not bear the interpretation that would support a political theology. The tension between the incarnationist tradition and the eschatological—between the focus on God's kingdom in this world and God's kingdom in the next—is held whenever the context is abstract and purely doctrinal, theoretical. In the context of concrete socio-economic conditions, the incarnationist perspective is relegated to the status of an ethic. The alleviation of human suffering in the economic sphere is seen as an urgent pastoral problem and Catholics who work for social reform are praised for their moral endeavours: 'Christians who take an active part in modern socio-economic development and defend justice and charity', reads the paragraph following the quotation above, 'should be convinced that they can make a great contribution to the prosperity of mankind and the peace of the world', provided, however, they observe 'the right order of values in their earthly activities'.[16] The weight of papal and episcopal pro-

---

[15] The Church in the Modern World, art.71.
[16] *Ibid.*, art.72.

nouncements on the subject from all parts of the Catholic world—including Latin America—confirms that the 'right order of values' subordinates the structure of human society to the individual's personal response to God.

The risk that political theology might destroy the psychological basis of religious organization by identifying the kingdom of God with the political kingdom and salvation with socialism—thereby relativizing the Church as an instrument of social change, like the Party in Marxist theory—that risk has never been lost on the Catholic hierarchy. Political Catholicism is permissible as an ethic—rather like civil obedience in the older tradition—not as a theology.

Catholics who seek an alliance of the Church with Marxism must inevitably fail since the ethic of liberation forms an inextricable part of the Marxist theory of historical materialism. The link between theory and practice is central, and Marxists view any attempt to separate them as part of the strategy of bourgeois imperialism. Marxists have little to gain from an alliance with a Church which is still fundamentally religious in the traditional sense and for which the social order is a variable in the process of realizing man's supernatural end. The Marxist antagonism to religion is not only historically conditioned; it is also theoretically grounded in the later writings of Marx. All religion is based on a theory of cultural determinism—that is to say, ideas about God and theology can and should determine the way in which we live. Marxism is based on a contrary theory of social and economic determinism—how we live determines our values and ideas. In the context of Marxism, theology loses its transformative power and becomes redundant as an agency of change; it becomes simply a useful indicator of vested interest. For this reason, Christian Marxism is not only implausible on historical grounds; it is an alliance of contradictions.

Charismatic Catholicism

A second group within the Church, which provides an alternative option for Catholics in search of a relevant commitment and community is Charismatic Catholicism. In some respects the Charismatic Movement is the polar opposite of Political

Catholicism and their co-existence within the same Church raises new problems of management for its leadership.

Charismatic Catholicism is a movement seeking to renew the Church by renewing its liturgical life and converting its members through the experience of their baptism. The origins of this approach to Christianity lie in Pentecostalism, an evangelical and anti-sacramental movement which emerged in the United States at the beginning of the twentieth century and survives in an alliance of various Pentecostalist denominations in Great Britain and in North and South America.[17] It is characterized by a distinctive style of worship—enthusiastic, spontaneous, given to tongue-speaking and other manifestations of the Spirit—and a distinctly negative approach to morality which rejects permissiveness and discourages liberal attitudes and concern about social issues. In its early stages, Pentecostalism was attacked by the mainstream Protestant churches from which it recruited, mainly on the issue of the excessive display of religious emotion which the movement encouraged and which stood in contrast to the sober and formalistic worship of the established denominations. The Baptist and Methodist congregations, which were the main source of membership for the new religion, had become uncomfortably middle-class for the mass of working-class men and women in their ranks, who resented the departure from the simple certitudes of faith and from the ethical rigorism of old-time religion and who felt themselves alienated from the worldly life-style which was pervading the churches, particularly Methodism.[18]

Since the 1960s, most of the major Christian churches have been visited by a form of Pentecostalism which derives from the classical American tradition, but which differs from it in some notable respects. The modern Pentecostalist or Charismatic movement is directed towards a transformation of the churches, not towards the establishment of new organizations; it is largely a middle-class movement, not one which as yet encourages working-class sympathies; finally, it rejects the ethical rigorism of classical Pentecostalism, thereby opening its

---

[17] See Quebedeaux (1976). For historical material I have also drawn from O'Connor (1971); McDonnell (1976).
[18] Damboriena (1969), pp.29–30.

membership to those of widely different cultural backgrounds. The modern Charismatics have no wish to flee the world and no intention of fleeing the churches in which their Christianity was basically formed and in which they can find the community of people of similar cultural background and interests. Classical Pentecostalism contained an affirmation of its own irrelevance to the modern world, or—to put it more sympathetically—of the world's irrelevance to the beliefs and attitudes of revivalistic religion:

Often with the revivals came a simplistic and individualistic Christ-ian ethic. The righteous life was characterized by clean living; therefore no smoking, drinking, dancing, makeup, theatre-going or other amusements were allowed. . . . In its own cultural setting and development, this religious style is quite beautiful, meaningful and relevant. But it is not essential to or desirable for the baptism of the Holy Spirit especially among people of far different religious back-grounds.[19]

Whereas the older Pentecostalists felt a double pressure to secede from their churches of origin and to establish organiza-tions specific to their needs—a sense of alienation from the dominant culture of their churches and, conversely, an attitude of intolerance to their beliefs and practices and a refusal to accommodate them on the part of the mainline churches—the new Charismatics are culturally at ease in their churches and their churches seem very willing to accommodate them.[20] It is not the style of life of their co-religionists which the Charisma-tics wish to change but the style of prayer.

Catholic Pentecostalism began modestly in Pittsburg about two years after the close of the Second Vatican Council. A small prayer group of academics at Duquesne University, influenced by accounts of the effects of charismatic renewal in other Christian churches, prayed for the gift of religious experience . . . 'that the Holy Spirit of Christ would renew in them all the graces of their baptism and confirmation'.[21] The movement rapidly spread to other universities and consolidated links with

[19] Ranaghan, Kevin and Dorothy (1971), p.129.
[20] Quebedeaux (1976), pp.36–42.
[21] Quoted *ibid.*, p.63.

evangelical Protestants whose example had been followed and whose help had been sought in the initial stages of spiritual renewal. There is no doubt that the growth of Charismatic Catholicism has been phenomenal by any standards of religious revival, but as yet, partly due to the loose organizational structure, statistics of membership can be no more than speculative. In the United States alone it is estimated that active participants in the movement had grown to 10,000 by 1970 and 300,000 by 1973. The movement today is spread throughout the Catholic world and appears to be growing also in the eastern Orthodox Church.[22] Pentecostalism is probably the only growth area in the Catholic publishing world today.[23]

The Charismatic faith can be summarized briefly: the ethic is love and the doctrine is the experience of Christ's presence. The rejection of the taboos of classical Pentecostalism is matched by an implicit rejection of the specific injunctions of traditional Catholic morality. This is not to suggest that Catholic Charismatics actively promote permissiveness against the norms prevailing in the rest of the Church. On the contrary, the Charismatic view of morality is fully in accord with the teaching of the Second Vatican Council, which stresses the primacy of charity over other commandments and does not legislate on its public or private expression. While this ethic is not in itself permissive, however, it does have an affinity with a permissive culture in the sense that it removes the traditional religious restraint on the practice of permissiveness. The shift of emphasis from public morality at the behavioural level to private morality at the intentional level which characterizes the new theology of the post-conciliar period effectively makes the individual autonomous in relation to the Church and prevents the Church from playing any formative role in the determination of culture. What is permissible behaviour and what is forbidden was formerly determined—in part, at least—by the commandments as interpreted and sanctioned by the Church. Under an ethic of love, as understood by the new theologians and within the Charismatic movement, the Church ceases to

[22] O'Connor (1971), p.17.
[23] A rough indicator can be found in the 28-page bibliography of Catholic Charismatic writings during the eight-year period from 1967 to 1974 in O'Connor (1975).

function in this role. Theologically—in theory, that is to say—it can be explained that the Church continues to influence public morality through its members who have been baptized in the Spirit and whose renewed commitment will affect their environment all the more. But individuals are never autonomous, even when theologians discover that they are. The moral gap left by the Catholic Church will be inevitably filled by the less formal institutions of class, or race, or nation, as determinants of ethical behaviour. The absence of any formal constraints on behaviour must pose a dilemma for any religious movement which claims to transcend political and economic boundaries. Either Charismatic Catholicism—or the Charismatic movement in general—will begin to develop ethical constraints in order to prevent its fragmentation as local groups begin to reflect their own peculiar class and culture, or the movement will become the preserve of the middle classes, just as classical Pentecostalism functioned to legitimate the life-style of the economically deprived.

On the ethical level, therefore, we can see the sharp conflict of opinion between Charismatic and Political Catholicism. The ethical core of Political Catholicism is not simply love but the facilitation of Christian virtue through the provision of social conditions which make it possible. The ethic of Charismatic Catholicism does not logically exclude such an orientation but its thrust is so individualistic as to reduce the possibility of social activism to the level of charitable works of a politically ineffective kind. 'Every one of us should be passionately concerned about justice, public morality, and the plight of the under-nourished and under-privileged,' writes Michael Harper, 'and a balanced spirituality should reflect really deep commitment to the cause of man's physical as well as spiritual well-being.'[24] Harper's concern to balance the spirituality of the movement is echoed by the Ranaghans, who insist that the Charismatics have a mission to transform the world 'shackled with poverty and disease, with racism and war, with lust for power and just plain indifference to the "other guy".'[25] These sentiments can be found scattered throughout the Charismatic

[24] Harper (1968), p.60.
[25] Ranaghan, Kevin and Dorothy (1969), p.212.

literature; but it is only in the literature that the record of Charismatic concern for the social order will be found as long as the theological and psychological foundation of the movement is the religious experience of the individual. Baptism in the Spirit is the basis of Charismatic theology, and it is interpreted, not as an alternative or rival to infant baptism, but as a manifestation of the Spirit in the consciousness of the individual. It requires, therefore, some expression, some proof of validity and this provides the characteristic joyful and loving behaviour of Charismatics. Social concern in the sense of working for structural change in society requires an entirely different focus on the nature of salvation and the ethical obligations which flow from it. A religious movement which attracts converts by the promise of immediate and personal rewards cannot be expected also to motivate its members for the sustained, collective action necessary to implement a programme of social change.

Of the major groups which emerged in the contemporary Church, Charismatic Catholicism is the most unlikely and remarkable. Pentecostalism embodies beliefs and attitudes which developed in opposition to Roman Catholicism, whose theology of priesthood, formalism of worship and centralization of control are the antithesis of the Pentecostalist approach. The enthusiasm and emotionalism associated with the movement, the anti-intellectualism and the substitution of experience for doctrine are characteristics of Pentecostal religion which make it a doubtful candidate for ecumenical dialogue with Catholicism, still more for full incorporation into the institution of the Church. One would expect, therefore, that a movement for the Charismatic renewal of the Church, sponsored by the laity, would be vigorously resisted by the Roman authorities and stifled by the hierarchy.

The response of the hierarchy, documented by Father Kilian McDonnell, has been little short of enthusiastic.[26] Beginning with the Report of the Catholic Bishops of the United States in 1969 and ending with Pope Paul's address to the International Charismatic Congress in 1975, McDonnell charts the course of the movement's assimilation into the Church, from cautious

[26] McDonnell (1976), ch.3.

approval to wholehearted welcome and the conversion of the Belgian Cardinal Suenens. On the face of it, this is consistent with the teaching of the Second Vatican Council on the role of the Spirit in the Church:

> It is not only through the sacraments and Church ministries that the same Holy Spirit sanctifies and leads the people of God and enriches it with virtues. Allotting his gifts to everyone according as he will, he distributes special graces among the faithful of every rank . . . These charismatic gifts, whether they be the most outstanding or the more simple and widely diffused, are to be received with thanksgiving and consolation, for they are exceedingly suitable and useful for the needs of the Church.[27]

But the conciliar documents are highly ambiguous, as we have seen, and while the passage quoted functions as a charter for the Charismatic Movement, it cannot be assumed that the intention of the Council Fathers included a mass organization of Catholics actively engaged in practices repugnant to traditional Catholicism. Why has the Roman Church tolerated and welcomed the Charismatic Movement?

Before attempting to answer this, one must first address the question it implies: does Charismatic Catholicism in fact represent a threat to the structure of Roman authority and doctrine? Frequent investigations by various national hierarchies have noted the attachment of Charismatics to traditional symbols of piety, such as the Rosary and the Real Presence in the consecrated bread of the Eucharist. They have also warned of certain dangers inherent in a movement which emphasizes experience at the expense of doctrine—the dangers of 'false ecumenism', of 'religious indifferentism'. Historically, the Church has acted swiftly to eliminate these dangers whenever they arose in movements of zealots and enthusiasts—particularly lay enthusiasts. It is certainly the case that Charismatic Catholicism, in practice, if not in theory, makes experience the crucial test of grace and orthodox relationship with God, thereby demoting belief. This means that there is no objective test of moral, doctrinal or sacramental validity and there is no longer a basis for the traditional disagreements between the

---

[27] Constitution on the Church, art.12.

Christian churches. Since experience is incommunicable, each individual must be his own judge of his standing before God. The traditional structure of the Roman Church is built upon a contrary principle: it is not experience which matters before God but the content of belief which can be expressed verbally, communicated, and tested for validity against the unerring measure of the Roman *magisterium*. It follows that the Charismatic Movement is incompatible with the structure of traditional Catholicism.

But the Roman Church today is in some respects incompatible with traditional Catholicism. The old structure of authority survives, but its theological legitimacy has collapsed. The dominant theology in the Church today is consistent with the Charismatic principle in that it empties theology of its content while retaining theological formulae as symbols of commitment and community. As Francis Shaeffer writes of modern theologians and Pentecostalists:

They are really existentialists using theological, Christian terminology. Consequently, not believing in truth, they can enter into fellowship with any other experience-oriented group using religious language.[28]

Provided no direct attempt is made to undermine the structure of authority, Catholic Charismatics cannot be considered a threat to a Church which has changed in accordance with the same theological principles. The theological difference between mainstream and Charismatic Catholicism is not one of content but of style and expression. The dangers of 'religious indifferentism' and 'false ecumenism' must be understood in the context of broad theological agreement. The indifferentism which threatens the Church is not a matter of doctrinal content but of authority and organization, of compliance with the rules of ecumenical dialogue formulated by clerical authority—and on that count, the Charismatics score rather higher than some other groups in the Church.

It is fairly clear, therefore, that the basic reason why Charismatic Catholicism is tolerated within the Church is because the Church which it threatens no longer exists and the dangers

[28] Shaeffer (1972), p.16.

which remain can be, and are, minimized by the appointment of clerical and episcopal supervisors. Charismatic Catholicism is acceptable, furthermore, because it is the weakest of contemporary 'heresies' in the Church, the least threatening of the groups which make up the new Catholicism. A movement which is anti-doctrinal and enthusiastic, but which is also compliant and, moreover, functions as a safety-net for fringe or lapsing Catholics, offering a continuing religious identity without specific obligations, and which creates no problems for the Church by threatening the established political order—such a movement is more likely to be encouraged than repressed even if its style is repugnant to the more traditionalist leaders.

The peculiar feature which distinguishes modern from classical Pentecostalism has been noted: the movement scattered throughout Christendom since the 1960s is largely middle-class and its members are concerned to retain their cultural identity within their community of baptism. The extraordinary and unprecedented nature of the Catholic movement raises the further and more difficult problem of explaining its attractiveness to Catholics in the 1960s. It cannot be explained simply in terms of general disenchantment with the new Catholicism of Vatican II. The Charismatics are not notably critical of the Second Vatican Council and their intellectual leaders frequently cite its documents approvingly. Secondly, a general disenchantment with the new theology and liturgy has already found its organizational expression in Traditionalist Catholicism, the members of which regard the Charismatic Movement with considerable distaste. (They have an old-fashioned Catholic language and readiness to communicate this repugnance which, characteristically, is not reciprocated by the Charismatics.)

Research on Charismatic Catholicism, however, does indicate an antipathy towards the Second Vatican Council and the type of religion to which it gave rise in certain specific respects.[29] The movement has attracted Catholics who share certain concerns and anxieties about the Church and the world: there is a general sense that society is in a state of crisis or moral decay; that the old certitudes have disappeared with the old

---

[29] McGuire (1975); Johnson and Weigert (1978); Quebedeaux (1976).

stabilities and that spiritual rather that social reform is the proper solution. There is a feeling of ambiguity about personal salvation in the post-conciliar Church and concern about the loss of a sense of mystery and miracle. These are sought and reaffirmed in a new way in the Charismatic Movement; the element of the mysterious is emphasized in the practice of tongue-speaking and in the cultivation of illuminating experience, rather than rational argument, as the means of conversion; the practice of healing and the fostering of a lively faith in the power of intercessory prayer serve to reintroduce the miraculous into a religion which tends to de-emphasize magic and the intervention of the supernatural. Finally, Charismatic Catholicism offers some compensation for the loss of a sense of the security of personal salvation—mediated through the sacramental system in the pre-conciliar Church—by restoring that certitude in the experience of being saved.

The restoration in new form of these elements of the old Catholicism does not explain why the Charismatic Movement appears to have attracted few adherents outside the middle class. If economic class position divides the secure from the insecure one would expect to find the middle class fortunately placed. As in classical Pentecostalism, one would expect to find a modern Charismatic Movement recruiting from the lower ranks of society and providing them with some religious substitute for their well-documented social and economic deprivations.

It may be, as Richard Quebedeaux postulates, that the Charismatic Movement tapped a modern phenomenon in the growing sense of frustration within a middle class whose values and attitudes, so long dominant in Western society, are today being rejected and whose confidence in themselves and in their status has been severely shaken.[30] But there are less speculative ways of linking class and religious enthusiasm; there are other factors which make the Charismatic Movement attractive to those who belong to the class of professionals, who are geo-

---

[30] *Ibid.*, p.230. Quebedeaux does not try to develop this hypothesis but modestly relegates it to a footnote. There is a sizeable body of speculative and empirical literature on capitalism, bureaucracy and trade unionism which might support it.

graphically and socially mobile and whose economic interests persuade them of the virtues of conservatism. Whereas classical Pentecostalism imposed cultural and behavioural constraints which integrated its members as a religious and social community and integrated the secular and religious dimensions of their lives, its modern Catholic form releases individuals from such constraints. It celebrates the end of the ghetto and with it the end of the Catholic type who could not be trusted to give full commitment to secular affairs. Like Unitarianism, modern Pentecostalism has nothing to say which will offend, nothing to do which will make others feel ill at ease and discourage their professional trust and confidence. Its theology is functional in a plural society for those best equipped to exploit the opportunities of economic advancement: it tolerates all, excludes no one; it guarantees salvation without demanding the social or economic price of idiosyncracy; it can move anywhere, since its mission is to change one's self, not one's environment. The Catholic Charismatics did not invent this type of religion to suit their needs; they discovered it in the dominant themes and trends of the new Catholicism, they packaged it and gave it a title.

Traditionalist Catholicism

The third group contending for recognition as the true and authentic Church is Traditionalist Catholicism. Traditionalism, like social concern, is an ideal shared by a far greater number of Catholics than those organized to fight for its principles and for the acceptance of its programmes by the official Church. It is impossible to make even an educated guess at the numerical support for a return to the traditions of the old Catholicism. Latin Mass societies in several Catholic countries, Tridentine associations and traditional Catholic Action groups sustain old-fashioned values in the new Church and provide a presumably extensive group of fringe supporters for the *avant-garde* of Traditionalism: the movement led by Archbishop Lefebvre.

Marcel Lefebvre founded the Fraternity of St Pius X in 1968 and opened a seminary at Ecône, in Switzerland, for the ordination of priests dedicated to working for the overthrow of the new theology, morality and liturgy. Initially, the strategy was to remain within the Church and to promote the counter-revolution by example and conversion. But the opposition of Rome, the threats of censure, even excommunication, soon made it clear that Traditionalism was even less welcome in the new Church than either of the other forms of Catholicism. In January 1975, Lefebvre's Profession of Faith was published in the French review, *Itinéraires,* and it contained his categoric rejection of the Second Vatican Council, whose reforms he regarded as heretical and therefore not binding on any conscientious and faithful Catholic. By 1976, Lefebvre controlled three seminaries and his active support—in Britain estimated at 2500—extended throughout North America, France, Germany, with some promise of a foothold in part of Latin America. The secular press and television exploited the drama of the struggle between the Archbishop and Pope Paul VI and the Catholic world waited for what seemed to be the inevitable outcome: excommunication and schism. In the event, the penalty imposed by the Pope was of a milder form—suspension—which the archbishop could, and did, ignore and which allowed his movement to continue in strained but not schismatic relations with Rome.

The main focus of Traditionalist Catholicism is the liturgy. Opposition to the abandonment of the so-called 'Tridentine Mass', published by Pope Pius V in 1570, and to the introduction of the vernacular by the Second Vatican Council forms the main thrust of the Traditionalist argument and the thread unifying the different groups of Catholics working for counter-reform. The unchangeability of the Eucharist had stood for many in the old Church as a symbol of the unchangeability of the Church and of the continuity of its teaching. Older Catholics were shocked by the speed of change and found it difficult to adjust to the new ritual. Traditionalists were shocked by the *fact* of change. For them, the ritual was a vehicle of doctrine and the Church's readiness to change it was an expression of its willingness to abandon all that was fundamental in response to public pressure to be relevant. The reform of the liturgy was symptomatic of the 'neo-modernist and neo-Protestant leanings' which had infected the Church of Rome, according to Lefebvre:

In effect, all these reforms continue to contribute to the destruction of the Church, to the ruin of its priesthood, to a negation of the Sacrifice of the Mass and of the Sacraments. . . . This reform, arising as it does out of liberalism and modernism, is entirely poisoned. It comes from heresy and will finish in heresy. . . .[31]

It does not require a flight of speculative fancy to link the conservatism of Traditionalist theology with political conservatism and opposition to the social and cultural changes of the 1960s. Perhaps only in France, and for peculiarly French historical reasons, has there developed an association between Traditionalist Catholicism and right-wing political movements of fascist persuasion.[32] There is no evidence that British followers, or Traditionalists in other parts of the world, explicitly connect their religious ideals with particular forms of civil government—apart from a general tendency to identify Communism as the major enemy of the Church. But it does appear that the central characteristic of Traditionalism—the rejection of the new theology and of doctrinal tolerance in favour of the dogmatic certitude and authoritarian government of the old Catholicism—has its social roots in a rejection of individualism and permissiveness at the moral level, of liberalism and democracy at the political. For the Traditionalists, it is not simply the Church that has gone astray but the world too in which the Roman Church once stood as a bulwark against the evils of modernity, identified as freedom of conscience and religious liberty. This is consistent with the estimate that half the British supporters of Lefebvre are converts to Catholicism, who were attracted to the authoritarian Church of Pius XII and felt betrayed by the apparent *volte-face* of Vatican II.[33]

There is a certain affinity between Political and Traditionalist Catholics which does not extend to the Charismatics. Both movements retain a strong sense of the relation between belief and action and of the possibility and the need to distinguish

---

[31] Archbishop Lefebvre in his 'Profession of Faith', 21 Nov 1974, published in *Itinéraires*, January 1975.

[32] Angevui (1976).

[33] Given by Rev. Peter Morgan, leader of the British Society of St Pius X in *Catholic Herald*, 27 Aug 1976. See also interview with Lefebvre in *Der Spiegel*, reported in *Catholic Herald*, 20 Aug 1978.

between statements which are true and those which are false if one is to justify religious organization. Both groups have an objectivist sense of morality which follows from this: some actions are good and some are evil and these actions can be specified without resort to intention-laden terms like 'love'. Finally, and for these reasons, both groups share a strong antipathy towards the Charismatic Movement, which empties belief of its content and ethics of their capacity to mobilize action for political ends. This common antipathy, of course, is mild by comparison with the mutual repugnance of Traditionalists and Political Catholics themselves. They may agree on certain philosophical conditions of meaning and morality but their disagreement on what is true and what is ethical could scarcely be more complete.

The fundamentalism of the Traditionalists is a response similar to that of Protestant fundamentalists who could not tolerate the moral and intellectual liberalism of their co-religionists and who formed their own communities to protect the fundamentals of faith and to preserve the ethical rigorism which was threatened by liberalism. The Catholics, too, found their Church leaders dismantling the ghetto in which a cultural and ethical rigorism was imposed and in which a kind of security was available at the cost of religious liberty. In the attempt to retrieve that security, Traditionalists have become more fundamentalist than the *magisterium*, more intolerant of doctrinal development than the Holy Office in the Curia of Pope Pius XII.

There is a certain advantage built into Protestant fundamentalism which makes one doubt the capacity for survival of its Catholic counterpart. The Bible as the unique source of revelation has always been a symbol of protest against Catholicism and conservative Catholics, in reaction, have stressed the Church's tradition as the source of true knowledge of God. It is easier to legitimate a schismatic or quasi-schismatic movement within Protestantism since it is a classical tradition of the Reformation to appeal over the heads of human authority directly to the Scriptures. Everyone is his own priest and has equal access to the word of God. It is partly for this reason that Protestantism, more than Catholicism, has given birth to so many sectarian movements, each of which could claim that it was returning to its biblical roots. Catholicism, on the other hand, has been identified for centuries with a two-source theory of revelation which, in practice, focused exclusively on tradition. The truth of doctrine is established, therefore, by its interpretation by those who follow in the Apostolic succession—believed to be the Pope and the bishops in council. Catholic fundamentalists face the particular technical problem of recruiting and holding members on the basis of an appeal to the truth of the Apostolic tradition against the statements of its present office-holders. 'It is not we who are in schism but the Pope,' says Lefebvre, echoing similar attempts by Protestant sectarians down the centuries to wrest legitimacy from their bureaucratic leaders. It is difficult to see how a fundamentalist movement can survive for long in opposition to the papal institution on whose sacred lineage and infallible pronouncements the fundamentalist faith is based.[34]

Theological Individualism

The emergence of Political, Charismatic and Traditionalist Catholicism in the wake of the Second Vatican Council has given to the Roman Church an organized form of the major tendencies of Protestantism: Social Reformism, Evangelicalism and Fundamentalism. These are the three major movements in the Church which specialize in one or other of the religious options now available to Catholics. Not all Catholics are specialists in this sense, of course. The majority remain unattached to any alliance, uncommitted to any doctrinal or ethical position other than that which they believe characterizes the universal Church, the *ecclesia,* and distinguishes it as a community of faith from other religious collectivities. We can

[34] Catholic fundamentalist literature frequently hints at a neat resolution of this tension. The alleged apparitions of the Virgin at Bayside, New York, since 1970, have provided a source of revelation for Quebecois and other North American Catholics in search of inspired guidance in the vacuum of infallibility left by the Second Vatican Council. The real pope, according to the apparition transmitted by the Bayside traditionalists, has been imprisoned and the voice which preaches ecumenism and condemns traditionalism in his name is that of an impostor, an agent of Satan.

speak, therefore, of a fourth option, of a residual group comprised of practising catholics who pursue no specialist interests or goals but who tolerate such interests and goals as a positive expression of 'pluralism'. For them, the Second Vatican Council has effected a renewal without a fundamental break in continuity, and the existence of different theologies and organizations is a key indicator of that renewal, manifesting the diversity of ideas and talents which signifies the unifying presence of the Spirit.

In the preceding chapter, we looked at the new theology which has dominated the Church since Vatican II and now at the new movements which have come to replace the old uniform structure of Catholicism. What kind of Church has emerged? In the light of the evidence discussed, how can we characterize contemporary Catholicism?

I argued in Chapter 7 that the dominant ideas which inform Catholic theology and morality today are not in any real sense pluralist. There is no commonly accepted boundary to their meaning; the consensus among theologians is restricted to their verbal form, and in that sense the unity of faith, unquestioned in theological circles, is an artefact of intellectuals. It is not grounded in the concrete beliefs and practices of Church members. It is a rhetorical device to facilitate discourse among theologians, not the verbal expression of a social mechanism to facilitate unity among Catholics. The major groups within the Church which have emerged in the wake of the new theology are not the manifestation of unity-in-diversity. They are not complementing one another within a common faith in any sense consistent with the conciliar ideal of pluralism or with the Pauline ideal of organic unity. They are not different parts of the same organism, working in different ways towards a common goal. They are different faiths, different churches, sharing a common name. Of the three major groups, only the Charismatics are tolerant of the beliefs of the other two and, as the others would argue, this is not a matter of tolerance but of Charismatic indifference to doctrine and ethics.

The actual state of Catholic doctrine and morality—as distinct from the idealized version of it routinely given by Church leaders and theologians—is not one of pluralism but of individualism. The evidence of a world-wide division of Catholicism into competing faiths is exactly what one would predict at the behavioural level as a consequence of the transition from theological uniformity to theological individualism.

Individualism in the secular sphere poses problems of management and control for political authority. Individualism in religion threatens the survival of the religious community. In the old Catholicism, tensions between doctrinal or ethical ideas and movements could be resolved by a religious authority which had the advantage over secular authority of being formally sacralized: the rite of ordination invested the incumbents of priestly office with a supernatural power over the distribution of grace and knowledge and this gave them a divine mandate to control the means of salvation. Technically, this priestly power—referred to in theology as the power of order and of jurisdiction—was unequally distributed within the priesthood and it was not officially interpreted as defining man's sole access to grace and revelation. In practice, however, the priesthood as such enjoyed the benefits of supernatural legitimation and the thrust of Church teaching discouraged the search for God's truth and grace through private enterprise. The belief in the sacred character of the priestly office gave to the Roman authorities a unique control over their subjects. Theological collectivism, or uniformity, was formally sanctioned by God.

Theological individualism, on the other hand, makes the individual responsible for his own path to salvation. Its effect is to fragment the religious community—not in the sense of creating individualists, each acting autonomously in relation to God and the supernatural. That is the myth of individualism and, for reasons given in Chapter 5, it is sociologically absurd to suppose that it could represent the reality. Individualism does not make people individuals, freed from the constraints of external authority. It merely releases them from those constraints in certain areas of thought and behaviour which are defined as significant, and shifts authoritative control to others. Theological individualism implies a change in the perception of authority of a kind similar to that involved in the secular sphere. But whereas secular individualism merely transfers the burden of social control from one aspect of secular life to another, theological individualism has the effect of desacralizing religious authority in itself. As a consequence, the function of determining the new alliances which must inevitably arise passes to secular agencies of political or economic control, such as race, class, nationalism. The desacralization of power in the Roman Church has liberated grace and revelation—the means of salvation—from the control of any visible authority, leaving the individual free, in theory, to follow his own lights and conscience. In practice, it makes him vulnerable to the conditioning of other social forces.

The basic sociological condition for the unity of faith is that there should be some institutionalized means of drawing and maintaining a distinction between truth and falsehood in the matter of belief. This condition was met in the old Catholicism—scrupulously, perhaps excessively—by the maintenance of credibility in the hierarchy's privileged access to grace and the knowledge of God. Theological individualism has undermined that belief by desacralizing the power of the priesthood and *magisterium*. While there are undoubtedly many Catholics who still retain the traditional belief in the divinely sanctioned authority of Rome, the condition for the survival of that belief no longer exists. There is no authority in the Church which can successfully arbitrate between truth and falsehood. Whereas Catholics were once united in faith by the teaching of the Church—a set of core beliefs which were seen to be defended against public denial—this is no longer the case. In this technical sense, the teaching of the Church has been cut off from the source of its strength and energy; it survives—if it does—by the inertia of secular social forces.

Theological uniformity—and theological pluralism, to a lesser degree—refers to a relatively authoritarian religious structure in which the beliefs, practices and alliances of members can be predicted from the publicly available statements of its leadership. Such an authority is, by definition, a sufficiently powerful determinant of consciousness to inhibit alliances formed on the basis of secular social or economic relationships. The structure facilitates the unity of faith. Theological individualism, by contrast, refers to a structure which is individualist in respect of doctrine and ethics and thus permits secular forces to determine the substance of beliefs and the nature of alliances. The individual Roman Catholic, whose access to grace and revelation was previously mediated through a visible authority which guaranteed their efficacy and validity, is now responsible for his own salvation. This means that there is no mechanism within the Church to resolve the tensions and contradictions which inevitably arise in theology and which previously were managed by religious authority. The major tensions in the Roman Church between the priesthood of all believers and the institutional priesthood, between Tradition and Scripture, and between private and public morality or commutative and distributive justice, which were held under control in the old Catholicism, are now released for personal resolution by the individual Catholic. But in fact the vacuum of religious authority is filled, not by the individual, but by politics, education, the economy—all the powerful secular determinants of values and attitude which were once transcended in Catholicism.

This, then, is the nature of the Catholic crisis. Theological individualism—not pluralism—is the reality of the modern Church but the unity of faith implicit in theological pluralism is still the myth cherished by theologians, embodied in their literature, the ideal that informs official policy. Pluralism is the ideal, too, which continues to define the Church in the consciousness of most of the Catholic laity, but their actions bear witness to the destruction of the conditions necessary to make that ideal possible. Modern Catholicism contains an internal contradiction between culture and structure, between a theological ideal and religious practice.[35]

There is now, albeit still in embryo, a Catholicism of the political left, which emphasizes public morality to the exclusion of private; a Catholicism of the middle class, which has developed a kind of *laissez-faire* religion by replacing public standards of truth and morality by personal experience, and a Catholicism of political conservatism, which struggles for the restoration of authoritarianism in doctrine and morality. In addition, there is the residual group—the Ecclesialists—com-

---

[35] No moral judgement is intended in proposing this description of the change in Catholicism. One may approve or disapprove of it while still recognizing its character.

mitted to the notion of continuity with the pre-conciliar Church and to the idea of a 'healthy pluralism' within the framework of a basic unity of faith. The leadership of the Church, which forms part of this group, has in practice abandoned all pretensions to legislate in the moral sphere and can therefore be described as ethically subjectivist or individualist. With regard to doctrine, it retains the old pretensions in line with the pre-conciliar ideal, but its capacity to legislate effectively has been eroded by the increasing exercise of the individual's authority to dissent which was the principal effect of the bishops' deliberations in the Second Vatican Council.

These are the main alliances in the Church which could not be predicted from an official statement of Catholic teaching and values, and this unpredictability is a consequence of the theological individualism incorporated in the documents of the Council and enshrined as a basic principle of Catholic theology by the new theologians. It is important to stress once again that the divisions in the Church discussed in this chapter are analytical categories—they do not represent tidy, organizational differences in the concrete world. Objectively, Catholicism is divided in far more complex ways than the observer could adequately describe. The groups discussed are models of Catholicism, made available by social and historical circumstances, which function as options for individual Catholics. But they are not 'models' in the sense sometimes discussed in works of new theology, that is to say, different ways of believing the same truths, different modes of orientation to the same reality. As we have seen, these are competing models—rather as communism and Christian Democracy are competing models of political commitment in modern Italy, for example. They exclude one another ideologically and only at the rhetorical level can certain symbols of common origin be marshalled to provide a link between them.[36]

It is still early to expect clear statistical corroboration of the

---

[36] A rough, schematic illustration of Catholic fragmentation may be obtained by noting where each of the major groups stands with respect to the interpretation of Scripture and Catholic tradition. It should be noted that for centuries before the Second Vatican Council Catholic teaching on doctrine and ethics was objectivist: beliefs were true or false and actions were objectively right or wrong. Today, a new situation obtains:

thesis that Roman Catholicism has passed from theological uniformity to individualism and that the control of beliefs and ethics has passed to the secular domain. This thesis is strictly about religious change, not about decline, and the numerical decline of Catholicism is not an immediate consequence which one should expect from the type of change described. While in the long run the change seems certain to result in a reduction of membership, there is no reason why individualism should not have the immediate effect of stimulating lapsed and fringe members of the Church to declare themselves for Rome and so inflate the statistics. (One can intuitively see why a sudden release from the constraints of a rigorous moral and doctrinal belief system should have the immediate effect of increasing commitment. The research of the American sociologist, Andrew Greeley, shows that the Second Vatican Council actually had an immediate positive effect on statistics of Catholic devotion.[37])

The signs from the developed European and North American countries are that there has been a steady decline in all the key dimensions of religious commitment. One should not read too much into such figures—their comparability between countries and between historical periods is suspect. None the less, it

| | | Doctrine | |
		Subjective	Objective
Ethics	Subjective	1 Charismatic	3 Ecclesialist
	Objective	2 Political	4 Traditionalist

Only the Traditionalists retain an objectivist view of doctrine and ethics, occupying the cell (number 4) within which the entire Church was defined before the Council. Even the Roman authorities (Ecclesialists) have vacated that cell; official pronouncements still emphasize the need for doctrinal unity and appeal for the authority to accomplish it, but they are tacitly abandoning an objectivist position on ethics. The Charismatics have moved furthest from a pre-conciliar position. Political Catholicism shares neither the ethical nor the doctrinal dimension with the official leadership of the Church. (The objective character of this group's *political* theory stands in contrast to a subjectivist attitude towards traditional Catholic theology.)

[37] Greeley (1976).

is difficult not to be impressed by particular tendencies which suggest that theological individualism is filtering through to the laity more rapidly than one might reasonably expect. Among the empirical consequences of theological individualism one would expect to observe a change in the pattern of recruitment to the Church. Where access to grace and revelation has passed to the control of the individual rather than the legitimate representatives of the religious collectivity, there is no longer any compelling reason to become a Catholic. If the Church offers no apparent advantages in the important matter of being saved why should one join? Most Catholics join the Church at birth and the record of their affiliation does not, therefore, reflect an awareness of the changed conditions. Adult conversions are a better guide to changing lay perceptions of the Church than baptisms, and these have decreased by about fifty per cent on average from the beginning of the 1960s until the early seventies; the trend is still downward in North America and in most countries of Europe.

One would also expect theological individualism to have some effect in liberating Catholics from such onerous obligations as may still remain on the statute books, even if these obligations still carry certain legal sanctions and their force has been reaffirmed by legal authority. If the desacralization of authority is a reality of the structure and not merely an idea in some theologians' heads then, at some stage, one should find concrete evidence of non-compliance in significant areas which previously were tightly and successfully controlled. A difficulty with comparative evidence of this sort is that too many factors are changing. For a valid comparison of the response of the laity to clerical authority over a particular period, one needs to assume that clerical authority remains constant—that Church authorities continue to command obedience in a similar manner and in matters which are comparable. In fact, clerical authority only remains constant if the lay response does so also. If the laity refuses to obey and thereby manifests its emancipation from religious authority, that authority is not likely to continue as if nothing had changed in the relationship. The Pope is not likely to risk another rebuff by making dogmatic statements about sexual morality. We can expect Church leaders to make it as difficult as possible for anyone to observe a decline of their authority—to seek to persuade rather than command, to be vague rather than specific, so that any resistance on the part of the laity can be interpreted as a healthy sign of pluralism, of spiritual maturity, of the responsible exercise of authority. None the less, there is evidence of desacralization which is striking, most notably the massive and much-publicized rejection of papal authority on the issue of artificial contraception in the years following the encyclical *Humanae Vitae* in 1968. In addition, the figures for attendance at Mass —probably the only serious obligation surviving the transition from old Catholicism to the new—declined dramatically during the period 1965–75, according to the official Directories and Yearbooks of France, Italy, Holland, Germany, Belgium and North America. Of these, the United States registered the lowest decline in Mass attendance at thirty per cent of its Catholic population.

Modern Catholicism, deprived of the means of controlling the beliefs and values of its adherents and ensuring a degree of consensus necessary for it to claim political significance and moral authority, is rapidly becoming an association of disparate groups and individuals whose affiliation to the Church is an expression of common origin rather than common commitment. Like the British monarchy, the Church functions as an important symbolic link with one's communal past; its functionaries still use the language of an age when authority was real and the power to set standards and initiate policy was manifest. The conflict with the world is now over, however—for monarchs as for Church leaders—and the control of beliefs and values has passed into other hands. Like one's ethnicity, the Church is one point of reference among many in establishing one's identity. It links individuals of radically different beliefs and multiple allegiances. It is fast becoming an object of nostalgia for modern Catholics whose lives are immersed in the temporal affairs of this world as they once were immersed in the business of the next. It is losing its effectiveness as a sign of grace and becoming simply the religious dimension of one's biography.

I am a Catholic, simply, neither Orthodox, nor Roman, nor Anglican, because the Catholic Church has preserved the anthropological, the folk religion, that engendered and nourished Western civilization. These are our own rites of passage and of the year. . . . Although as a corporation it [the Church] defines faith as belief and excludes the disbeliever, it can still nourish faith as life in an age of faithlessness. Religion is something men do, not something they believe.[38]

---

[38] Kenneth Rexroth, quoted in Marty and Peerman (1971), p.76.

9
Summary and Conclusion

The account of Roman Catholicism given in the preceding chapters is, like all historical accounts, selective. It is for the reader to judge whether the selection and the omissions provide a coherent and interesting interpretation of the development of modern Catholicism. Unlike most conventional history, however, this account has focused less on the details of the Church's past than on the significance and interrelation of the events selected for discussion. The book has been an exercise in what may loosely be described as Weberian social theory. In the work of Max Weber, ideas are not simply the reflection of material interests, nor is social change simply the consequence of ideas and policies formulated by intellectuals. Ideal and material factors are dialectically related. In the sphere of religion, theology reflects the political and economic interests of the group which has the power to formulate it and, in turn, it acts upon those interests and tends to transform the structure of the Church in which they arise.

At a less abstract level, the Church and secular society stand in a relation of similar interdependence, each tending to modify the other and to fashion it, if not always according to its own image, at least according to its own interests. This dual interdependence is not something which can be observed; it is not a fact which happened and for which there is documentary proof of a kind which would satisfy the criteria conventionally employed in historical studies. On the contrary, it is an interpretation of the past which, in a sense, transcends the concrete facts and events and which is not likely to find favour with the people involved in those events—particularly the intellectuals, who, of their nature, have a tendency to elevate the status and exaggerate the autonomy of ideas. One would not expect Luther or

Calvin to accept Weber's ironic interpretation of Protestantism as the agent of capitalism and secularization. Similarly, one would not expect Pope Leo XIII or Pope John XXIII to accept that each, in his own way, was the unwitting agent of a process culminating in the individualism of contemporary Roman Catholicism. The Reformation contributed to the rise of capitalism and Protestantism was fundamentally changed in the process. Capitalism, in its turn, has transformed Catholicism, forcing it to conform to a pattern congenial to its efficient functioning and to discard elements of its organization and teaching which might inhibit that end.

If social theorizing is necessary in order to provide a coherent account of any particular process of social change, and if it is therefore necessary to transcend the concrete facts of history, this does not relieve the theorist of the obligation to ground his interpretation in the historical data. The reader is not invited to assent to the argument on the basis of whatever aesthetic merit it may have but on the basis of the concrete evidence from which it is drawn. On empirical grounds, critics have demolished all but the broadest features of the thesis contained in Weber's *The Protestant Ethic and the Spirit of Capitalism,* but few have questioned its intellectual merit or denied the cultural importance of constructing interpretations of history at this level of generality. Explanations of social change can never be more than speculative and tentative. The complexity of the variables involved and the temporal distance which separates the theorist from the events and processes under examination make it impossible to establish definitively a specific causal link between them. None the less the attempt must be made because such explanations of our past are inescapably part of our culture. We are constrained by history and—however unwarranted it may be—it is from our understanding of the past that we learn the lessons which shape our social and political policies for the future.

The problem which emerged at the beginning of the period under consideration and which provides the main focus of attention throughout this study is the problem of relevance. Implicit in the popular conception of 'relevance'—and even in theologians' usage of the term—is the notion that relevance is an objective fact, a property of ideas which can be measured rather as one might measure a person's wealth or height against a given standard. But there is no such standard by which we can measure the relevance of an institution or set of ideas. Relevance is not a property of ideas; it is an accomplishment of idea-mongers, of intellectuals. To say of a policy or institution that it is irrelevant is not to characterize it objectively but to claim that it no longer serves a desired function. To speak of a church as irrelevant is to claim that it has lost—or perhaps never possessed—the power to set the standards which govern people's desires. Modern Catholicism is not in itself relevant or irrelevant to the modern world. The world is not a unitary concept and it is strictly nonsense to speak of any institution as being relevant to it. The Church may accommodate its teaching to certain values and goals which are characteristically modern and secular. In so doing, it becomes relevant for those who subscribe to those values and irrelevant for those who do not. At any period of its history, Catholicism was relevant for those who felt that it served their interests.

In examining the Church's response to the problem of relevance, we have seen the effect on Church doctrine and organization of the struggle for power between the religious and secular world since the French Revolution. What was at issue was the power to dictate the style, the trend, the attitudes, for the whole society. Many of the values of Western society —democracy, individualism, women's rights—are today widely accepted within the Catholic Church. These values were generated within the secular world, not the Catholic, and their acceptance by the Church carried with it the risk of compromise—the risk that the Church might lose its identity and legitimacy in the eyes of its own members. To the extent that this might occur, the question of relevance would lose its urgency and significance—any church which simply mirrored the values of the wider society and had no power to influence them would be literally irrelevant to that society; it would no longer serve any useful purpose and, in the long term, society would not be affected by its disappearance. It would be ironic if such a state of affairs were to occur in the pursuit of relevance. From the analysis of contemporary Roman Catholicism, it is difficult to resist the conclusion that such an irony has been at work.

I have distinguished three stages in the Church's relations with the world as a rival political force. In the first stage, which lasted from the French Revolution until the death of Pope Pius IX in 1878, the Church was committed to a policy of rejection of the world and Catholics were encouraged to organize their lives in a way which best protected them from the influence of non-Catholic ideas and attitudes. It was the period of the ghetto, and its remarkable achievements by the end of the nineteenth century in re-vitalizing and expanding the Church were due mainly to the efficiency of the bureaucracy set up by Pius IX and to his own passionate commitment to other-worldly Catholicism.

The policy carried certain risks. In his concern to strengthen the spiritual authority of the Church and to focus the eyes of Catholics on Rome and upon his own person as Christ's Vicar, the Pope committed the Church to a dangerous theological position. The dogmas of the Immaculate Conception and Papal Infallibility were peculiarly Catholic beliefs, not shared by most other Christian churches, and they were highly contentious even among Catholic theologians. The Pope's decision to resolve these issues was part of his total policy of rejection of the world. If that policy failed and if a decision were taken in the future to dismantle the ghetto, then the Church would be seriously compromised. The Pope had left considerably less room for theologians to negotiate doctrinal change within that framework of doctrinal continuity on which the identity of Roman Catholicism depends.

The ghetto fulfilled the important function of disseminating orthodox beliefs and controlling dissent. In a ghetto, the individual's life is lived, more or less totally, according to community norms. There are few if any relationships available or roles to play which are not part of the community network and where the tacit sanctions of the community do not operate as controls on behaviour and attitudes. The Catholic ghetto of the nineteenth century made life difficult for deviants and potential heretics. One could not be seen to abandon Catholicism or to question its beliefs and practices unless one was prepared to pay the penalty of exclusion from the only group whose culture was familiar enough to make social life tolerable. Excommunication was not then a purely theological matter which the individual Catholic could incur in relative privacy. It was a death sentence in the spiritual and the social order, cutting the individual off from the source of grace and, by the public character of its execution, ensuring that its victims were treated as social outcasts.

The second stage of Church-world relations began with the accession of Pope Leo XIII in 1878. His attitude was no less antagonistic towards the new values and institutions which challenged the Church, but his policy was competitive and manipulationist in style and intent. Catholics were encouraged to understand the modern world in order to bring a Catholic influence to bear upon the major problems of the time, particularly the social problem. This policy risked dividing the loyalties of Catholics, particularly of intellectuals whose contact with secular ideas could not easily be monitored like physical contact. Catholic academics, thoroughly socialized into their religious community and hitherto discouraged from knowing anything of secular philosophy and non-Catholic theology except the formal proofs of their absurdity, were now permitted to work with and among non-Catholics. In effect, this was to permit intellectuals to undergo a double socialization into worlds which, at that stage, were still seen as incompatible. Protestants were still heretics; the Catholic Church was still necessary for salvation and this was the fundamental fact when it came to discussing the problem of relevance. Clearly, Catholic academics and intellectuals could not sustain this simplistic level of hostility if they were to answer the call to make the voice of truth heard in the world. Dialogue in some form was necessary.

Beginning with the modernist movement, the response of intellectuals to the Leonine strategy was to bring increasing pressure on the Church to take seriously the problem of relevance—relevance to the world of secular science and to the world of other Christian churches. Changes were proposed and questions raised whose implications were not clearly visible—the ecumenical, the liturgical and the worker-priest movements were channels for new ideas in their early stages—and a new theology came to prominence in which the dilemma of intellectuals was resolved by distinguishing the substance of faith from its form. Thus the Church was provided with an instrument of relevance—a means of reconciling Catholic doctrine and practice to features of the modern world—in order to prepare the way for change in the Church in response to the pressure of changing social and cultural conditions in secular society.

The growth of affluence and individualism, the fragmentation of society in terms of the units and categories in which it was organized, the appropriation by secular agencies of most of the functions previously carried out by the Church, the relativization of ideas and values by radio, television and the press, the exposure by social scientists of the weakness of Catholic commitment even in Catholic countries—these social changes in Western countries, which grew to revolutionary proportion after the Second World War, created conditions which placed the continuation of Leonine Catholicism under increasing strain.

In the third stage, beginning with the end of the Second Vatican Council, the Church entered into a relationship of partnership with the secular world. In the Council documents and, more important, in the later interpretation of them which rapidly gained prominence throughout the Church, Catholicism was brought up to date—in the sense usually given to this expression. The documents and the post-conciliar commentaries on them are a triumph of relevance: the fundamentals of Catholic faith are reaffirmed but their meaning is largely optional, relativized to secular cultural experience.

In the contemporary Roman Church, theology, morality and liturgy reflect more and more the major characteristics of the secular world on which they were modelled: individualism, science, therapy. Theological individualism is the reality disguised by the term 'theological pluralism' and it replaces the dogmatism of the old Church. Scientific morality similarly replaces the objectivist morality of traditional Catholicism. Sin is a defect of environments or institutions, not of individuals, whose moral status is determined not by what they do but by their intention. A therapeutic liturgy, finally, has shifted the emphasis from the action performed by the priest to the experience of the participants sharing in it. The Mass is no longer the objective source of unity and continuity throughout the Church but a means of celebrating and stimulating the unity, friendship, camaraderie of groups within it. Whereas theology, morality and liturgy in the old Catholicism were intended and structured to foster the unity of the whole Church and to inhibit the expression of disunity, all three dimensions of modern Catholicism serve to manifest the fragmentation of the Church.

The condition of the Roman Church today can best be described as one of theological individualism. This is evidenced by the proliferation of theological and moral dissent on fundamental questions of faith discussed in Chapters 7 and 8 and by the fact that there is no longer any authority in the Church which can prevent the public expression of beliefs and actions known to be opposed to its *magisterium*. The state of theological individualism means that the Church can no longer be identified by its continuity with a recognizably Catholic tradition and its members are no longer united by common beliefs. Catholics are united, not by a bond which imposes common obligations of beliefs and practices, but by their common origin in a religious tradition which has ceased to function as a communal system constraining the ideas and behaviour of its members. As in a race or ethnic group whose recent past has united its members in the pursuit of a common political goal, Catholics will continue to exhibit similar cultural features and to favour similar symbols of communication which lend an identity of sorts and give the appearance of continuity with their religious tradition. But the community no longer exacts a high price for deviation. Like lapsed Jews who are still inhibited from eating certain foods, it is force of habit rather than religious conviction or social pressure which will continue to provide a semblance of unity and community among Catholics.

Theological individualism describes the structure of Catholic beliefs since the Second Vatican Council. It is not a description which can be verified by surveying the actual practices of individual Catholics. These still conform to a general pattern which, while it indicates considerable change from the orthodoxy of the pre-conciliar Church, is still Catholic to all appearances, facilitating a plausible case to be made for its consistency with the pre-conciliar tradition. Most Catholics do not manifest and are probably not even aware of the extent of their religious freedom—their freedom to think and act according to their own judgement. But, as the analysis in Chapter 8 shows, that freedom is built into the new structure of beliefs which has replaced the authoritarian structure of the old Church. The new democracy has, as yet, wrought little change at the organizational level: the allocation of power and responsibility in the Church is still accomplished in the traditional authoritarian way, with little more than rhetorical concessions to participatory government. The faith which supports that authoritarianism, however—the belief in the supernatural power of the hierarchy mediating grace through the sacramental system—that faith is no longer subject to authoritarian control. The relativity of faith, proposed in general terms by Pope John XXIII, embodied in the documents of the Vatican Council and successfully defined as official teaching to the exclusion of absolutism by the interpreters of that Council, has now been publicly tested and—by default, at least—approved as orthodox. In the emergence of certain movements, in the utterances of certain theologians, and, notably, in the contraception affair surrounding the encyclical *Humanae Vitae*, the authority to dissent, sanctioned by the Vatican Council, has been effectively granted and manifested. It is a matter of time before this freedom expresses itself in a general and more visible fragmentation of Catholic beliefs and the Church of Rome acquires the doctrinal and moral tolerance of a religious denomination. The observation, then, that the condition of the Church is one of theological individualism refers to the fact that Catholicism is no longer organized to defend its beliefs against public denial or modification by its own members; and this state of affairs is not the consequence of planned theological development but, on the contrary, has arisen despite the opposition of the Pope and Curia and against the expressed intentions of most Catholic bishops and theologians, even those who contributed to the victory of progressive theology. Catholicism can no longer be defined by the beliefs and ethics of its adherents; the structural conditions of doctrinal and moral unity no longer exist.

It is not the author's wish in this study to pass moral judgement on the general or particular developments of Catholicism. Whether theological individualism is a good or a bad thing is a question which is not here a matter of primary concern. Some regard the changes in the Church as the sign of its imminent collapse. Among these, some are conservatives, for whom the collapse is a disaster; others are more theologically progressive and regard Catholicism as redundant—an obstacle to Christianity. Most progressives, however, tend to see in modern Catholicism the beginning of a renewal which will preserve the essentials of the Catholic tradition and eliminate those elements which are no longer functional. Within the theoretical framework of this book, one cannot dispute the moral and theological elements of these judgements. But one can raise issues of a sociological kind which theologians need to bear in mind in considering the social implications of holding particular doctrinal positions, and some of these have already been discussed in Chapter 7. If, as I have claimed, theological individualism is the reality behind the rhetoric of pluralism now current in the Church, it is difficult to see how Catholicism can still make credible its claim to be a coherent, moral force preserving and preaching to the world the truth—as opposed to the fallacy—of the gospels. What kind of Church is envisaged by theologians like Dulles, Schillebeeckx, Baum and others who advance doctrinal relativism as its underlying principle in a form which inescapably entails theological individualism? The question is critical if one is to understand what is meant by describing the present state of the Church as a renewal, an *aggiornamento,* and the answer needs to be spelled out in considerably greater detail with regard to the practical social consequences of doctrinal change than is customary among theologians. It is clear that theological individualism was not on the agenda of the renewal programme when the Church officially embarked on it at Vatican II; and it is clear also that it contradicts the aims and aspirations of the theologians who made it possible.

It is impossible to offer a watertight explanation of what caused the changes in Roman Catholicism which have culminated in its present condition. What can be attempted is an interpretation of the historical process, both within the Church and in the secular society of which it formed a part, which created the conditions in which the victory of progressive theology was finally assured. There can be no general explanation which

would account for the decision of Pope John XXIII to convene
the Second Vatican Council. There is evidence that those in
power in the Church experienced increasing pressure after the
Second World War to accommodate Church teaching to ideas
and social conditions summarily termed 'the world'. But from
what we know of the election and background of Pope John,
there is nothing to suggest that he was in any sense representative of that pressure. John XXIII was not necessary or inevitable. If the Second Vatican Council was, as I shall argue, a key
link in the historical developments which converged to produce
fundamental change in Catholicism during the 1960s, that does
not make it inevitable that the Church should have changed at
that time.

It is quite conceivable that the pre-conciliar Church in all its
main features could have continued for decades to resist the
pressure to change, or yielded to it only superficially. What is
puzzling about Catholicism is not only why it changed so
radically when it did but also why it survived unchanged for so
long despite the pressure to conform, to be relevant. Since the
nineteenth century, and particularly since the death of Pope
Pius IX and the failure of his policy of resistance and antagonism towards the world, the Catholic Church has been engaged
in a struggle for the survival of its structure. It has stood almost
alone in the twentieth century as an institution at once powerful
and archaic, a bastion of medieval values and outdated ideas, a
source of consolation and suffering for its members, of outrage
and envy for others. For all those who struggled for freedom
and tolerance within the Church in the 1950s, there were others
who saw it as the only relevant institution in a runaway world
and could be moved to immoderate prose in describing their
admiration and their fears:

. . . haunted by many recurring conflicts and crises, skilled in states-
manship, enriched by an unfathomable memory, [the Roman
Church] is a vigilant Mother-Confessor and a wise Director of Souls.
A candid Protestant or an honest humanist will find himself at last
asking—what, in a world rocking in helpless indecision and revealing
ominous cracks of threatened collapse, will become of our Christian
heritage and traditional culture should that Church compromise its
sense of divine commission, or if, bribed or tortured by lust of power,

it should tremble to impose its own discipline, lose its nerve and snap under the breaking strain?[1]

Before the Second Vatican Council, Catholicism was united by common beliefs in the sense that the Pope and his Curia enjoyed legitimate authority and, through the episcopacy, controlled the faith of Catholics, successfully preventing public challenge to the Roman definition of orthodoxy. After the Council, Catholics began to demonstrate their religious freedom for the first time and to express their emancipation from clerical and Roman authority. What happened between times was that the Church committed itself publicly and officially to doctrinal relativism in order to resolve the problem of relevance which had occasioned the Vatican Council. Theological individualism is the consequence of the Council, which, in turn, was the product of the demand for the accommodation of Church teaching to the scientific, economic and political realities of the secular world.

It is not inconsistent with this interpretation to observe that the immediate effect of Vatican II was a resurgence of devotional practices among Catholics and a general renewal of interest in the Church and of enthusiasm for the changes in attitude and liturgy announced by the Council Fathers. As Andrew Greeley has shown with reference to devotional practices in American Catholicism, the decline in the Church was not correlated with the Vatican Council but with the encyclical on birth control, *Humanae Vitae*, which followed it in 1968. This does not mean that the Council was less significant than the encyclical in bringing about that decline. The fact that *Humanae Vitae* contained unpleasant news for Catholics does not explain why they responded by withdrawing their commitment to the Church. They received unpleasant news from the Vatican before; why only now should they resist lawful authority?[2]

[1] Lloyd Thomas (1951).
[2] Greeley (1976). Greeley presents the evidence for a correlation between devotional decline and the contraception issue. He does not satisfactorily establish a causal link between them, nor does he convincingly argue the case that Vatican II had a positive rather than a negative effect on religious practices and devotion. In addition to the observation made above—that the public resistance of Catholics to a papal encyclical itself requires an expla-

The simple answer and, I believe, the correct one, is that the same authority which now commanded them to desist from the practice of artificial contraception had, during the Council, effectively released them from the obligation of submitting their consciences to the judgement of Rome. The encyclical *Humanae Vitae* was a remarkable document, not because it caused dissent among so many Catholics throughout the world, but because it manifested the emancipation from authority which had been accomplished by the Second Vatican Council. Suddenly, after the Council, Catholics found it legitimate to act in a range of different deviant ways without suffering the social or ecclesiastical consequences which previously inhibited deviancy and ensured compliance. The attraction of particular deviant actions, such as refusing to accept papal authority on the birth control question, leaving the priesthood, divorce and remarriage, does not explain why it suddenly became possible, even fashionable, for so many to perform them. They were presumably no less tempting before, but those who yielded were forced to act *as deviants* and to feel the full psychological force of their crime. The Vatican Council legitimated dissent. This was a consequence of the doctrinal relativism adopted by the Council, whict made beliefs and morals relative to social and cultural environment, and it was structurally embodied in the Church by the proliferation of competing faiths in the years immediately following.

But what caused the Vatican Council and what caused the

---

nation—it could also be argued that initial enthusiasm for the change of attitude of Vatican II was a prelude to devotional decline, not an expression of renewal. Historically, release from doctrinal and moral rigidity has had the immediate effect of creating a semblance of religious vitality. From a wider historical perspective than Greeley employs, that vitality can be seen to cover a latent secularization—see, for example, Gilbert (1976).

Furthermore, post-conciliar Catholicism so expanded the definition of the Church as to make it, in some countries, as unthinkable and unnecessary to define oneself as a non-Catholic or a lapsed one as it was previously unthinkable to define oneself as a non-believer or an atheist. In the United States in particular, one would predict an enthusiastic welcome for a Council which promised an end to divisions among Christians, increased participation in secular affairs and closer identification with one's fellow-Americans of whatever creed. It would be rash to infer that such enthusiasm was durable and religiously motivated.

participants in it to express themselves so radically and with such revolutionary consequences? Before attempting to amplify the explanation, it must be repeated that the revolutionary character of Vatican II was not intended or anticipated even by those who pressed for radical change. It is clear from the documents and from the evidence of theological and pastoral writings after the Council that no one foresaw theological individualism as the outcome of the relativity of faith. That relativism was proposed and adopted as the only possible solution to the dilemma of modernizing the Church without abandoning its doctrinal continuity with the past. The search for relevance was conceived in terms of accommodating Catholic teaching to a secular world and to the need to heal the divisions in Christendom which were seen as increasingly irrelevant in societies which posed political, social and economic questions outside the framework of scholastic and Reformation theology. What caused enthusiasm among so many Catholics during the Second Vatican Council was the prospect of a Church renewed by a sense of moral urgency for the solution of problems of social justice, divested of its archaic language and symbols, and revealing to the world its heritage of inner truth and moral rectitude which had been hidden by centuries of papal imperialism and theological obscurantism. It was to be the same Church, holding the same beliefs formulated in a new way adapted to the changed conditions of secular society, and uniting its members in a common mission to subvert the world and to transform it according to the Christian ideal.

Ironically, the efforts to renew the Church have resulted in its fragmentation, and the attempt to make it relevant has resulted in conforming it to ideas and values generated within the world without giving it power, status, or a credible missionary role in secular society. As a Church which defines itself in terms of its missionary function to evangelize the world, Catholicism is probably less relevant now than before the Council. Catholic teaching and symbols are useful in mobilizing political support in certain countries against authoritarian, capitalist regimes. For the leaders—and the led—of liberation movements in Latin America and elsewhere, the Church has a highly significant ideological role to play. But there are no indications that the political definition of Catholicism can survive the particular conflict to which it relates and, in time, establish itself against rival definitions of the Church. In modern Catholicism, the co-existence of contradictory ideologies and incompatible movements is not an indicator of relevance in the sense anticipated by the new theologians but of the impotence of the ecclesiastical authorities to halt the process of fragmentation facilitated by the Second Vatican Council. In the contemporary Church, one man's orthodoxy is another man's heresy and between them there is no effective court of appeal, no effective mechanism of reconciliation.

The Vatican Council was the climax of pressures upon the Church, both secular and religious, to abandon its absolutism in favour of doctrinal relativism, thereby releasing Catholics from hierarchic control of their beliefs and consciences. One can trace the convergence of influence in this direction since the Restoration at the beginning of the nineteenth century. But it is in the years following the Second World War that these pressures developed to a pitch which makes it difficult to believe that the Council, the confrontation and the result could have been avoided. Pope John's decision amazed the world; but sooner or later the Church would have been forced to resolve the problem of relevance—through another Pope, at another time, undoubtedly with similar consequences.

One can distinguish three ways in which the secular world influenced the Church in the direction finally taken at the Second Vatican Council. The first was the direct attack on Church property and competence. In the nineteenth century, Pope Pius IX and Pope Leo XIII could not conceive of the health of Catholicism except in terms of its temporal power and they defined the success of ecclesiastical policy primarily in terms of the defence or recovery of the Papal States. Secular attack on these territories, which culminated in the humiliating defeat of Pius IX by the Italian nationalist forces in 1870, was accompanied by the gradual shift of the boundary between Church and state competence, particularly in the field of education. The civil authority could not tolerate the extent of Church control and began the task of redefining certain areas of social life as secular, rather than religious.

From the beginning of the twentieth century, the growth of the welfare state in most Protestant European countries signalled the end of Catholic influence over a wide area of individuals' lives and the end, too, of an important structural feature of the Catholic ghetto. From now on, Catholics in these countries needed to make a more positive commitment to the Church in order to live their lives under its care and patronage; the state had opened an escape route from the ghetto by making schools, health and welfare generally available in irreligious form. Radical advances towards the welfare state were made after the Second World War as state planning and involvement touched the lives of every individual and the Church's area of competence and its power to influence legislation rapidly diminished. Religion became a private and specialized affair, one set of role relationships and social obligations among many others, creating moral dilemmas when its demands conflicted with those of business, health, education or civic duty. The best-known exemplar of this post-war Catholicism was President J. Kennedy, who successfully demonstrated to a still-suspicious American public that the life of a Catholic can be compartmentalized and that the values and obligations it entails need not transgress the boundaries of a well-defined ritual context. It was only by means of an elaborate casuistry, accomplished by theologians and moralists, that the actual teaching of the Church could be accommodated to this new way of life. Catholic doctrine and morality, formulated before and during the ghetto period of the nineteenth century, still posed embarrassing difficulties for millions of Catholics living, like Kennedy, in countries where Catholicism was not the established religion. Official teaching about the nature of the Church, about the status of non-Catholics and about sexual morality placed modern Catholics at a disadvantage in their increasingly complex and extensive secular areas of activity, marking them in the eyes of the world as being potential infiltrators, less than loyal to the secular institutions which now housed them, fed them, educated them and defended their rights as individuals.

Related to this structural change in post-war society were two cultural factors which impressed themselves on the theologians and Church leaders in the pluralist societies of Northern Europe. First and foremost was the advancement and prestige of science, notably the human and social sciences. In

the major and victorious confrontation with the modernists at
the beginning of the twentieth century, the Roman authorities,
by their action, demonstrated the force of the threat represented by the infiltration of science and the scientific ethos
into Catholic theological circles. Catholic intellectuals,
attempting to recover prestige after half a century of intellectual poverty enforced by the policies of Pope Pius IX, looked to
historical and textual criticism to save the Church from the
ridicule of non-Catholic scholars and non-Christian scientists.
In the conditions facilitating easier contact with non-Catholics
which began after the Leonine period, their search for an
accommodation of Catholic teaching to the findings of science
continued, despite the warnings and purges of the anti-
modernist campaign. The rise of the social sciences offered a
new challenge and opportunity to intellectuals. The traditional
conception of the Church was untenable in the light of Marxist,
Freudian and sociological analysis; on the other hand, the
social sciences offered the possibility of a 'deeper' understanding of the Christian message—one which saved the traditional
teaching of the Church by relativizing it to past ages and
cultures and which, at the same time, opened up Catholic and
non-Catholic teaching to the possibility of a new synthesis at a
more profound and more human level.

The scientific analysis of society since the middle of the
nineteenth century exposed all traditional institutions to
attack. The bewildering pace of social change in the post-war
years was hastened by the development of social science which
undermined institutions by explaining their human origins and
revealing the vested interests they served. In this context, the
Church stood condemned with the rest of society as the ideology of conservatism, the bond which held together a now
discredited social order. During the modernist crisis, that social
order was still sufficiently stable, sufficiently protective of
ecclesiastical interests to afford the Church the luxury of
crushing the incipient social science which encouraged some of
its intellectuals to explore new ways of thinking about God and
religion. By the 1960s, social science had achieved wide recognition and respectability; social change had become virtually
the norm and conditions were ripe for a new exploratory
theology which would recover a role for a Church left stranded

by the institutions which had protected it and for which it provided an integrative function. Nothing was fixed or certain; nothing was immune to questioning, and theologians could find no better discipline to exploit the ambiguities of the social order in the 1960s than social science, which enjoyed the status of an empirical science and, at the same time, the freedom to speculate in the manner of old-fashioned social theorists and metaphysicians. The Roman authorities were ill-equipped and could ill afford to dismiss the new theological experiments as they had stifled the old, with all the new theology's apparent sophistication and cautious lack of precision and with all its manifest concern for the Church at a time when the old traditional ideas had lost their social roots.

Intellectuals had direct access to the new ideas in science through their improved contacts with non-Catholic scholars and literature. But an indirect channel for the communication of social scientific ideas in particular was made available through the structural changes discussed above. The encroachment of the secular world upon the Church's domain of competence brought with it competition between clergy and lay professionals for the provision of welfare. The Church, through its ministers, continued to feed the poor and to educate their children long after the state had begun to establish secular institutions to perform the same function. The sociological principles which informed the organization of the social services also stimulated new thinking about poverty, injustice, educational opportunity within the religious ministry and furnished clerics with sophisticated methods of data collection and analysis which revealed a considerable gap between the appearance and the reality of religious commitment. The information thus acquired exposed the critical situation of the Church, even in Catholic countries, and encouraged the view that radical changes of attitude and teaching were needed.[3]

---

[3] This is not surprising. At any time in the Church's history, the employment of a social science methodology to collect information and statistics of membership and beliefs would have revealed a crisis. The methodology is linked to a theoretical system which *presupposes* a gap between individual beliefs and their public expression. This is not to suggest that the information acquired by surveys of religious commitment was incorrect. But the crisis lay more in the shock of discovery than in the facts themselves.

The second cultural factor facilitating the critique of traditional Catholicism was the ideology of individualism and what I have termed the cultural fragmentation related to it. It is a paradox of capitalist societies that as pressure for human rights increases, so too does the size of the bureaucracy which is apparently required to promote and protect them and which, in turn, poses a new threat to individual freedom. Both individualism and bureaucracy were well advanced by the time of the Second Vatican Council, large bureaucratic organizations operating mainly in the field of welfare to supplant the traditional function of the Church. The concern for individual rights and freedom is as old as modernity and could be called a constituent feature of the world in opposition to the Church, to its collectivism, to its absolutism, and to its consistent alliances with illiberal and authoritarian states. The Second World War is frequently linked with increased sensitivity towards human rights. Whatever the cause, it is clear that affluence and the expectation of continued economic growth which followed the war are a necessary condition for an ideology of individualism to take root. Affluence, in turn, requires and creates conditions which are inimical to the traditional organization and teaching of the Church: high geographical and social mobility, openness to innovation and intolerance of tradition, reliance on observation and experiment rather than supernatural intervention.

The fragmentation of old categories of thought, systems of ideas, forms of expression, reached rampant proportions in the 1960s, when it became almost mandatory on artists, journalists, even philosophers, to distance themselves from their traditions and to seek new forms of communication. These had the common property of rejecting the pretensions to categorize reality in the old systems of thought and of respecting the individual, the unique. The central focus was not on objective reality but on language as a problematic medium between the knowing subject and object. One might say that twentieth-century thought can be characterized by its concern with language—as a means of knowledge and a distortion of it, as a vehicle of communication and an obstacle to it. Traditional theology was premised upon language as transparent, unproblematic, capturing the objective reality and communicating it without bias. Theologians in tune with secular trends found themselves analysing theological language and asking questions about the meaning of its terms and expressions, which led inexorably to the principle of doctrinal relativity.

The three factors noted as providing the conditions for the emergence of a new theology and influencing theologians in the direction finally taken at the Second Vatican Council—the development of secular welfare, the prestige of science and the growth of individualism—cannot of themselves explain the victory of the new theology and the shift from traditional to contemporary Catholicism. The Church, after all, has for a long time withstood severe pressure to accommodate its teaching and structure to the conditions of secular society. Why could it not continue to do so, to reject the world as Pope Pius IX insisted or to manipulate it to the Church's advantage as Leo XIII intended? Faced with the early signs of theological individualism, why could Church leaders not silence dissenters and expel the rebellious from their ranks in the same authoritarian way that had been one of the marks of Catholicism even up to the eve of the Vatican Council? In the decade following the end of the Council, the instances of doctrinal dissent, indiscipline, clerical defection and other unacceptable practices dramatically increased. To say that it was now legitimate to act in these ways simply raises the question of why this was so when the sanctions inhibiting such behaviour were clearly successful previously. There is no evidence that the Roman authorities willingly, even reluctantly, tolerated this state of affairs. On the contrary, all the indications show that the Pope and the Curia struggled to recover their traditional authority but were impotent to act decisively as they wished. What made the Catholic Church in the mid-twentieth century so vulnerable to secular pressure?

Part of the credit must go to the change in policy initiated by Pope Leo XIII and continued, albeit warily, by his successors. The effect of Leo's directives was to create an elite of Catholic intellectuals, living and working on the fringe of the ghetto, mixing freely with Protestant and non-Christian intellectuals and assimilating in part their ideas and attitudes. After Leo, a channel of communications was opened up and institutionalized, creating an ambiguous situation for a relatively small number of intellectuals in Protestant-dominated countries of

Europe. This nucleus of the Catholic elite, doubly socialized into Catholic and non-Catholic ideas and attitudes, continued to expand throughout the twentieth century, their numbers enlarged by the expansion of state-controlled education and by the accidents of two World Wars which gave first-hand experience of the fringes of Catholicism to many more clerics and laymen. It was this elite which acted as the mechanism of change in the Catholic Church.

Could not the Roman authorities expel the dissident intellectuals, despite their numerical strength, and remove their influence over the rest of the Church? A critical factor in the development of modern Catholicism is the role of the media. Television, radio and the press were cumbersome vehicles of ideas and values even up to the beginning of the Second World War. Since then, their range and influence have multiplied.

The effect of our international system of mass media is not to draw peoples together in some form of 'global village'; it is not to make societies more communal but to make them more similar and to relativize their cultures. The media tend to destroy ghettos—hence the need for rigorous censorship in countries where cultural isolation is required for ideological reasons. Television thrives on cultural differences and, in societies where censorship is minimal, its short-term effect is to accentuate those differences, stressing their 'interesting' features. The aim is to convey a quasi-anthropological experience and tolerance of different cultures and values to those who are prevented from doing so at first hand and to display alien beliefs and practices, not as true or false, but as expressions of a different way of life, a different point of view.[4]

The long-term consequence, however, is the progressive destruction of differences through exposure to the media. Societies whose cultural distinctiveness once expressed the distinctiveness of their economic and political structures without any great effort on the part of their tourist boards now find that it is increasingly difficult to preserve their cultural heritage and increasingly necessary to set up agencies specializing in this peculiarly modern task. We cannot attribute this effect to

---

[4] The ideal of balance in television journalism is a particular internal form of relativization.

the media alone. It is clearly functional in societies where the economic system is international capitalism that ideological differences, articulated by culture, be minimized and prevented from overflowing into the economic sphere. The imperialism of the media in tending to destroy the distinctiveness of cultures and make them conform to an international standard is consequent upon the imperialism of international capitalism[5] This long-term erosion of differences by the media has little to do with universal harmony. It does not make societies more tolerant but—in both senses of the word—more indifferent.

A small group of Catholic intellectuals scattered throughout Northern Europe could hardly have succeeded in exerting pressure for change and carrying the weight of episcopal opinion in the Vatican Council if they were not representative of a much wider body of opinion. Their ideas were already in harmony with those disseminated by the media to a wide Catholic audience in their own societies. It is impossible to be precise about numbers in this case, but there is clear evidence, for example, that the views on Christian unity of Congar and de Lubac in France, Rahner and Küng in Germany, were considerably better known and more acceptable to French and German clerics and seminarians in the 1950s than they were in the more Catholic countries of, say, Ireland and Spain. The changes of the Vatican Council created less problems of adaptation for Catholics in Holland and Belgium, who were well exposed to the ideas of their theologians beforehand, than for the Catholics of Italy or the largely Irish Church in Great Britain. The media, together with an enlarged state education sector, thus expanded the Catholic intelligentsia, giving its spokesmen a sizeable constituency vote, so to speak, to carry with them to the Council. In the eyes of the intellectual elite of the late 1950s, the Catholic was hopelessly out of touch with the world as it was successfully defined in the media—tolerant, pragmatic, concerned with social justice, pluralist, suspicious of ideologies and claims to divine mandate. Progressive theologians had the advantage of speaking two languages: the language of Catholic tradition and the language of the prestig-

---

[5] This joint role of capitalism and the media is particularly well exemplified in the spheres of popular music and tourism.

ious world of science and non-Catholic biblical scholarship which was already well-known and respected in their own countries and was already infiltrating the rest of Europe through the medium of television.

Another reason why the Roman authorities could not silence dissidents was that the erosion of the ghetto accomplished by state bureaucracy, welfare and the mass media opened up a refuge for potential rebels. Hitherto, the expulsion of the dissident had potentially devastating effects on the individual involved, entailing removal from the community in which his life was totally immersed. The cloth-capped outcast of Graham Greene's novels was not only a figment of Greene's imagination; priests who defected from the ministry, particularly in Catholic countries, were in fact demoted to pariah status. Now the sanction is no longer available to the Church. Since the Second World War, less and less areas of a Catholic's life are controlled by religious authority and the expansion of Church-neutral areas has opened up opportunities for contacts which form no part of the sanction system; the potential dissenter has somewhere to go and dissent is less perilous for that reason. Moreover, the secular media have consistently viewed theological dissent as a noble expression of the value of individualism. Even before the close of the Vatican Council, public dissent became positively attractive for Catholics who felt so inclined.

The media further aided the victory of new theology by its investigative role during and after the Council. It was the press and television which exposed the fallibility of the bishops during the Council debates. Most Catholics are aware that infallibility does not mean omniscience. But the daily and dramatized display of episcopal skulduggery, which was rich fare for the television producers, did nothing to enhance the credibility of the Church's *magisterium* except in the eyes of intellectuals. It was the press and television which prepared the Catholic world for a papal statement permitting artificial contraception, thereby contributing to the furore among liberal Catholics when their practices were condemned and to the increased disenchantment with the Church noted by Greeley.

A third reason why Rome could no longer silence dissent is that the ambiguity of the new theology made it virtually impossible to decide on its implications for the structure and teaching of the Church. The Church in the nineteenth century was forced by the rapidity of social change to make theological decisions which ultimately proved compromising. Capitalism, liberalism, democracy, socialism, nationalism—all presented themselves as images of the world, demanding that the Church should accommodate itself to each. In the mid-twentieth century, the speed of social change had accelerated to proportions, highlighted by the media, which made it difficult to characterize any particular society, much less the world. What could it mean to be relevant to a kaleidoscope of interesting cultures and shifting allegiances, a world where values and attitudes were held on approval, as it were, never absolutely? The task of the new theologians was to find a statement of Catholic teaching rooted in no particular culture and open to all.[6] It needed above all to be ambiguous—a theology which respected the other point of view, never certain, seldom clear, always open to different interpretations. Such a theology does not easily leave itself open to the charge of heresy.

After over a century and a half of resistance, the Church finally emerged from the Second Vatican Council with a positive commitment to the world and a theological principle—the relativity of faith—which seemed to promise ecumenical and missionary success. But the world of the 1960s was no longer that which demanded a relevant theology ten years earlier. It was a runaway world, and the Catholic Church was fundamentally transformed in the search to locate it and run with it.

---

[6] On the wall of an American campus lavatory, an amusing—if exaggerated—version of the statement was inscribed: 'And the Lord said to them: "Who do you say that I am?" They replied: "Thou art the eschatological manifestation of our being; the reality of existential awareness; the kerygma in which is grounded the ultimate meaning of interpersonal relationships." And the Lord said to them: "WHAT?"'

Epilogue:
The Church of John Paul II

The accession to the papacy of the Polish Karol Wojtyla in 1978 was warmly welcomed by most sections of Catholic opinion. The Traditionalists, predictably, reserved judgment until such time as the new Pontiff made it clear, within their uncomplicated frame of reference, whether he was with them or against them. The other three major groups in the Church saw no reason to suppose that the spirit was not blowing in their direction and that Wojtyla's election was not a continuation of the renewal of the Church as they variously interpreted it.

Approaching the third year of his pontificate, the picture looks somewhat different. The close contact with Communist countries and ideas and his outspoken criticism of the repression of freedom under Communist rule were qualities of Wojtyla's experience and personality which, in the eyes of progressive Catholics, augured well for the Church in the modern world. 'The one who voices his opposition to the general or particular rules or regulations of the community,' he had written, 'does not thereby reject his membership.'[1] In 1969, Karol Wojtyla saw this kind of opposition as 'essentially constructive'. Ten years later, those who expected a similar approach to the internal problems of the Church were to be disappointed. If the Pope's experience under Communist rule has modified his thinking on community and authority, it is in the direction of firmer control and closer monitoring of opinion rather than decentralization and encouragement of constructive criticism. The repression of thought and action which Catholics suffered under Polish government and against which the Pope campaigned as archbishop appears to be a tolerable

[1] Wojtyla (1979), p. 286.

necessity of life from the perspective of the Vatican. Of the groups which emerged from the crisis of Catholicism in the 1960s, it is the Traditionalists who have most cause for optimism. In the view of one victim of papal policy, the current trend in Rome is not towards the continuation or expansion of Pope John's Church of openness and dialogue but towards the closed and repressive Church of Pope Pius XII.[2]

If this fear is confirmed and if Vatican policy is successful in restoring the old Catholicism of the pre-Conciliar era, the central thesis of this book will have been invalidated. For it has been the concern of the author to demonstrate that the Church has *fundamentally* changed and that the conditions in which it functions today are such that there can be no return to traditional Roman Catholicism. It is as impossible for the Roman Church to recover its past cohesiveness and social significance and for the Roman authorities to recover their past control of the consciences of clergy and laity as it is for European monarchs to recover their political power over their so-called subjects. For good or ill, Catholicism has lost its status as a universal Church and joined the Episcopalians and Anglicans, Baptists and Presbyterians as a denomination. Its leadership has yet to acknowledge this change and, in the symbols of ritual and organization, the old claims to universality are still pressed by Pope and prelates as if the Second Vatican Council was no more than a routine crisis in the history of the Church. Theologians will play their traditional role in defining the change as a development of the same fundamental teaching and values which characterized the old Catholicism. But the conditions which facilitated their successful management of change in the past no longer exist. With the cooperation of the Vatican, but not by its dictate, the laity has tasted the pleasure of dissent and the secular world, which created the impulse towards this emancipation, is no longer under the control of the Church.

The passage of time will manifest the change in Roman Catholicism in the same way that time made visible the shift in power from monarchy to elected assembly throughout Europe. Pope John Paul II has inherited a Church which still com-

---

[2] Küng (1980).

mands the allegiance of millions of Catholics and enjoys a measure of moral authority in the secular world as a consequence. He recognizes the point consistently made throughout this book—and the crucial role of theologians in realizing it—that the ideological strength of the institution lies in the maintenance of a sense of tradition and continuity of faith.

For the soundest sociological reasons, therefore, the Pope is leading a vigorous retreat from the Second Vatican Council as it has been successfully interpreted by the new theologians. Their arguments for freedom of conscience, freedom of thought, lay participation in the priesthood and the restoration of Christian unity are difficult to challenge, even for an infallible pope. But it is understandable if the consequences of embodying these ideals in the organization of the Church cause more alarm at the centre of power in Rome than the long-term consequences of ignoring them.

In the few years of his pontificate, John Paul II has made it clear that he will not tolerate the continuation of the Conciliar renewal of theology, morality and liturgy in the direction set by the new theologians. Unlike Pope John XXIII, he is not prepared to gamble the future of the Church as an institution for the dubious benefits of secular approval and esteem. Unlike Pope Paul VI, he is not prepared to languish impotently as if the fate of the Church had been irreversibly settled by the spirit of the age. He has re-asserted the Church's traditional teaching on the Eucharist and the doctrine of transubstantiation; he has reaffirmed the traditional ban on artificial methods of contraception—though he has not been so rash as to make the point a test of his infallible moral authority. By a number of strategic episcopal appointments in Holland, he has succeeded—for a time, at least—in halting the progress of experimental ecumenism and liturgy which had made that country the model of new theological renewal. He has acted most decisively in the area over which he exercises bureaucratic—rather than merely moral—authority, curbing defections from the priesthood by refusing permission to marry and curbing deviations from doctrinal orthodoxy by threatening to remove the deviants from their teaching posts in Catholic institutes. (The case of Hans Küng, who was dismissed from his chair at the University of Tübingen in 1980, is a warning to all theologians, whose careers depend on episcopal approval, to return to the pre-Conciliar policy of judicious self-censorship if they wish to remain in employment.)

While a sociologist cannot but commend the present papal policy as a short-term solution to the organizational problems of the Church, its certain failure in the long run must make one question the wisdom of attempting it at all. It is easy to reconstruct the appearance of the old Catholicism and give the impression of a restoration of papal authority by limiting freedom of thought and action in the area of bureaucratic control. At this level, the Pope enjoys a similar kind of power to that exercised by President Carter, Mrs Thatcher or any other bureaucratic leader whose sanctions are supported by law. It is not that kind of power which characterized the old Catholicism. The medieval pontiffs and their successors up to Pius XII exercised it, to be sure, but it was secondary to the charisma of authority which they acquired *ex officio* and which guaranteed the unity of the Church by ensuring the allegiance of Catholics to their commands, to their teaching and to their person. Even a charismatic leader in the popular sense of the word could not restore the charismatic authority of the Roman pontiff in the peculiarly Catholic sense. The traditional power of the pope—and the traditional Catholicism which was organized around it as its core—depended on belief in the continuity of faith, and that, in turn, depended on the capacity of the Pope and his *magisterium* to impose a unity of faith by distinguishing between truth and falsehood and by preventing the public denial of the official interpretation of Catholic doctrine. Now the breach of continuity has been displayed and, more important, the disunity of faith also. The authority to dissent has become, paradoxically, an article of faith—not officially defined, but effectively internalized in the lives of the clergy and laity throughout the Catholic world.

In this light, the chances of re-establishing continuity with the old Catholicism in anything but name and organizational trappings are as slim as the chances of restoring the power of the European monarchs or of reviving religious fervour in secular Britain. In effect, Catholics choose to obey or disobey papal directives on morality, to accept or reject papal interpretations of orthodoxy, implicitly recognizing that their moral status is not determined by compliance with a collective norm. In varying degrees, the secular structure of Catholic life is a positive inducement to emancipation from ecclesiastical control and this new situation is reflected in the increasing unwillingness of the Vatican to put Catholic allegiance to the test in the manner of Pope Paul VI's command on contraception. This attempt to re-establish ideological, as distinct from bureaucratic, control over the Catholic world was disastrously unsuccessful. The current policy of asserting papal authority at the bureaucratic level is timid, by contrast, and unworthy of a pope who found the same reliance on repressive bureaucracy in the Communist world so distasteful and immoral. Such is the physical and cultural isolation of Communism from the rest of the world that—ethical considerations apart—one could appreciate the need for repressive bureaucracy. In the contemporary Catholic world, however, its political effect is more likely to be negative.

Excommunication by apathy is the new mode of detaching oneself from the Church and the Pope appears to be set on a course which will ensure its popularity in the future. The inquisitorial control of theologians could only have the desired effect of restoring unity to the Church if the theologians themselves were the source of disunity and their dissident views had not yet been internalized by the laity. That was broadly the situation in the modernist era at the turn of the century. Theologians today are not working in the same conditions, engaged in the same intellectual disputes with their peers in the Catholic and non-Catholic churches. They no longer have the autonomy vis-a-vis the laity which the Pope's disciplinary policy implies. Penalizing theologians for the disunity in the Church is rather like penalizing the supporters of a football club for the poor performance of the team. Their role today is to articulate the dissent implicit in the lives of the Catholic laity, the source of which lies in the social and cultural conditions over which neither they nor the Pope have any control.

A vigorous thrust in the direction of renewal set by Pope John XXIII and continued by the new theologians would appear now to be the only option open if Roman Catholicism is to retain a mass membership and to recover a measure of prestige and social influence. This is a vague aspiration, admittedly, and one whose realization is unlikely to be testable in any satisfactory way. Short of a divine intervention of cataclysmic proportion, the traditional Church has disappeared and a new institution is taking its place. The Roman Church has enough reserves of moral authority to lead the Christian world into a new and, as yet, unknowable form of religious commitment. Despite the risks, it would surely be a wiser strategy for the Pope to act positively towards this end. To employ the nautical metaphor hallowed by Catholic tradition, there must come a time in a long voyage when the replacement of the ship is the only guarantee of moving in the right direction.

References

Except where otherwise stated, all quotations from the documents of the Second Vatican Council are taken from Abbot (1966).

Abbot, Walter M., ed. (1966), *The Documents of Vatican II*, Geoffrey Chapman, London.

Alexander, Edgar (1953), 'Church and Society in Germany', in Moody, Joseph N. (ed.), *Church and Society: Catholic Social and Political Thought and Movements 1789–1950*, Arts Inc., New York.

Angevui, Jean (1976), *Le Drame d'Econe*, Sion.

Arroyo, Gonzalo, S. J. (1974), an interview in *New Blackfriars*, November 1974.

Bainvell, J. (1924), *Devotion to the Sacred Heart of Jesus: the Doctrine and its History*, Burns, Oates & Washbourne, London.

Barraclough, Geoffrey (1968), *The Medieval Papacy*, Thames & Hudson, London.

Baum, Gregory (1971), *Man Becoming*, Herder & Herder, New York.

Berkouwer, C. (1965), *The Second Vatican Council and the New Catholicism*, Eerdmans, Michigan.

Bettenson, Henry (1963), *Documents of the Christian Church*, Oxford University Press, London.

Bouyer, Louis (1969), *The Decomposition of Catholicism*, Franciscan Herald Press, Chicago.

Brugerette, J. (1935), *Le Prêtre Français et la Société Contemporaine*, Paris.

Butler, B. C. (1967), *The Theology of Vatican II*, Darton Longman & Todd, London.

Camp, Richard L. (1969), *The Papal Ideology of Social Reform*, Brill, Leiden.

Caporale, Rocco (1964), *Vatican II: Last of the Councils*, Helicon, Baltimore.

Century of the Sacred Heart (1924: author unknown), Burns, Oates & Washbourne, London.

Chadwick, Owen (1964), *The Reformation*, Penguin, London.

Chenu, M.-D. (1969), *La Foi dans l'Intelligence*, Paris.

Congar, Yves (1965), *Lay People in the Church*, Geoffrey Chapman, London.

Connolly, James (1961), *The Voices of France*, Macmillan, New York.

Corbishley, Thomas (1976), in *Catholic Herald*, 28 Nov 1976.

Damboriena, Prudencio (1969), *Tongues as of Fire: Pentecostalism in Contemporary Christianity*, Corpus, Washington.

Danielou, Jean (1958), *The Lord of History*, Regnery, Chicago.

Daniel-Rops, Henri (1963), *Un Combat pour Dieu*, Paris.

—— (1965), *The Church in an Age of Revolution 1789–1870*, Dent, London.

Dansette, Adrien (1961), *Religious History of Modern France*, Nelson, London.

Davies, Christie (1975), *Permissive Britain: Social Change in the Sixties and Seventies*, Pitman, London.

Dawson, Christopher (1972), *The Gods of Revolution*, Sidgwick & Jackson, London.

De Kadt, Emmanuel (1970), *Catholic Radicals in Brazil*, Oxford University Press, London.

Dellhaye, Philippe (1972), 'The Contribution of Vatican II to Moral Theology' in *Concilium*, Vol. 5, No. 8.

De Lubac, Henri (1946), *Catholicism*, Sheed & Ward, New York.

Delumeau, Jean (1978), *Catholicism between Luther and Voltaire*, Burns & Oates, London.

Denzinger-Rahner, eds. (1957), *Enchiridion Symbolorum*, edition 31.

Dewart, Leslie (1969), *The Foundations of Belief*, Herder & Herder, New York.

Dulles, Avery (1973), *The Survival of Dogma*, Image, New York.

Ellul, Jacques (1969), *Violence: Reflections from a Christian Perspective*, Seabury, New York.

Fletcher, Joseph (1966), *Situation Ethics: The New Morality*, Westminster Press, London.

Fletcher, Joseph (1965), *The Christian Century,* Vol. 82, No. 13.

Garrett, William R. (1973), 'Politicized Clergy: A Sociological Interpretation of the New Breed', in *Journal for the Scientific Study of Religion,* Vol. 12, No. 4.

Gellner, Ernest (1974), *Legitimation of Belief,* Cambridge University Press, London.

Gilbert, Alan D. (1976), *Religion and Society in Industrial England: Church, Chapel and Social Change 1740–1914,* Longmans, London.

Gilson, Etienne (1944), *La Philosophie au Moyen Age,* Paris.

—— (1960), *La Philosophie et la Théologie,* Fayard, Paris.

—— (1954), *The Church Speaks to the Modern World: The Social Teaching of Leo XIII,* Doubleday, New York.

Goldmann, Lucien (1973), *The Philosophy of the Enlightenment: The Christian Burgess and the Enlightenment,* Routledge, London.

Graef, Hilda (1965), *Mary: A History of Doctrine and Devotion,* Sheed & Ward, London.

Greeley, Andrew (1976), 'Council or Encyclical?', in *Review of Religious Research,* Vol. 18, No. 1.

Groethuysen, Bernard (1968), *The Bourgeois: Catholicism versus Capitalism in Eighteenth-Century France,* Cresset Press, London.

Gurian, W., and Fitzsimmons, M. A. (1954), *The Catholic Church in World Affairs,* University of Notre Dame Press, Indiana.

Gutierrez, Gustavo (1974), *A Theology of Liberation,* SCM, London.

Hadden, Jeffrey (1969), *The Gathering Storm in the Churches,* Doubleday, New York.

Halmos, Paul (1970), *The Personal Service Society,* Schocken, New York.

Hampson, Norman (1970), *The First European Revolution 1776–1815,* Thames & Hudson, London.

Häring, Bernard (1971), *Morality is for Persons,* Farrar, Strauss & Giroux, New York.

—— (1974), *Sin in the Secular Age,* St Paul's Publications, Slough.

Harper, Michael (1968), *Walk in the Spirit,* Logos International, New Jersey.

Haughton, Rosemary (1966), *On Trying to be Human*, Geoffrey Chapman, London.

Hay, Denys (1966), *Europe in the Fourteenth and Fifteenth Centuries*, Longmans, London.

Hebblethwaite, Peter (1975), *The Runaway Church*, Collins, London.

Heyer, Friedrich (1969), *The Catholic Church from 1648 to 1870*, Adam & Charles Black, London.

Hitchcock, James (1971), *The Decline and Fall of Radical Catholicism*, Herder & Herder, New York.

Houtart, François, and Rousseau, André (1971), *The Church and Revolution*, Orbis, New York.

Huizinga, Johan (1972), *The Waning of the Middle Ages*, Penguin, London.

Hyma, Albert (1924), *The Christian Renaissance: A History of the Devotio Moderna*, The Century Co., New York.

Jacoby, Henry (1976), *The Bureaucratization of the World*, University of California Press, Berkeley.

Jedin, Herbert (1960), *Ecumenical Councils of the Catholic Church: An Historical Outline*, Nelson, London.

Johnson, C. Lincoln, and Weigert, Andrew J. (1978), 'An Emerging Faithstyle: A Research Note on the Catholic Charismatic Renewal', in *Sociological Analysis*, Vol. 39, No. 2.

Jungmann, Joseph A. (1959), *The Mass of the Roman Rite*, Burns & Oates, London.

Kernberg, Otto F. (1976), *Borderline Conditions and Pathological Narcissism*, Jason Aronson, New York.

Küng, Hans (1967), *The Church*, Burns & Oates, London.

—— (1971), *Infallible? An Enquiry*, Collins, London.

—— (1972), *Why Priests?*, Collins, London.

—— (1980), 'Open Letter from Hans Küng', *The Tablet*, 22 March.

Laurentin, René (1962), *L'Enjeu du Concile*, Paris (5 vols).

Leclercq, Jacques (1949), *L'Enseignement de la Morale Chrétienne*, Vitrail, Paris.

Lewy, Guenther (1974), *Religion and Revolution*, Oxford University Press, New York.

Lindbeck, G. A. (1965), *Dialogue on the Way*, Minneapolis.

Lloyd Thomas, J. M. (1951) in *Hibbert Journal*, April 1951.

Loisy, Alfred (1931), *Mémoires pour servir à l'histoire religieuse de notre temps,* Nourry, Paris.

Lucacs, John (1970), *The Passing of the Modern Age,* Harper, New York.

Manning, Cardinal H. E. (1877), *The True Story of the Vatican Council,* London.

Marsden, George (1977), 'Fundamentalism as an American Phenomenon: A Comparison with English Evangelicalism', in *Church History,* 1977.

Martimort, A. G., ed. (1961), *L'Eglise en Prière,* Desclée, Tournai.

Marty, M. and Peerman D., eds (1971), *New Theology,* Vol. 8, Macmillan, London.

McDonagh, Enda (1975), *Gift and Call: Towards a Christian Theology of Morality,* Gill & Macmillan, Dublin.

McDonnell, Kilian (1976), *Charismatic Renewal and the Churches,* Seabury, New York.

McGuire, Meredith (1975), 'Towards a Sociological Interpretation of the Catholic Pentecostal Movement', in *Review of Religious Research,* Vol. 16, No. 2.

Mersch, Emile (1939), *Morality and the Mystical Body,* Kennedy, New York.

Nierman, P. (1968), *Liturgy in Development,* Newman Press, Glen Rock.

O'Brien, Elmer, ed. (1965), *Theology in Transition,* Herder & Herder, New York.

O'Connor, Edward D. (1971), *The Pentecostal Movement in the Catholic Church,* Ave Maria Press, Notre Dame.

—— (1975), *Perspectives on Charismatic Renewal,* University of Notre Dame Press, Notre Dame.

O'Dea, Thomas (1968), *The Catholic Crisis,* Beacon Press, Boston.

Oraison, Marc (1952), *Vie Chrétienne et Sexualité,* Lethielleux, Paris.

Outka, G., and Reeder, J. P. (1973), *Religion and Morality,* Anchor Press, New York.

Pelikan, Jaroslav (1959), *The Riddle of Roman Catholicism: its history, its beliefs, its future,* Abingdon, New York.

Poulat, Emile (1962), *Histoire, Dogme et Critique dans la Crise Moderniste,* Tournai.

Quebedeaux, Richard (1976), *The New Charismatics: The*

Origins, Development, and Significance of neo-Pentecostalism, Doubleday, New York.

Quinley, Harold E. (1974), *The Prophetic Clergy: Social Activism among Protestant Ministers*, Wiley, New York.

Rahner, Karl (1966), 'On the Theology of the Incarnation', in *Theological Investigations*, Vol. 4, Darton Longman & Todd, London.

—— (1961), 'Theological Concept of Concupiscentia', in *Theological Investigations*, Vol. 1, Darton Longman & Todd, London.

—— (1964), *Visions and Prophecies*, Herder & Herder, London.

Ranaghan, Kevin, and Dorothy (1969), *Catholic Pentecostals*, Paulist Press, New Jersey.

—— eds (1971), *As the Spirit Leads Us*, Paulist Press, New Jersey.

Reardon, Bernard (1975), *Liberalism and Tradition: Aspects of Catholic Thought in 19th Century France*, Cambridge University Press, London.

Rieff, Philip (1973), *The Triumph of the Therapeutic*, Penguin, London.

Ruether, Rosemary (1968), 'The Free Church Movement in Contemporary Catholicism', in *Continuum*, Spring.

Rynne, Xavier (1966), *Letters from Vatican City*, Farrer, Strauss, Giroux, New York (4 vols).

Schoof, Mark (1970), *A Survey of Catholic Theology 1800–1970*, Paulist Newman Press, New York.

Shaeffer, Francis (1972), *The New Super-Spirituality*, Inter Varsity Press, Illinois.

Stierli, Josef (1956), *Heart of the Saviour*, Herder & Herder, New York.

St John, Bernard (1903), *The Blessed Virgin in the 19th Century*, Burns & Oates, London.

Tavard, George H. (1966), *The Dogmatic Constitution on Divine Revelation of Vatican Council II: Commentary and Translation*, Darton Longman & Todd, London.

Teilhard de Chardin, Pierre (1959), *The Phenomenon of Man*, Harper, New York.

The New Catechism (1970), Search Press, London.

Thibault, Pierre (1972), *Savoir et Pouvoir: Philosophie thomiste et politique cléricale au XIXe siècle*, Les Presses de l'Université Laval, Quebec.

Thils, Gustave (1940), *Tendances Actuelles en Théologie Morale*, Gembloux, Paris.

Thomas, Keith (1977), *Religion and the Decline of Magic*, Penguin, London.

Thomas, O. C. (1972), 'Where are We in Theology?' in Marty, M., and Peerman, D. (eds), *New Theology*, Vol. 9, Macmillan, London.

Thorlby, Anthony (1969), *The Romantic Movement*, Longmans Green, London.

Vallier, Ivan (1970), *Social Control and Modernization in Latin America*, Prentice-Hall, New Jersey.

Vassall-Phillips, O. R. (1920), *The Mother of Christ*, Burns & Oates, London.

Verheylezoon, L. (1955), *Devotion to the Sacred Heart: Object, Ends, Practice, Motives*, Sands, London.

Vidler, Alec (1969), *A Century of Social Catholicism 1820—1920*, SPCK, London.

—— (1970), *A Variety of Catholic Modernists*, Cambridge University Press, London.

—— (1971), *The Church in an Age of Revolution*, Penguin, London.

Vogel, C. (1972), 'An Alienated Liturgy', in *Concilium*, Vol. 2, No. 8.

Vollert, C. (1951), 'Humani Generis and the Limits of Theology', in *Theological Studies*, Vol. 12.

Von Aretin, Karl Otmar (1970), *The Papacy and the Modern World*, Weidenfeld & Nicolson, London.

Weber, Max (1966), *The Sociology of Religion*, Methuen, London.

Weigel, G. (1951), 'Commentaries on Humani Generis' in *Theological Studies*, Vol. 12.

Wells, David (1973), *Revolution in Rome*, Tyndale Press, London.

Wills, Gary (1972), *Bare Ruined Choirs*, Doubleday, New York.

Wojtyla, Karol (1979), *The Acting Person*, Reindel, Boston. (Polish edition, 1969.)

Woodward, E. C. (1963), *Three Studies in European Conservatism*, Cass, London.

Index

DATE DUE